Contents

FEMONOMICS

About the Author

Corinne Low, PhD is an Associate Professor of Business Economics and Public Policy at the Wharton School, where she teaches an award-winning course on the economics of discrimination. Her research has been published in journals such as American Economic Review, Quarterly Journal of Economics, and the Journal of Political Economy. She regularly speaks to and advises companies on their practices, and her research has been featured in media outlets from Vanity Fair and the Guardian to the Harvard Business Review. She received her PhD in economics from Columbia University and her BS in economics and public policy from Duke University, and formerly worked for McKinsey & Company. She lives in Philadelphia with her family.

FEMONOMICS

What Data Tells Us About
Women's Lives and Getting the Most
Out of Yours

Corinne Low

hodder
press

The names and identifying characteristics of some persons described
in this book have been changed.

Femonomics was first published under the title *Having It All* in the United States of
America in 2025 by Flatiron Books, 120 Broadway, New York, NY 10271, USA.
First published in Great Britain in 2025 by Hodder Press
An imprint of Hodder & Stoughton Limited
An Hachette UK company

Th e authorised representative in the EEA is Hachette Ireland, 8 Castlecourt Centre,
Dublin 15, D15 XTP3, Ireland (email: info@hbgi.ie)

1

A CIP catalogue record for this title is available from the British Library

Hardback ISBN 9781399737609
Trade paperback ISBN 9781399737616
Ebook ISBN 9781399737623

Hodder & Stoughton policy is to use papers that are natural, renewable
and recyclable products and made from wood grown in sustainable forests.
The logging and manufacturing processes are expected to conform
to the environmental regulations of the country of origin.

Hodder & Stoughton Limited
Carmelite House
50 Victoria Embankment
London EC4Y 0DZ
www.hodderpress.co.uk

For the women who just can't do it anymore.

Introduction

In 2017, I gave birth to my son, and also a midlife crisis. Suddenly, my two-hour commute from our home in New York City to my job at the University of Pennsylvania went from inconvenient but sustainable to the bane of my existence. And my marriage, which had seemed flawed but in a cute, work-in-progress kind of way, suddenly seemed to be falling apart at the seams. At the same time, in my academic career, rejections were stacking up, and I couldn't shake the feeling that my male colleagues, some of whom were going up for tenure years before I was, simply had more time in their days. Nor did I feel like I was at the top of my game in other domains, constantly observing how much nicer other people's houses looked, how much better dressed their little bundles of joy were, how much more time they seemed to have to juggle motherhood, work, and coordinate everything therein.

Perhaps the nadir of this period was when track repairs were taking place on my train line, and I spent a total of six hours commuting, only to work in my office for four. I pumped in the Amtrak bathroom, crying, because I wouldn't make it home in time to put my son to bed. I not only felt as though I didn't "have it all"; I felt like I didn't have *anything.* Not the successful career I wanted, not the thriving family and homelife I wanted, and I wasn't even the fun person I used to be, who traveled and laughed and enjoyed things. Most of all, I was So. Darn. Tired. All the time.

It's a refrain I've heard time and again from working women, who feel like they're constantly juggling and constantly dropping each ball, one by one. A lawyer friend tells me all she does is work, parent, and sleep. "I'm so tired," she confides, "and I'm so busy, and I don't have time for anything, but I can't afford to make less money, so I can't leave corporate law!" Another says she's so burned out she doesn't enjoy the career she once loved, and she finds herself snapping at her husband and not being the kind of mom she wants to be with her kids. When Mother's Day rolls around, her greatest wish is to rest, away from her family. A young mom on a high-flying career track laments, "I haven't gone for a run in four years, since my son was born," causing me to do a double take, having just overheard her husband say he swims for an hour every day.

These women are accomplished. They are competent. They are fierce. How did they end up in such undesirable, unmanageable situations? How did *I* end up there?

And they aren't the only ones struggling with how to manage all the things in a world that seems to be stacked against them. During office hours, a student asks, "Should I break up with my boyfriend? He barely does any of the housework, and we don't even have kids yet—is it going to get worse?" Another one worries aloud, "I want a career like my male classmates are dreaming about. But I know I also want kids. If I become a mother, will I just be signaling to everyone that I'm not serious about my career?" Her classmate declares, "I actually never want kids." Then asks, "Is there a way to communicate that to my bosses so they won't treat me differently from men?"

While these may not be the kinds of questions most economics professors receive, for me, they are common. My research is focused on the decisions that shape women's lives and the economic and societal constraints they face when making them. Because I talk about my research in class, the conversations in my office are generally not limited to the latest assignment. My students—undergrads and MBAs—often come to me in search of advice. Which is why it was so shocking to realize that I had somehow managed to chart my life so badly off course.

Navigating my way out of that dark place—out of the metaphorical Amtrak bathroom I was stuck in—added insight to the research I've done since my time as a PhD student at Columbia. I started thinking not just about the unseen economic forces influencing women's lives but about how we could shape our lives around and in spite of those forces. And the requests for advice kept coming. Not just from students, but from peers, navigating career, relationships, fertility, and more.

In this book, I hope to open up the conversations I've been having with women of all ages and all walks of life to a broader audience. I want you to know that you are *seen* and *not alone* in facing these challenges. And that you are not doing anything wrong, though society can sure make it easy to feel that way. We'll talk about just how many of our societal systems and workplace norms were created either without the needs of women in mind or specifically to exclude them. But I will also provide you with research-backed tools you can use right now to reclaim your agency and improve your life, even while we continue the longer fight for systemic change. On a personal level, this work starts with stepping back to assess what improving your life really means, identifying what will bring you the most happiness and security over the long term, and learning to let go of the notions of "having it all" that we've been conditioned to believe we must strive for, but that, in fact, only offer false or short-term payoffs in exchange for an incredible amount of time, effort, and stress.

We have been sold the idea that optimizing our lives means being able to *do* the most things in a day or *have* the most items in our possession. But I'd argue that the most optimal life choices are those that your future self—five, ten, twenty years down the line—will be most grateful for. My research highlights just how many additional factors women must consider when trying to build that happy future. Because of

3

a few biological realities and a lot of imbalanced cultural and institutional norms, men simply do not face the same level of complexity and potential repercussions when making major life decisions, such as whether or not to obtain an advanced degree, what type of career to pursue, when or whether to get married and/or have kids, if they should get divorced or end a partnership that isn't working, or even where they should live.

Yet somehow, most conventional advice for women still seems to center on the idea of contorting ourselves to fit into corporate and cultural standards that simply don't align with our reality: lean in. Stop apologizing. Habit stack. Nice girls don't get the corner office. Airport shelves are lined with books telling women how to get ahead in business through changing their approach, making smarter choices, finding the right style. If you're unhappy with your career or your life, the underlying messages of these books tells you that you can always buckle down, change your attitude, and *work harder.*

I reject the premise that the barrier preventing women from living optimally—or even just happily—is our failure to try hard enough to have it all or do it all. In this book, I will present a radical framework for understanding the lives of women, and improving yours if you happen to be one: acknowledging women as *economic agents*, making choices to improve our lives given the constraints we face. What does that mean? It means the same models economists use to study *people* broadly should be used to study *women* specifically. It means we can understand women as rational entities doing their best to optimize in a world where options are often limited and odds are stacked against us, no matter how hard we work or how far we lean in. This book asks the question: what would it look like if we stopped assuming the problems in women's lives are caused by women's choices and started looking instead at the structural, economic, and biological factors that are forcing and constraining those choices in the first place?

Women today face unsustainable demands on our time and efforts largely because economic forces have created an environment where gender roles have converged in the workplace and yet have not converged at home. Whereas the division of labor in a marriage was once clear and structurally reinforced throughout society—one person worked and one person managed the household—the wave of women entering the workforce upended that tidy arrangement. In theory, women becoming economic agents outside of the home promised a more equal division of labor and opportunity on both professional and domestic fronts. But the reality hasn't matched this promise. In the professional realm, what initially seemed like a revolution of women earning their own incomes and making strides in wages and management representation has turned into a stalemate: women's wages have plateaued, and our percentage in the upper echelons of management and pay grades has stalled. And in the domestic sphere, women are still tasked with the majority of housework, regardless of whether they earn more or less than their male partners. We believed in the promise of having it all—at work and at home—but for many women, what we have instead is just exhaustion.

As an economist, I think the rationale for a lot of our decisions can be boiled down to a simple question: *Am I getting a good deal?* You make a deal when you accept a job, enter a marriage, or decide to have kids. For each deal, you are contributing time, money, and effort for a perceived payoff. In combination, these deals, with their payoffs and sacrifices, form the experience of your life.

At work, women's financial deals all too often do not match men's: they are discouraged from pursuing lucrative STEM jobs, are shuffled into less prestigious roles, are asked to take on important but less promotable responsibilities,[1] face hiring discrimination, have to change careers or go part-time in order to parent, are overlooked for promotions . . . and then find mid-career that for some reason they are making substantially less money than their male peers. At home, the old marriage contract was flawed but clear: one person's job was financial production, the other's was home production. While women have faced economic pressure to take on more of the financial share, men have not faced similar pressure to take on more of the home production. In fact, women in heterosexual marriages who are the primary breadwinners do almost twice as much cooking and cleaning as their male spouses.[2]

For too long, women have been expected to accept unfairly labor-intensive, functionally unsustainable deals in all areas of work and life and to somehow just make up the difference by working harder, optimizing better, and, when that fails, "self-care". But it's not working for us—women's happiness and mental health are cratering. We see the signs of strain across the world, and across women of all socioeconomic backgrounds. We cannot keep going in this direction. Something has to change.

Even before our work–life boundaries were destroyed by the pandemic, finding balance at the intersection of work and life has long been a struggle for women. We want productivity and purpose, connection and success, and the leisure time to actually enjoy the lives we've worked so hard to build. The study of this quest for happiness and fulfillment has popularly been the domain of behavioral psychologists, with previous bestselling books encouraging us to nudge our subconscious into better decisions through choice architecture, or more intentionally balance our fast-thinking "lizard brain" with our slow-thinking analytical brain. But while we've invested plenty of resources in understanding how people make mistakes at the bank or the grocery store based on behavioral biases, there's been precious little space devoted to exploring how much the most significant decisions in our lives, particularly women's lives, can be shaped by deeply seated impulses that too often leave us depleted and unhappy when we thought we were doing just the opposite. We make deals based on what feels right in the moment—meeting the needs of the demanding job we love, taking on extra responsibilities to help out a family member—but don't fully consider the long-term impact of those choices on our lives.

I want to look at how our lives can be improved by taking an evidence-driven approach to these deals. I want to look at the small print of every contract we enter into and consider why we so often make choices that feel right in the moment but don't serve our longer-term goals. Part of this investigation involves understanding the ways that love and caring are evolutionary forces that have an outsize effect on women, functioning much in the same way "temptation" and "present bias" cause people to mis-optimize in financial matters.

I know this is not as straightforward as it sounds. While I've always prided myself on using a hyperrational approach to modeling women's decisions in my research and carefully poring over the data, somehow in my own life, I ended up in an epically bad deal. I was working so hard, at every margin—trying my best to squeeze blood from stone. The unhappier I felt, the harder I worked. On myself, on my career, on my relationship.

It took a major wake-up call for me to finally decide to make some drastic changes—in my case, end my marriage, move to Philadelphia, and trade a two-and-a-half-hour train ride for a seven-minute commute by bike. In Philly, I was able to afford enough space to have a live-in au pair, which meant having *real* help with my son for the first time. Even when it was clear that my marriage wasn't working, I had been so scared of the prospect of single parenting that I was willing to accept a bad deal. Imagine my surprise when, instead of getting harder, things actually got easier. I had more time, more energy, new work ideas. I daresay I was even . . . well rested? The data validates my experience here—divorced mothers sleep more than married ones.[3]

Another change made in the wake of my divorce was more central to my identity. When I was young, I defaulted to dating men but had never truly felt "straight". Over the course of my marriage, I started to see how much heterosexual gender roles were taking from me. Why on earth was I the one keeping track

7

of school events and writing long emails to childcare providers and painstaking instructions on how to grocery shop or cook dinner when I was also commuting to another state and the primary breadwinner? *Gender* was making decisions that I thought I got to make for myself. After I got divorced, I had no desire to be with a man again. My theoretical bisexuality had calcified into certain queerness. I started dating women.

Two years after leaving my marriage, with tenure in hand, I sat on a sunny porch, surrounded by friends and neighbors, my son happily running around with other children, and wondered: what took an economist like me so long to negotiate a good deal for myself at work and at home?

Which brings us to this book, which I'm writing because I want to help other women be as relentless in finding good deals for themselves as we are in trying to make everything work for everyone else all the time. I want to encourage you to think like an economist as you make life decisions. Part of that entails identifying your *personal utility function*—a term economists use to capture the idea that individuals have unique definitions and means of maximizing personal "profit" in their lives, in the same way that a business maximizes profit in dollars, euros or pounds. I sometimes encourage my students to think of their utility as a personal video game score, with points allocated by category. Only you know how the points are earned and in which category. Some of those points might accrue from dollars earned, but not all of them. That's often where I find people go wrong or end up getting into deals that are going to make them unhappy in the long run. They either focus too heavily on one category (like financial earnings, sacrificing time with family), or they prioritize things that feel like they're paying off in the short term (being the best team player! Going into debt to keep up with the Joneses! Chasing a relationship that never seems to love you back!), but don't add any utility "points" to their lives in the long term. This is especially true for women, who face unique pressure to prioritize caring for others over finding what brings them satisfaction and enduring happiness.

I want to offer readers an opportunity to step back and ask if they're truly getting the "points" they want, based on their most dearly held values. This means that the changes I made may be totally different from the ones you choose in your life—your utility function is unique to you. I will suggest though, that if you live with a partner, this is a joint problem: this book is not going to put even more pressure on women to solve everything on their own. For instance, ask yourself (and your partner): do you *as a household* need to figure out ways to increase earnings with the goal of providing you a little needed wiggle room to spend money on creating time? *If* you had the ability to delegate some key responsibilities or tasks to others, what possibilities would open up for you? There are also strategies for freeing up your time even if paying for things truly isn't an option: can you trade tasks with friends, create car pools, or just invest in simplifying your life so that certain obligations are no longer a consideration? These are the types of questions this book will prompt you to ask yourself, based on where your time is being squeezed to the point of distress, and where you might find more joy instead.

This book is my guide to getting the most happiness and satisfaction from your life and career in a world full of constraints. It is a manual to using the latest research and data to create strategies that empower you in every sphere. It is also a call to action for firms, policymakers, and anyone else with an iota of power to get to work on the tough job of *changing* these constraints instead of the easier one we seem to default to: criticizing women. It redefines the concept of "having it all" to be about finding out *what you need* and how to get it in a reality that too often lets women down and implores us to do more while settling for less.

This book isn't just for women in corporate careers, although we'll certainly cover those domains, and it also isn't just for mothers or those who want to become them, although we'll talk plenty about juggling the demands of parenting alongside everything else. This book is for anyone who is struggling with the balance of being a woman in a world set up for men. It draws upon research conducted across the globe, in North and South America, Asia, Europe, Africa, and Australia. It is for women in medicine, law, academia, the tech and business worlds, and those working in education, health care, and everything else. This book is for women just starting out on career paths and trying to chart the beginning of their course, and for women who are looking to make changes mid-career after not getting what they want from their current jobs. It's for women who are considering relationships or children in the context of planning careers, and it's for women who already have kids and are looking to make the impossible puzzle pieces fit, and for those whose kids have moved out of the house and are wondering what's next. And it's for women who are looking for a partner, trying to make a marriage work, and those that are newly divorced. Because in all these stages, women face unique constraints from an economic system that devalues their contributions and their well-being.

You will find in these pages lots of infuriating evidence of the forces making our lives hard, but I'm not going to gaslight you into thinking that you are the thing that needs to change. *You* are doing more than enough—literally, you are doing it all. So instead, I'm going to share some practical advice on how to work around the constraints, and arm you with the tools to get more of what you need: from your partner, from your boss, and from the system itself. Consider this the essential economics textbook for life as a woman, but hopefully a little more fun.

Chapter 1

Winning the Bread and Baking It Too

AS A GROUP, women are very good at "making it work". Human beings are naturally adaptable creatures, but women—we are great at coping. When faced with hard things, we try harder. We find margins to shift, we devise creative solutions, we make time and space where there is none. It's like scrimping on your daily coffee to save up for vacation, but the thing we scrimp on is our happiness—our souls.

Here's the thing: women can't bend anymore without breaking. We can't tweak or life hack our way to more hours in the day or around the major structural issue that's making our lives impossible: that there is simply no way to juggle a fifty- to eighty-hour career with full-time housework and—for those of us who are mothers— the parenting load (and all the emotional and mental labor that comes with it).

That's the real story, to me, of the past seventy years of economic change, which is often depicted as a happy tale about women's empowerment and the feminist revolution. But I see a much darker subplot.

A Revolution for Women?

Between 1955 and 1985, American women's participation in the workforce skyrocketed, from 35 percent to 55 percent,[1] mirroring a broad trend in other OECD countries. Specifically, *married* women's workforce participation doubled. Single women already had high rates of workforce participation. And, in fact, so did women of color, something we'll revisit in a moment. It was married white women who tended to not provide work in the market during the middle of the century, as part of an arrangement economists call *marital specialization,* where one partner works for pay while the other puts their labor into housework and raising kids.

The famous economic model of marriage, for which Gary Becker won the Nobel Prize, involved two people forming a household unit to take advantage of different types of efficiency.[2] One was *returns to scale,* which is that it's more efficient to have two people cleaning just one living room and mowing just one lawn rather than each caring for their own home (and paying their own rent on that home!). The second is *specialization.* Specialization is the ability to focus on just one type of task, and presumably do that task more efficiently than trying to split your time between two tasks. In a household, that used to mean one person going to work and one person taking care of . . . everything else (i.e., housework, chores, parenting, and even those things sometimes called *adulting*). In the field of economics, this type of domestic labor is referred to as *home production,* which recognizes that it contributes value to the household just as a paycheck does.

In this model, the person who went to work was typically the man, and the person who focused on home production was typically the woman. Now, I think there were a lot of downsides to this arrangement, and I'm not arguing for a retro social order. But it's also important to note that, for a lot of women, this setup was a privilege and an aspiration. In fact, poorer women and women of color typically did not have households that followed this model, because their households simply couldn't afford to have only one person work. So, while some aspects of this deal were problematic, it also *was* a deal— one with very clear terms and that gave women both financial security and, often, a lot of leisure time.

Our mental model for this arrangement, the 1950s in the US, was a specific moment in history where the population was urbanizing, the postwar economy was booming, and new, time-saving home technologies—like baby formula and vacuum cleaners—were being introduced,[3] all leading to lower working hours for women. I always side-eye claims that women "just started working," when in any agrarian economy, women obviously supply a tremendous amount of labor! Work by economists like Valerie Ramey and more recently Rachel Ngai, Claudia Olivetti, and Barbara Petrongolo shows exactly this—documenting that in historical time-use surveys, rural women were often working sixty-hour weeks.[4] But in the '50s, for urban, married, white women, division of responsibility was the ruling economic system.

Doing the shopping, the cooking, the paperwork, the housecleaning . . . waiting for the electrician, walking the dog, taking the car in for repairs, calling about a bill . . . plus raising children and the myriad responsibilities that entails— some households were privileged enough to essentially have a full-time home-management professional in the role of wife, while the husband could focus on having a career. Because if the breadwinner had to share that work, he might be able to have a job, but not a career. High-paying jobs required "human capital investments" that meant working nights and weekends and whenever your boss called, which just wouldn't be possible without someone else investing in making everything operate like clockwork at home. These types of jobs have come to dominate the high-paying workforce as America, the UK and other developed countries transformed into service-based economies. But today, there are fewer and fewer "housewives" to pick up the domestic burden.

There are many theories as to why married (white) women started entering the workforce in such high numbers in the 1960s: feminism and cultural change, technology, a decline in discrimination, the spread of birth control and liberalization of abortion, gender integration in higher education, the list goes on. But another trend was also driving this change, highlighted in Georgetown economist Mary Ann Bronson's cleverly named paper "Degrees Are Forever".[5] The rise in easier divorce. The introduction of unilateral divorce laws in many US states meant that men could walk away from their marriages, taking their paycheck with them (the classic trope—the husband falling in love with his secretary—was popularized during this period, for good reason). Wives could have spent years investing in home production and easing the path of someone else's career that they now couldn't benefit from. A host of research demonstrates that during this period, women ended up financially worse off after divorce—they went from an even split of the household's joint resources to making do with whatever sum the court offered in child support and alimony / spousal support.[6] One reason women started to enter the workforce, then, was to protect themselves. Bronson's research shows that women earning college degrees, eventually outpacing the level of men, follows the rollout of unilateral divorce laws. And it wasn't just in the United States—divorce skyrocketed around the world at the same time, whether spurred by legal changes, such as the UK's 1969 Divorce Reform Act, or social ones, threatening previously certain marital security.

I picture young women growing up hearing cautionary tales about their aunts, and mothers' friends giving their "best years" to marriage and "ending up with nothing"—learning about women who spent countless hours creating a home, raising kids, and making sure that Dad's suit was always freshly pressed, only to be left considering part-time work at forty while he moved on with someone fifteen years younger. Specializing in home production while your spouse builds his career is only a good deal as long as the relationship stays intact. These young women, Bronson's research tells us, didn't want to hedge their futures on that uncertainty. Degrees, after all, are forever.

I tested this theory in my own research with my frequent collaborator Jeanne Lafortune in a paper we call "Collateralized

Marriage".[7] We show direct evidence that women are more willing to specialize when their marriages feel more secure. To do this, we exploit the fact that US marriage law specifies that assets accumulated during the marriage are to be divided upon divorce. As nonmarital child support enforcement has increased and divorce has become easier, this remains one of the few sources of relationship security that can be attained only through marriage.

The implementation of unilateral divorce laws were a double-edged sword. While they enabled women to leave abusive and untenable situations, as documented by economist couple Betsey Stevenson and Justin Wolfers, who show that changing divorce laws decreased women's mental health distress and suicide, they also left women whose husbands were the ones who wanted to leave in a much worse financial position, as discussed above.[8] Getting more into the details, prior to this change, a partner who wanted a divorce had to gain the other person's assent—which often meant writing them a hefty check. There's a scene in *Mad Men* depicting this period where one of the named partners tells his wife he wants a divorce, and she says, "I know, but it's going to cost you," to which he pulls out his checkbook. In a unilateral divorce, on the other hand, there's no need to gain this agreement. One party wanting to divorce is enough, and a couple can either reach a financial settlement through a mediator or have one determined via a judge. If a woman invested more resources in home production and child-rearing over the course of her marriage, and thus earned less money, court-mandated alimony and child support are unlikely to make up the difference.

But with assets to divide, she would get a one-time lump sum that would help soften this blow. If that asset is a marital home, in addition to getting half the proceeds when it was sold, she would often be granted the rights to stay in the home until the kids grew up (a great quote we unearthed while writing this paper, attributed to various comedians and Rod Stewart: "Instead of getting married again, I'm going to find a woman I don't like and just give her a house"). Thus, we call marriages with assets, especially homes, *collateralized*, because they're a contract with financial collateral to back it up. I know, very romantic.

We then looked at the difference between people nudged into home-owning at the time they were married, who thus end up accumulating marital assets, and people who were more likely to rent. Housing markets go through cycles, and so some people got married in years where houses happened to be more affordable in their state and were more likely to buy a home. We use this variation in prices rather than just looking at who owns and who rents because couples who make that choice themselves may be different from one another, whereas this method allows us to compare two couples who are otherwise similar but just happen to be facing different housing prices and thus have a different probability of owning.

Consistent with our theory that "divorce insurance" matters to women when choosing how much to specialize, we found that couples who were more likely to own tended to have a more "traditional" division of labor. She worked less, earned less money, and spent more hours on home production tasks. Revealing just how valuable this deal could be to both parties, we found that the men in these "collateralized" relationships work more and earn more money—her time investment at home, by freeing up his time, is essentially an investment in his career.

In the couples we studied who didn't win the "home price lottery" and were more likely to end up as renters, we observed that the wives not only worked more hours outside the home and earned more money but invested less time in parenting and other home production tasks. Not having security in the case of divorce meant she had to look out for her own bottom line, just as Mary Ann Bronson's paper speculated.

We think this is one of the reasons why people with fewer assets are also marrying at lower rates (while marriage rates remain high for richer people, who are able to "collateralize"), and tend to choose the more flexible approach of nonmarital fertility. Marriage is offering less value to people than it once did. Marriage is in part a contract to protect women who specialize in home production, and when divorce exposes them to a possible raw deal, they have more incentive to "lean in" at work rather than make so many investments at home, and by proxy in their husbands' careers. So the feminist revolution was really, in part, the bottom falling out of the marriage economy. Married women rushed to the workforce so they could bring home a paycheck that would always be there for them, even if their romantic fortunes changed.

When "Having It All" Is Too Much

For a while—throughout the '70s and '80s—it looked like *that* new social order might work. Those time-saving home technologies—everything from dishwashers to frozen meals and the microwaves to heat them—had made it easier to get things done at home and be able to put in a shift at the office, too, earning them the moniker "Engines of Liberation" from economists.[9] The gender wage gap started to close. Was there a new future where men and women could be equals in the workplace *and* at home?

Unfortunately, the '90s told a different story. Women's workforce participation rates plateaued. So, too, did the gender wage gap, not just in the US, but also in the UK, Australia, France, South Korea, and more. And for the first time, home production got harder instead of easier. Why? Because, as documented in Valerie and Garey Ramey's work "The Rug Rat Race,"parents, particularly mothers, and specifically college-educated ones, started pouring their time into their kids.[10] Between 1993 and 2003, the amount of time college-educated mothers spent with children nearly *doubled* from around twelve hours to over twenty-two hours a week. That's right—this time-intensive and often guilt-ridden model of raising children—where you invest hours a day in talking to your baby, breastfeeding, babywearing, then putting them in "baby and me" classes, tot activities, and three sports by the time they're seven, spending hours chauffeuring them to different activities by the time they enter middle school—literally didn't exist thirty-five years ago. It used to be perfectly acceptable to hand the baby a bottle and leave them in the crib, except for the occasional stroller walk, and then park a toddler in front of the TV. Many Gen X and millennial adults fondly recall their childhoods freely roaming the neighborhood until sunset, eating whatever was in the cabinet, and watching TV in the basement. Which meant their parents—mothers— were somewhere else—having *time*.

I remember reading Anne-Marie Slaughter's viral *Atlantic* article, "Why Women Still Can't Have It All" in 2012, and celebrating its truth-telling as I juggled the competing demands in my life.[11] Her acknowledgment of the difficulties and contradictions women face shaped the way I would think about the idea of "having it all" from that moment forward: maybe the generation before us, who had seen sacrifice as the path to success, was wrong. But there was also a structural force that had shifted in the background, as Slaughter felt the urge to leave Washington to provide support for her teenage son: the time parents spend on childcare had changed.

I created my own graphs of these changes, using data from the Panel Study of Income Dynamics for changes in working time and housework hours, and the historical American Time Use Survey, a nationally representative time diary study, for changes in childcare time. The graph shows that the changes in labor-market work (from around twenty to around thirty hours a week) and housework (from around twenty-five to around fifteen hours a week) for women exactly offset each other, but then the surge in childcare time is unaccounted for (this is averaging across all women—for mothers, it would be even bigger).

Changes in Women and Men's Time Use Over Time
25–45-year-olds

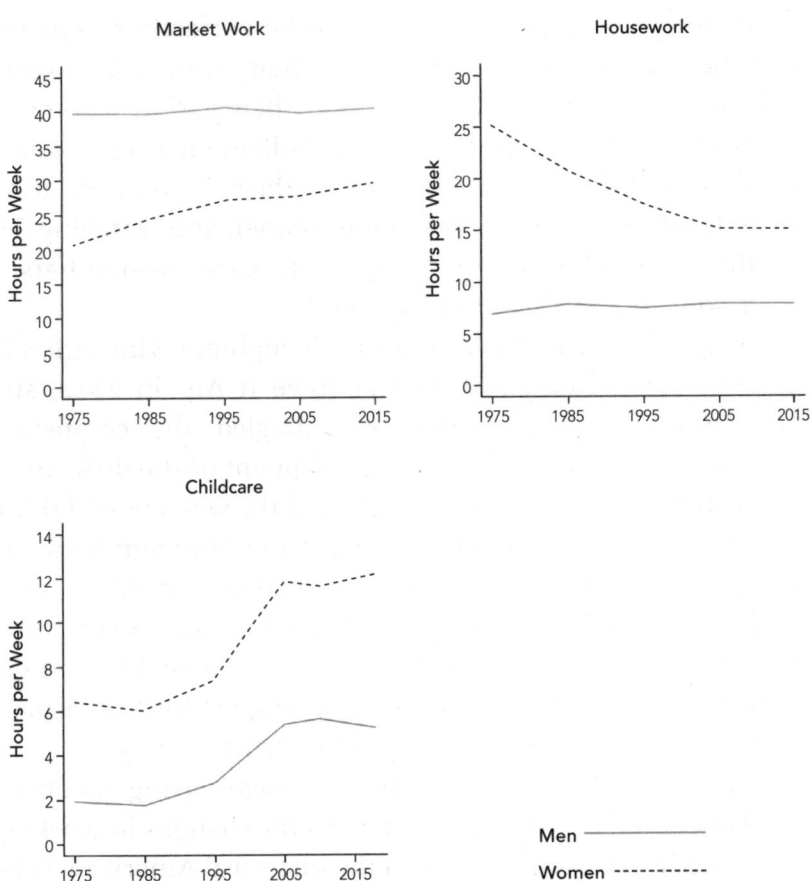

Source: Panel Study of Income Dynamics (market work and housework); American Heritage Time Use Study (childcare); men and women 25–45[12]

And so, as shown by Ilyana Kuziemko and coauthors in "The Mommy Effect," women entering the workforce in the 2000s ended up in their thirties working *less* than they expected to when they had been teens and young adults, and they found being a parent more taxing than the groundbreaking generation before them.[13] After all, they had seen their moms *actually* have it all, and they expected they could, too. But instead of powdered formula and TV dinners, this generation became parents in a world of extended breastfeeding and screen-time limits. And even more intensive, a world where playing with your child on the floor, saying two thousand words to them an hour, tutoring them at the kitchen table, and enrolling them in countless activities meant that an increasing number of child-rearing tasks *could not be outsourced*. Kids in this new model required investment in "building their human capital," which was something impossible to outsource—group day care where twenty kids watch TV might be accessible to most, but one-on-one childcare with a college-educated provider isn't.

It was a mean trick that parenting became monumentally more intensive just as the structure of specialization that created time for women to invest in home production collapsed. And maybe it still could have worked if, as the feminist fantasy of what was to come envisioned, willing spouses who wanted to act as equals at home had taken over this growing load. But in reality, while gender roles converged in the workplace, they did not converge at home.

Specialization means one person does labor-market work, the other person does home production, so as women's earning power grows, men are supposed to do more home production. Instead, the data shows that while many women now earn as much—or more—than their spouses or cohabiting partners, men's home production time hasn't kept pace with women's wage growth. As the above graph shows, men's housework time hasn't budged over forty years of drastically changing time use for women. As a result, many women are now in the position of "winning the bread and baking it too," the title of my paper with Jeanne Lafortune and Kyle Hancock.

Using data from the American Time Use Survey, where individuals are interviewed about their time use in very detailed increments, we found that in heterosexual relationships, men's housework time doesn't move an inch, no matter how much his wife makes compared to him. A man who earns only 20 percent of the household income does about the same amount of housework as a man who earns 80 percent! In heterosexual relationships with a male breadwinner, the non-breadwinner naturally does more housework, and the breadwinner does less. The same, it turns out, is true for same-sex relationships. For both gay male and lesbian relationships, whoever is the primary breadwinner on average does less housework and the non-breadwinner does more. But heterosexual relationships with a female breadwinner violate this pattern: the woman does more housework even though she is the primary breadwinner. A *lot* more. These differences are not only driven by taking care of the kids or even the labor of household management. Women do twice as much *cooking* and *cleaning* in the household, a fact that shocked me when I first encountered it. (When I present this graph, I often joke that, for an economist like me, being a lesbian is an *evidence-based* decision.) This phenomenon is broader than the US: we see a similar pattern in time use data in Australia and the UK, and recent research has found the same phenomenon in Germany.[14]

So, if women have been stepping into previously male shoes in the workplace, but we haven't seen that same convergence in men taking on more labor at home, then women are being expected to compete professionally with a half deck of cards. Women in the workforce simply have a different time budget constraint from men. And time is only one resource; women's mental, emotional, and physical resources are already depleted by the tremendous amount of work they're doing at home by the time they clock in to work. On average, men are married to someone who makes less money than they do (and thus whose career is perceived as less demanding), whereas women are married to someone who makes more money. And even regardless of earning split, men in heterosexual marriages have a partner who does more of the home production, while their wives have a partner who does less (a lot less). If we're looking for someone to "lean in" to advance women's careers, I'd start by looking at men at home, rather than the women at the office already doing everything they can (chapter 8 will discuss in greater detail how to have this conversation in your relationship).

The problem with marriage today is that it has retained the same social role, while having a completely different contracting structure and a totally different value proposition to women. These are major cultural shifts that have wide-reaching implications beyond married couples. The changes that altered married life have impacted single life, too. Along with the revolution in workforce participation for women came a revolution in reproductive control that promised women freedom to pursue longer periods of career investment without needing to get married just to access contraception (or avoid the stigma of unwed births), as documented by Claudia Goldin and others.[15] And of course, greater reproductive control is important—*crucial*, in fact—for women to fully participate in society. But greater access to birth control has also allowed heterosexual couples to spend longer periods of time dating, which is much costlier to women with a shorter period of fecundity than it is for the men. And while relationship structures like ethical non-monogamy and polyamory offer women more options, I've also heard so many young heterosexual women on the dating market complain jadedly that while offering putative freedom, these labels seem increasingly like pretexts for men to have sex with multiple people while being accountable to none of them.

Amid all these challenges, women who recognize what a struggle it is to find an equitable relationship, or to juggle a career and family—and therefore choose to stay single or not to have children—face a constant blaring societal disapprobation telling them they need to get married and are responsible for the falling birth rate that will lead to the collapse of society.

Meanwhile, at work, women face discrimination, harassment, microaggressions, and other forms of bias that make ascending the career ladder a steeper climb. In this perfect storm of circumstances, it is structurally *impossible* to succeed (at least, with our well-beings intact) in any domain. And yet, the advice we receive from experts of all varieties implores us to do more or work harder or get up earlier or be more organized, as if we aren't already extended beyond our capacity and feeling guilty about all the ways we still come up short.

And *that's* why we're so goddamn tired all the time.

All our lives, we've been told we can do everything men can do, that we should hold ourselves to their same standard of achievement. But not only are we being graded on different tests, we are given a fraction of the time to study for it. In the next chapter, I'll share more about my "so tired" story and how making big changes in my life made me realize that we don't have to put up with this unsustainable status quo.

Chapter 2

Leveling Up Instead of Leaning In

THE COVID-19 PANDEMIC was a tragic, devastating crisis in New York City and across the world, with profound, life-changing impacts that continue to endure. For me, it also served as an important wake-up call. Working from home without childcare for thirteen weeks, I had no choice but to let go of the drive to make academic progress (and with it, accept that I might not get tenure at my current job) and simply spend time taking care of—and more importantly being with—my then two-year-old. We went to Central Park every day. We watched the very first flowers bloom, then blossom, then give way to other colors. We watched leaves bud and then open, like a Robert Frost poem, the palest green, with the light filtering through the woods, before turning into full, leafy lushness. We saw fish protecting nests in the pond, then tiny squiggling black lines that turned into guppy-size creatures a few weeks later. And I watched my son, K, as he turned from two to three, learn language, express himself, grow slightly slimmer in the legs and face, grow more restless with carrier walks, eager to be free. And I realized just how much I was missing by commuting and juggling so much all the damn time.

When in-person work sprang back with a vengeance, I returned to carrying the breadwinning load and the home production load and feeling like I was failing at everything all at once. But this time, I knew that Something. Had. To. Change.

My marriage hadn't started out like this. Or maybe it had, but I just hadn't realized. I didn't see the seeds being planted that would necessitate me taking on more labor as our lives grew more complex. I thought I had married a feminist, but we got together when I was twenty-one—what did I know? At the time, like so many of my students, I was focused solely on career plans. I didn't know if I ever wanted kids, and I certainly hadn't thought about what sharing that load would look like. I had just graduated college and was working at McKinsey, a top global consulting firm, when I started dating my future ex-husband, who was employed by a rival consulting firm. We both worked a lot and traveled a lot. I was out of town Monday through Thursday, so there was no need to think about weeknight meals, and we mostly ate out with friends on weekends. When we moved in together, sure, we had to navigate keeping the place clean, but considering I was making what felt to me like a *fortune* and living in an affordable neighborhood, we sprang for a house cleaner. He had a child from a previous relationship and flew to see them (I'll call them A), every six weeks or so. I had grown up with divorced parents and knew how hard it was for me that my dad was absent for important milestones. So when I decided I wanted to go to grad school, I talked to my then boyfriend about moving someplace closer to A so he could be more present in their life.

Suddenly, with a young child regularly staying in our home, weekends were about more than just hanging out with friends. There was a lot of work to be done . . . and I noticed I was the one doing it. Buying clothes, creating a cozy space for A, preparing healthy meals and snacks. In addition, without the consulting travel lifestyle, we were spending a lot more time at home, and that meant needing . . . groceries. Laundry. The mundane chores that make everyday life possible. The inequalities started to pile up. I blogged about "useless man syndrome," where men plead incompetence to avoid tasks that aren't actually skill-based. We fought. Grudgingly, he took on more tasks. At this time, balancing out the reality that I was doing more of the home production was the fact that he was making more money. I was living on a grad student stipend, while he had continued working at a corporate job. He paid for dinner out. Instead of doing the laundry, he paid for dry cleaning. It felt like enough. We got married.

My friends remind me I almost called it off, taking an emergency trip to visit my two best friends from college when he failed to do his assigned wedding-planning tasks while I was doing fieldwork in Zambia. But I was distant from my natal family and felt, for the first time, between him and A, that I had a little family of my own. I was in love—we could figure the rest out, right?

I graduated and accepted a job at Wharton, commuting from Jersey City (essentially a borough of Manhattan) so we could stay close to A's mom. Always the feminist, I bristled when people asked if I was commuting for my husband's job. "No! I have a stepkid," I replied. Then, with an ironic chuckle . . . "If it were his job, he'd be the one on the train!" There was another period of adjustment, since my commute meant I wasn't around to handle the daily cooking duties. But meal kit services were just gaining popularity, and we happily paid the premium so we could share that task. We were both working, life was still relatively cheap, and we found ways to solve many of our problems with money. My commute was tiring, but it felt doable.

Then, all at once, like someone had flipped a switch, I felt ready to have a baby. I couldn't picture juggling an infant and commuting to another state every day, so first I tried to find a job at NYU or Columbia. When that didn't work, we briefly considered buying a second place in Philly, with the idea that we'd live there during the week and maintain a weekend place in New York. But I could see that A needed more from us than that. So we bought a condo in Manhattan, I got pregnant, and I redoubled my efforts to find a new job.

I liken what happens next to the experience of turning up the difficulty level on a driving video game. At slow speeds, you're able to take the turns, avoid your opponents, and navigate safely to victory. Then you get cocky, turn up the speed, and are suddenly careening wildly off the track and exploding into a fireball.

Around the same time my son was born, A began living with us full-time, so we went from having zero full-time kids to two. I found my brain, my heart, my very being irrevocably transformed by the experience of having a newborn. I was attuned to his every need. Stressed beyond measure by his smallest discomfort. And . . . sleep-deprived, painfully learning to breastfeed, and recovering from childbirth. My husband seemed relatively unaffected.

Perhaps we had never been the seamless unit that I'd imagined (or wanted so much I'd hallucinated its existence), but we suddenly felt out of step on *everything*. I needed someone to move with me in unison, to contribute to the functioning of our family because we were supposed to be in this together. To see that the baby needed to be held and pick him up. To see that I was struggling with laundry and fold what was in the basket. To read the book on infant sleep and share the advice with me.

The books . . . there were so many of them. On pregnancy, breastfeeding, starting solids, baby motor development. I joined the Facebook groups, too, on every aspect of newborn life. And in all of them were other women, other moms. There were no men for miles around.

The theory of feminism that I had been so devoted to was crumbling down around me. I had rejected gender roles. Clung to the belief that men and women could be equal if we only tried hard enough. That marriage could be equal. That my career could be equal to my male colleagues'. But giving birth was not a gender-neutral event. (Note: because this book deals with data, and thus averages, it will at times be cis and heteronormative, but all the things written below could apply to anyone who gave birth.)

My husband and others with pregnant wives weren't dealing with physical exhaustion and nausea or physical therapy because their pelvic bones were separating too much. They didn't have to recover from perineal tearing or a C-section and rebuild their bodies. They didn't have to learn how to breastfeed, call lactation consultants, get a new wardrobe. My male colleagues would be back to work as usual within a week of their partners having a baby. I didn't see any dads racked with guilt about returning to work and leaving their infants in day care, as I was. And when they returned, they didn't have to schedule meetings around pumping or find small rooms with electric outlets and a door that would lock so that they could produce sustenance for their babies—while also checking email. The new mom support groups I went to were, of course, all women . . . desperately trying to navigate being in charge of another life. Meanwhile, our husbands continued to be the centers of their own universes.

The Squeeze

A little less than a year after K was born, my husband left his job to start his own business. In theory, this might have made things better—more flexible hours, more time to help at home—but the reality was the opposite. He didn't stop working or requesting (feeling entitled to?) equal time to work; he just stopped earning money. Suddenly, I was doing the majority of the home production *and* was the sole breadwinner. I wanted to be supportive—I wanted him to follow his dreams and find his own success. But I also couldn't shake the growing sense of unfairness, or the deep-in-my-bones weariness from the load I was carrying. Commuting, parenting, trying to publish and keep my job, remembering things either kid's school needed from us, making sure we ate healthy food that managed everyone's dietary preferences and sensitivities, fighting the entropy of four people in an NYC apartment, returning Amazon packages, protecting against bedbugs, trying to recycle or give things away so as not to create waste, *composting.*

I did what most women like us do when we encounter difficulties—what we've all been trained to do. I tried harder. I leaned in at work—writing research papers through my maternity leave. I made appointments for couples therapy. I made chore charts. I made lists. I tried life hacks and workarounds. Every day became a battle to try to claw back a little bit more time—for work, or just for myself. We fought. He said I was being "transactional" about time. That we were supposed to be a team, not keeping score.

Living on one salary with financial decisions we'd made when we had two, I stressed incessantly about money. I became angry. Then numb. I felt disbelief that *this* was my life. That as someone who had always seen myself as intellectually equal to men, here I was on the brink of losing my career, and my sanity, because I didn't have any frickin' *time*.

I was experiencing something that I didn't yet have a name for but now call "the squeeze". This isn't just something we feel—it is a phenomenon backed by data. It's where home responsibilities peak at a time where our careers aren't yet where we hope they'll eventually be, so our time at work is also crucially important, but because our incomes haven't reached their peak yet *and* we're often paying for full-time childcare (before kids enter public school), we can't "throw money at the problem."

The graph below is a visual representation of the squeeze. It shows women's time in housework and childcare from the American Time Use Survey, juxtaposed with their income. Time expenditure peaks before income. And when home time is at its peak, women's income growth slows down (while their spouses' continue to grow steeply)—they're making investments, but not at work. The graph shows an average of lots of women's experiences—so the timing won't line up for everyone. But it made me feel validated—things really *were* that hard at that point in my life.

Women's Time and Income over the Life Cycle

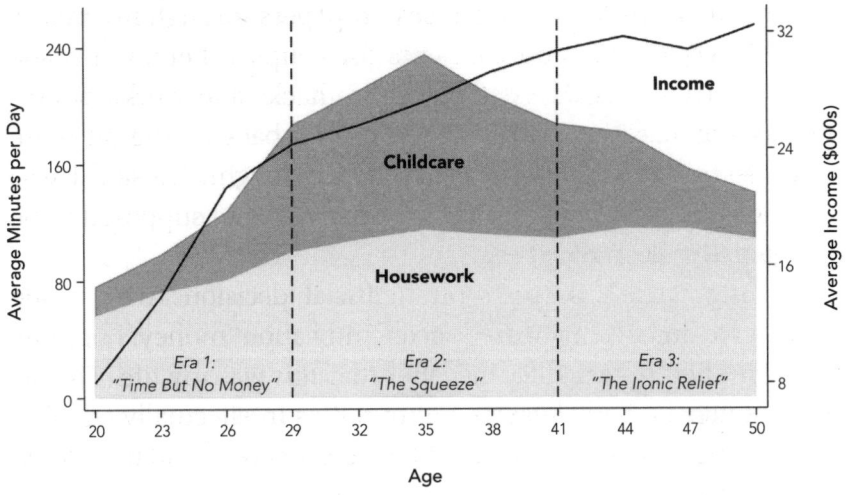

Source: American Time Use Survey (2018–2022, excluding 2020)[1]

In the past, women alleviated this squeeze for men. First, of course, by taking on the lion's share of the home production and caregiving, allowing men to eliminate the time squeeze that happens when young children and career coincide. But secondly, by helping to eliminate the *money* squeeze that could happen with early career investments that haven't yet paid off, like higher-level degrees. Research by my coauthor Jeanne Lafortune and family economist Murat Iyigun shows that women in the 1960s would often work while their husbands went to school, a phenomenon widely referred to as "putting the husband through." Jeanne and Murat documented extensive evidence, showing not just the high labor supply for women with husbands in school but also historical records like universities offering "PHT" degree ceremonies for wives.[2] My own grandmother had worked as a secretary while my grandfather pursued his law degree, a story I shared excitedly with Jeanne when she told me about the research. I had no idea my grandmother's story was so common; that it was part of a broader pattern.

But now, with women in the workforce making investments of their own, the squeeze doesn't have a release valve.

The squeeze will hit different people at different times. It might be earlier for people who have children in their twenties, or later for people who have kids at an older age or whose squeeze comes from caring for elderly parents or from teens with learning challenges or mental health needs. It might hit unexpectedly because you or a spouse loses a job, and so spending money to make things easier isn't a viable solution, or build over time as childcare, the rising cost of living, and other expenses add up to something unsustainable. But I think when you're in the squeeze—or maybe you prefer to call it *the suck*—it can feel so unrelenting and overwhelming that you are often forced to contemplate making a major change.

When you're in the squeeze—pushed to every limit with no end in sight—it can also be hard to identify exactly *what* isn't working. And it can be harder still to actually make a change. In my case, exhausted, depleted, commuting, and pregnant, then breastfeeding, I began to assume that my life would always be hard. That maybe the fun part was over.

But months of pandemic-induced lockdown brought with it a clarifying force.

I *knew* that if my and my husband's genders were reversed, if the one on the tenure track at Wharton were the male spouse and the one dabbling in starting a business were the female spouse, that the *paying* career that promised long-term job and thus financial security and health care benefits would take precedence. I didn't have to guess: I watched as my male colleagues' wives absorbed the burden of disrupted childcare while their husbands continued to work. And I realized that for me, maybe life really was that hard, maybe when you're in the squeeze, you are never going to sleep enough or feel like you're on top of everything, but nonetheless, the structure I had chosen for myself to weather this all—my marriage—wasn't working.

Leveling Up

Even though I knew I needed to make a change, that didn't mean that the idea of leaving and uprooting my and my son's life was appealing. How would I do everything on my own? How would I work and keep the house clean and the light bulbs changed and the toilets flushing and do bedtime every single night by myself? Leaving felt impossible, but staying felt worse, and so I went. I rented a house in Philadelphia. On a friend's recommendation, I got an au pair, which was a revelation. *Is this what life is like for people with equal partners?* I wondered. I called my landlord when things broke. I got an accountant to do my taxes and sucked it up and plunged the toilet and lugged out the trash (my later time use research revealed that while men indeed take on more of these tasks, they represent a very small portion of overall home time use). And much to my surprise, I was *fine*.

I made new friends, I had more energy, I spent more time with my son, and I had new work ideas for the first time in a long time. Perhaps most perplexingly, I didn't wake up every morning feeling achingly, unceasingly exhausted. Was this possible as a single mom of a young child on the tenure track? Life wasn't simple—I still had mountains of papers to try to get published, and I was navigating the conflict between a newfound desire for a second child and my suddenly salient advancing age—but it was . . . happy.

I built a beautiful life with K, filled with friends, community, time outdoors. Things I had felt like I had to fight for living in New York City, where your backyard is made of concrete and owning a car (or at least having somewhere to park it) is nearly impossible. A year after moving, I got tenure at Wharton, in the job I'd taken right out of grad school that I'd never really believed could be permanent for me. And much to my surprise, I rediscovered *myself*. I found who I had been before I became a stressed-out, angry, rapidly aging person. I was fun! I was creative! I could relax. I could stop feeling like I was failing at everything, all the time. My heart began to heal from the walls I'd built to protect myself from a never-ending loop of disappointment. I could love and be loved.

That was my big shift. And I write to you from the other side of it. It's not going to be yours—I'm not advocating that everyone who reads this book should leave their marriage and move to a new city. Your relationship problems might be solvable, or it might not be your marriage at all—maybe other forces are squeezing you. But I share all of this to show you just how stuck we can get in something that doesn't serve us. How much all my feminist theory and household economics data was useless in the reality of a deeply unequal marriage, and how I stayed in a cycle of a commute that ate up all my time, without the support I needed, trying to survive, but falling far short of happiness.

So what took a data-driven rationalist like me so long to make the big change my life desperately needed? Put simply: we have status quo bias. We acclimate to the way things are and work on adapting and changing ourselves to make the pieces fit. We even change the facts, or choose which ones to focus on, to support the decisions we're making, something behavioral scientists call *motivated reasoning*. And stagnation *is* a decision. Sticking with things that aren't working is a choice we're making, one that so often robs us of the happiness, joy, and fulfillment we could have if we were willing to take a risk of leaving the comfort of the familiar but unworkable. *Freakonomics* author Steve Levitt has shown that when people make decisions via coin flip, they end up happier when the coin comes down in the direction of change.[3] In other words, we're often stuck in decisions that aren't serving us. I don't think it's that we don't want change—I think it's that it often feels so difficult as to be out of reach, so instead, we stay. Stay stuck, stay unhappy, and stay in a series of bad deals.

I want you to understand that change *is* within your reach, and I hope this book will help you achieve it. I am going to challenge you to rethink the parts of your life where you're not getting the deals you deserve, and navigate to better ones. Because when we have the courage to ask for more, it can mean unlocking new possibilities, new horizons, that might let us see just how much happiness is out there for the taking. In my case, life was squeezing me from all sides, but there was a particular structure—my marriage, commuting from New York—that wasn't working. This couldn't be solved by simply working harder, trying harder. I needed to do something different. I needed to *level up*—the video game term for when your character gets new abilities and strength.

I've seen so many other women, as they encounter the squeeze, figure out how to do their own leveling up. One friend, burned out from corporate law and tired of its incompatibility with her kids' schedules, left her job to become a certified midwife, creating a career that was not only meaningful to her but also allowed her to make a good living with the ability to pick up her kids from school. Another friend yearned for easy access to the outdoors after years of city living and so found a job where she could work remotely, moved to a cheaper area near the mountains, and now gets to hike all summer and ski all winter. Yet another switched from her passion job as a labor organizer—which was fulfilling but depleting—to a more practical field where she could clock in and clock out, and now spends the evenings and weekends she got back investing in the causes she cares about. Creating a better deal for yourself might mean making changes like these, or it might just mean rethinking the terms of an existing deal and charting a new path to ensure you're getting what you need.

My move happened because I chose to end my marriage, but the truth is, we could have, and should have, moved earlier. It seemed like reasons always popped up for us to stay . . . reasons that made sense for everyone but me. But a location choice, as I found out, carries with it a whole bundle of possibilities. My move brought me not only closer to my job, which gave me back countless hours previously spent on commuting, but it also meant being somewhere with a lower cost of living—day care was *half* the price in Philadelphia as in Manhattan—which opened up possibilities like getting extra help. I also found that my neighborhood in Philadelphia came with a lifestyle where I felt more supported. In Manhattan, it often felt to me that everyone was so wrapped up in their own lives—in their own survival of the squeeze— that no one had anything left over to act as a "shock absorber" for friends and neighbors. In my new community, I was able to alternate school pickups with friends, there were constant neighborhood activities in the park, and my son could find plenty to do with kids on our block. My move was a structural change—a level up—that made everything in my life work better.

If you identify with any of the stories I've shared and are beginning to feel as though your life is in need of a level up, you're not alone. Birth rates are plummeting around the world, and people are sounding the alarm about what this means for the future.[4] And marriage has declined as well, not just in the US, Europe, and East Asia, where it's most hit the news, but other places—89 percent of the world's population lives in a place with falling marriage rates.[5] When I see these falling birth and marriage rates, I see women pushing back on a system that isn't working for them.

In South Korea, where the decline in fertility has been recently most precipitous, women report feeling like they need to choose between careers and marriage and family—it's not socially acceptable for women to work certain types of jobs after getting married.[6] In Japan, where the percentage of women working is higher than ever, and men perform the lowest share of home production among the world's richest nations, women increasingly choose to remain unmarried.[7] When forced to choose between having children and being a full member of society, women seem to be choosing the latter. In the US, since the overturn of *Roe v. Wade* in 2022, a small but growing contingent of young women are seeking permanent fertility control—tying their tubes or even getting hysterectomies,[8] convinced that the modern offering of marriage and motherhood isn't what they're seeking. In Europe, the fertility decline persists in spite of "family-friendly" policies and even financial incentives for having children.[9] In Germany, recent research showed eighty thousand fewer children born in 2022 and 2023 than anticipated.[10] In the UK, about 40 percent of thirty-two-year-olds report wanting children, but only 25 percent of them are trying to conceive, citing not feeling ready for children, financial pressures, career considerations, and lack of suitable partners.[11] Italy and Hungary have both implemented family-growth policies, providing tax breaks, liquid assets, or forgivable loans to young couples for having children, which so far have failed to reverse falling fertility.[12]

In the 2024 book *Holding It Together*, sociologist Jessica Calarco interviewed 250 working-class American families, documenting the way the system is failing them. She found that in the absence of a governmental social safety net—unemployment insurance, affordable housing, public childcare—women, across race, social class, and educational levels, are the ones picking up the slack and running themselves ragged while doing so. There's Akari, who's working three jobs since her husband's death, wishing that she could spend more time with her children. Patricia, who relates how when COVID hit, it was assumed she'd be the one to take on full-time childcare, despite being the family's breadwinner. And Chloe, who describes in detail how being in charge of the "worry work" of running a household was breaking her, while she tries to appear unbothered at work, fearful that showing any weakness would set back not only her career but those of future generations of women. "I knew it was going to be hard," Calarco quotes her, "but I don't feel like you can really fully wrap your head around wanting to be in two places one hundred percent at the same time."[13]

Economists Betsey Stevenson and Justin Wolfers, who documented the importance of divorce for women's mental health, have now shown a crisis of female happiness: just as women's earning power was growing, their happiness cratered in the early 2000s.[14] This decline has been in absolute terms—women's happiness is lower than it was twenty years ago—but it's even larger when considered relative to men, whose happiness has been improving. The authors speculate that one force may be exactly the irony of the opening up of possibilities leading to burnout and dissatisfaction: "The increased opportunity to succeed in many dimensions may have led to an increased likelihood of believing that one's life is not measuring up." And while the lack of a safety net documented by Calarco may make this appear as a uniquely American problem, I'd argue that it is more universal, reflecting just as much inflexible gender norms that have failed to adapt to the roles women are actually playing, at home and at work. Other research using data from the UK and around the world finds that women have long had worse mental health than men across a variety of measures, including anxiety, depression, anger, and now, for the first time, rate lower on subjective overall well-being, too.[15]

We know the deal we currently have isn't working. In the following chapters, I hope to give you both the science and the tools to identify the kinds of changes that will allow you to thrive and not merely exist, and work through some of the constraints holding you back. And if you're someone who manages women, loves one, or is raising a member of the next generation, I hope this book inspires lots of little shifts in your thinking that will help us create a more equitable, and less exhausting, society together. We can't keep leaning into a system that's failing us. It's time to *level up*.

Chapter 3

Love Is the Epsilon

THE RADICAL FRAMEWORK of this book—treating women as economic agents who are making rational decisions to optimize their lives within externally imposed constraints—can provide you with a way to seize some control of your life when you're getting squeezed from multiple sides. It can, I hope, help you find the places where you can reclaim a little bit of your time and energy and start to better protect your sanity and, dare I say it, joy. But first we need to figure out how you got into this situation in the first place, which is why, in the next few chapters, we will take a hard look at the evolutionary, biological, cultural, and institutional forces that have all had a hand in limiting women's potential joy in life.

Of course, economists rarely use zingy words like *joy*. Instead, we reference terms like *optimization* and *utility*. We've already covered the basic definition of *utility function*, but to truly appreciate how it can reframe our choices, we need to go a little deeper. How can we apply this dry academic idea to our messy, rich, lived experience, full of emotions and needs and conflicting desires?

The same way for-profit companies are assumed to be making choices to maximize their bottom line, economists view human beings as agents who maximize their own personal "profit" function: utility. But unlike dollars and cents that can be counted, utility is a much more amorphous concept. I sometimes describe it to my students as "jollies", but of course, that doesn't fully capture it. Because we can do something that doesn't necessarily feel joyful in the moment—like turning off Netflix to work on a project—but which can be a utility-maximizing move nonetheless. So one way to think of utility is as your personal video game score at the end of your life. Except you decide what gives you points, because only you know your values and priorities.

So, first, we're going to work on figuring out what your utility function actually is and how to ensure you're maximizing it within the bounds of the constraints you face—and where those constraints are stopping you from getting what you need to be happy, we'll also look at whether any of those can be moved, too. Figuring out your utility function is crucial, not just because it's your North Star in terms of orienting your values and guiding the decisions you make but also because it determines *how you should feel* about the choices you're making and the resulting outcomes.

Importantly, you cannot compare yourself to people who don't have the same utility function as you do. That's so essential that I'll say it again: *Do not compare yourself to someone who does not have the same utility function as you do.* It sounds obvious, but we fall into this trap all the time: you might find the greatest utility in volunteer work or travel, activities that don't leave you with a lot of time at home, or that lead you to deprioritize decorating or other homemaking activities. There's absolutely nothing wrong with that. But—and this is the trap—suddenly, when you visit a friend who finds great utility in homemaking, bespoke décor, and from-scratch cooking, you start to feel like you are failing in some aspect by not having a home that is "as nice" as your friend's, or not entertaining your guests "as well" as she does. This is not a failure—it is a difference in utility function. In the same vein, we all too often fall into the trap of comparing our career accomplishments against whoever is the best in our fields. We ignore the fact that that person might *just* value career, while we put our energy into taking care of extended family, doing community organizing, or being a present and involved parent. Your utility function is unique to you, and thus how you optimize your life will look different from other people. No one is supposed to or can have the best of everything—that is the damaging and unobtainable version of "having it all." What you should seek to have, instead, is a life that reflects your unique needs and wants.

Evolution Leading Us Astray

When it comes to figuring out your personal utility function, let's first talk about what *shouldn't* go into your utility. For a while now, it's been a hot topic in economics—in particular, the burgeoning field of behavioral economics—to focus on the mistakes, or mis-optimizations, that people make. The basic idea is that human brains weren't created to dispassionately maximize utility but to instead respond to a series of biological payoffs and triggers that helped keep us alive so that we could propagate our genes back when we were cave people. Nobel Prize-winning economist Richard Thaler and legal scholar Cass Sunstein describe in *Nudge* a contrast between "homo economicus", the ideal rational person, and homo sapiens as they are.[1] Psychologist Daniel Kahneman writes of the two-brain system—the lizard brain that makes instinctual, impassioned decisions ("system one") and the more rational brain that thinks about the big picture and the long term ("system two").[2] None of these behavioral theorists have written about how these insights might be applied specifically to women, but there's a natural extension there to talk about why we so often make choices that seem and feel right but leave us depleted and exhausted. I think that one of the ways women get bad deals is by responding to our primal instincts for *love*— as applied to our jobs, our families, our communities—rather than a more calculated optimization.

When behavioral economists talk about the human tendency to make irrational decisions, they often cite that the reward levers in our brains get triggered by actions that aren't necessarily best for us holistically. Much of this conversation is focused on primitive drives. For example, because food was once scarce, our brains urge us to consume high-fat, high-sugar foods whenever they're available. We feel an intense desire and need for these foods—the dessert at the potluck that we know will only taste so-so—because our genes shaped by millions of years of evolution don't know that our colleague's box-mix brownies aren't actually essential to our survival anymore. Likewise, we might spend too much money on things we don't really need, or procrastinate from engaging in effortful activities (like exercise) because our instincts prioritize momentary survival or conservation of energy over long-term thriving.

Often missing from these conversations are what I consider some of the most influential evolutionary forces pulling on our decisions, and especially shaping the choices of women: *caring* and *love*. These forces can sometimes lead us in exactly the right direction, but can also just as easily mask other needs or even be exploited. For the survival of genes, love is essential. We're evolutionarily conditioned to act out of love, to ensure that our genes in our children, and grandchildren, propagate. And that impulse extends to our partners, because pair bonding is good for child and self survival, as evolutionary psychologist Alison Gopnik has described.[3] When women are pregnant and give birth, they and later their newborn are incredibly vulnerable. Evolution selected for partnership and caring that was more likely to ensure survival of the young and the mother, hence the preoccupation with romantic love in our human experience (unlike other species whose young are more numerous, and thus less individually precious to survival, where the strategy is to fertilize and run). These evolutionary pathways continue to influence our behavior, even while many of the dangers that shaped them are no longer a primary concern. Biochemically, we get a "ping" of positive feelings from neurotransmitters like dopamine and oxytocin when we act out of love or care. And believe me, I think that a lot of times, responding to this reward system is perfectly compatible with happiness and a life well lived. I've told so many young women who were shocked at how hard it was to return to the office with a breastfeeding infant that millions of years of evolutionary selection infused in their DNA in every cell of their body was fighting their decision, and it made sense that all they wanted to do was snuggle their baby. And then gently, I would add that it's also okay to acknowledge this tremendous force, accept our feelings, and then go to work, anyway.

Love is a tricky thing because it both helps us find incredible joy, and yes, utility in our lives, and sometimes can compel us into situations that fail to meet our needs or provide the long-term fulfillment we seek. We fall in love with the wrong partner. We compromise on everything to make the relationship work. We sacrifice for our kids until we have so little left to give that we end up short with them. And we mistake the commitment we feel for our jobs for *love* and run ourselves ragged trying to meet other people's needs, other people's deadlines, and other people's desires. We're taught to pursue our passion, and to "love" our work, instead of asking what our work is giving us, most importantly in the form of a paycheck that can be used to meet the needs and wants that actually bring us utility.

We'll discuss more about career in a few pages, but for now, let's stay focused on that most traditional form of love: romantic love. I know women who have planned their careers with the utmost fastidiousness. They invested. They climbed. They negotiated. They set goals and they achieved them. And yet, almost none of us, and I'll include myself in this, chose our partners with the same care. We just . . . fell in love with someone. And then, when we could "make it work," we married them. *Him*—it was usually *him*.

Choosing a career *feels* like the most important financial decision you can make, but I think choosing a partner is even more impactful. And just like love can lead us astray in career choices, hoo-boy, can love derail us in choosing a partner. I know what you're going to say—isn't love *exactly* how one should choose a partner? But the thing is, it already *isn't* how we choose. At least not in isolation. People are much more likely to choose partners who are similar in age to them and similar in income and who go to the same college or live in the same city. Love makes us fall for some particular person within a category we're searching for, but it doesn't determine the parameters of our search. If it was all just wild, passionate love, when I graph spouses' incomes against one another, we would see a big cloud. Instead, we see a very clear correlation, with more matches happening when income is closer together and fewer as it's further apart.

I'll never forget giving a lecture on how people match based on income and age, and getting a question from the audience: "Do you really believe it can all be reduced to an equation? What about *love*?" I pointed on the slide to the tiny cursive ε, the Greek letter epsilon, that economists use to represent the error term in an equation—the statistical noise around a mean—and deadpanned, "No, love is here—love is the epsilon." And *nothing* has ever been truer in my life than that line. It could be the title of my autobiography. Because love is the *chaos*—the *noise*—around our sound decisions. When it comes to partner choice, it is the evolutionary, gravitational pull that moves us away from our best interest. It is also full of lots of joy—it can jack up our video game score like nothing else—but all too often *temporarily*.

A good friend is a finance executive who is also the CEO of how to pack the kids' lunches and book their summer camps, because her husband, who earns about a quarter of what she does, just can't. He is less capable than she is in every dimension of the joint business they are in: raising human beings; running a household. And I think, why would she choose this in a partner? But she didn't. None of us did. We dated until we found a "nice guy" we "loved". Our lives at the time involved career ambitions, friends, and a healthy dose of fun. We weren't yet chief executives of child-rearing operations that would consume our leisure time and mental capacity. And so, we didn't ask—the way we surely would have asked a business partner—is he *better* than I am at a number of things that we will be doing in our joint venture?

Your partner can make huge contributions to maximizing your utility function by helping you have time to do the things you love, by also bringing in money, and by lightening your domestic load. Loving you helps, too, but it's only one way in which they can make you happy. Just like I don't want you to focus exclusively on money for your job, you can't focus exclusively on love for your relationship.

You have to recognize here, too, how evolutionary instincts can do you wrong. We're drawn to prestige, and having a high-earning partner probably activates something primal about them being a great provider—but is that what actually helps make the most surplus in our lives now? For example, a friend's parents gave her a hard time about marrying her husband, a lawyer who isn't particularly ambitious. But now they have two kids, and he stays home to take care of them while her career thrives. For her utility function, it's a great deal.

Now, the deal I don't want you to ever accept is the spouse who earns less money and still does less domestic labor (let my auto-biographical oversharing, and the experience of the millions of women I see in the data both winning and baking the bread, be a cautionary tale). But if a potential partner's less lucrative work correlates with a genuinely commensurate level of investment in the work of living—gardening, taking care of aging parents, shopping and cooking, always doing day care pickup or walking the dog—I want you to ask yourself how much of your internal value assessment is influenced by evolutionary and cultural forces telling us we need to find the best provider, instead of the forces that actually shape our happiness today.

These forces don't just influence how we choose a partner; they can also lead us to make a common mistake in our professional lives: an obsession with *accomplishment*. The pursuit of accomplishment can be just as misguided as focusing only on love in relationships. It can cause us to work tirelessly toward goals that might not be maximizing our own utility, to the detriment of our well-being. Social dominance and prestige are very important for evolutionary survival, which means our brains have evolved a reward system for achieving them. And so, we seek endless accomplishment through "careerism" at the expense of more holistic happiness. The systems we exist within—capitalism, for example—function, in part, because these mechanisms give them sway over us, always keeping the feeling of accomplishment just out of reach, always presenting one more brass ring to grab, so we continue to work ever harder.

The need for social prestige chips away at our personal time, too, urging us to make hand-decorated cupcakes for children's birthday parties instead of picking up cookies at the grocery store. How much of the exhaustion that so many women feel can be attributed to following instincts to care, care, and care more, even if it leaves them with nothing left to give? If we're endlessly, ceaselessly unhappy, we cannot be maximizing our utility. And thus we must make different choices.

Finding Your Unique Utility Goals

When I talk about utility, it's a reframing of the terms of our decision-making to include our own big-picture needs and wants, which certainly can include love, accomplishment, and financial success but can't be driven by these things to the exclusion of *happiness*. Sometimes the big picture will require sacrifice and pain in service of those we love. But what I want for you is to take a step back and consider if you're truly optimizing, based on your most dearly held values, versus just acting from evolutionary compulsion. And when you seek out the momentary satisfaction of accomplishment, of "winning" at the game of social comparison, I want you to stop and ask yourself, *Is this happiness? Is this time well spent optimizing my life? Or am I seeking rewards that provide a momentary payoff, while detracting from what I need to actually be happy and fulfilled over my lifetime?*

Let's take a moment to consider your unique utility function—the needs and values you hold most dear. If you've never asked yourself before, I urge you to now ponder: what brings you profound and meaningful joy? Grab a notebook and write down six things that are deeply important to you. These ideas can be focused on your family life, your career, your leisure time, or how you interact with the world at large. Importantly, they aren't intermediate or material things like money. We need to go deeper to find the *why* behind intermediate wants like that. (If you've taken a negotiation class, this is similar to the step of finding the "interests" behind your positions.) Money becomes: affording the home I want for my family, and the education I want for my children (or the help I want to give my parents, or the vacations I want to take, or the philanthropy I want to do, or the hobby I want to pursue).

Here are some examples to get you started.

Family / homelife:

Giving my kids a quality education and home and community where they can thrive.

Feeling on the same page as my partner, and supported in my goals and values, while also having time for fun, romantic connection.

Having a warm, organized space where everything works and I can find what I need.

Career:

Earning enough money that I can afford to live where I need to and have a certain amount of ease in my decision-making (not fretting over every cent).

Earning enough money that I can take care of my needs while also helping to support my elderly parents.

Feeling valued, getting to learn, contributing to something I find important.

47

Personal time:
Eating healthy, nourishing food and spending time outdoors.
Getting enough sleep and taking care of my health.
Being connected to friends and family, and being able to spend time sharing experiences together.

You can come back to these ideas and revise them as you keep reading. Try to get really clear on separating what you truly want and value from the predetermined, socially reinforced ideas of what we're supposed to want, evolutionary instincts that lead us astray, and short-term rewards that leave us empty in the long term. As you write down each item on your list, ask yourself *why* it's important to you—why is this something you value? That question will help you get to the deeper driving interests behind your surface desires. Instead of "living in a good neighborhood," it becomes: "my children having access to a quality education" or "feeling safe, supported, and connected to others as a woman living alone." By getting a little deeper than the list of things you're supposed to want, we'll be able to identify the things that need to change. You can't shift your life in a positive direction if you're staying anchored to decisions that don't serve you because you've been programmed—by society or evolution—to think they are the "right" choice.

Inherent in our utility function are the trade-offs between different goals. In the next chapter, we will examine exactly these trade-offs and constraints. Identifying these conflicts can help us think about changes we may need to make in regard to our careers, partnerships, and overall life setups. The values and priorities you've identified now will serve as your North Star as you begin to recognize the pain points and obstacles that are keeping you from living a life aligned with these deeper needs.

Chapter 4

Maximizing Subject to Constraints

WHEN I WAS one semester away from college graduation, I shared with a female professor that I was hoping to pursue an economics PhD, but first, I had taken a job with McKinsey and Company. Her aghast expression surprised me. "No," she said, "you can't do that. Two years at McKinsey, six-year PhD, two-year postdoc, seven-year tenure track—". Then, with great urgency, *"You're never going to have kids!"* At the time, I felt taken aback, and maybe even a little offended, but also knew she was right. If I wanted to have kids, I had to think about how it all added up, in a way men just didn't need to consider. Years later, I authored a research paper that showed when Israel made IVF free, Israeli women delayed marriage and invested more time in their education and careers. When I presented it, many male economists questioned whether young women would really behave so strategically. Would the biological constraints at thirty-five or forty really be on a woman's mind at twenty-two? *Yes*, I and every woman in the room insisted, knowing how much reproduction is a part of women's life planning at every stage.

In this chapter, we're going to take a closer look at the various constraints that influence and sometimes limit our decision-making. I want to start with the constraints that are specific to women: fertility planning and reproductive control.

Reproductive Capital

In our teens and twenties, reproductive control is about trying not to get pregnant. Nobel Prize-winning economist Claudia Goldin and Larry Katz (a very well-known—and incredibly kind—economist in his own right, who was referred to in Goldin's Nobel announcement caption as "her husband, Lawrence," delighting me to no end) found that the introduction of the birth control pill, which allowed women to delay marriage and pregnancy, was pivotal for women to go to college and participate in the workforce.[1] Later, economist Caitlin Meyers (who spearheaded an amicus brief from economists in the Dobbs Supreme Court case) showed that abortion access had also played a substantial role in offering women the control over their reproductive timing that they needed for their lives and careers.[2]

Reproductive control also means being able to choose with whom to have children. In fact, evolutionary biology is rife with examples of the war over reproductive control in the animal kingdom (for an amusing overview, see *Dr. Tatiana's Sex Advice for All Creation*).[3] Why is being able to control reproduction so valuable? From an evolutionary perspective, eggs are metabolically costly, while sperm is cheap. This "large versus small" gamete divergence is the most common form of sexual reproduction. But it has deep implications. Because sperm is cheap, the male of the species can fertilize many eggs, whereas the female can't so easily make another set of eggs and so must be careful about who she lets fertilize hers.[4] This sexual dimorphism then creates an evolutionary force that encourages the female of the species to make other investments in her precious few offspring—such as, for example, the female incubating the eggs, either internally or externally, and feeding the baby through breastfeeding. All of these investments are reasons to be choosy about the genetic material one is dedicating that time to, and this choosiness creates a form of economic power for women: the male of the species tends to compete via economic resources to "win" the rights to fertilize the female's eggs. In the animal kingdom, this competition could take the form of shows of strength to represent both genetic fitness and the ability to provide protection and sustenance later. In the human world, it often takes the form of financial support in marriage. Economist Lena Edlund brought knowledge of this biological influence into economics, pointing out that the marriage contract was essentially an exchange of economic support for parental rights.[5]

I coined the term *reproductive capital* to describe the economic resource that fertility represents. Precisely because reproductive capital carries economic power—being able to decide who gets to fertilize their eggs gives women access to resources—one can also note that societies that attempt to limit women's power tend to take away their right to decide whether, when, and with whom to have children. One way is by giving these rights to parents or village elders: letting others make marriage decisions for women, in which case they often reap the economic rewards in the form of bride price. Another is by limiting women's access to contraception, so she cannot engage in free selection between multiple partners. Because if women have full reproductive control, they will also have the full economic power of the enormous value reproductive capital provides to society.

Later in life, a different form of reproductive control becomes salient: after delaying starting a family to make career investments, some women find it challenging to become pregnant. As we discussed at the start of the chapter, Naomi Gershoni and I used the world's most generous free IVF policy, the one passed by Israel in 1994, to test the impact on young women of having the reproductive time constraint extended. We showed that up until 1994, men's and women's age at first marriage moved very closely in parallel to one another. But in 1994, women's age at marriage increased substantially and then continued on an upward trend relative to men's. We also found that they made greater educational investments, completing college and graduate school at higher rates, and being more likely to become doctors, lawyers, professors, and other careers requiring substantial career investments.[6] The biological time constraint on childbearing was incredibly salient to young women's decision-making, just as it became to me when I was a college student considering a PhD.

But despite many advances in reproductive technology, women still hit a fertility wall that men do not face. Evolutionary biologists think that this might also be about the greater cost of reproduction to women—at a certain point, the trade-off in having another kid isn't worth it for our genes' survival compared to the benefit of investing in the children we already have, and their children (our grandchildren). For men, because there's no opportunity cost—or physical harm—associated with fertilizing additional eggs, there's no need to shut down the reproductive system. But for women, it actually meaningfully increases survival to not be able to get pregnant anymore, as each pregnancy is not only metabolically costly but medically dangerous as well.[7] Sadly, this time constraint is often a mismatch for our modern life paths, where we're unlikely to have birthed a half dozen kids well before we hit the fertility wall at forty. When I was writing about the impacts of free IVF, I was on the cusp of turning thirty, far from ever needing it myself. But a year after getting separated, as I neared my thirty-eighth birthday, I suddenly had a deep, persistent yearning for a second child, coupled with the fear that it might not be biologically possible anymore, or at least by the time I could find a suitable partner. This urge suddenly became an omnipresent intrusion into my dating life, coloring every decision and conversation. I remember looking jealously at single or divorced late thirties and early forties men, knowing that they could navigate new relationships, and the journey of finding themselves, without such a stark biological constraint.

Family planning isn't the only part of women's lives impacted by a reproductive deadline. My research shows that this biological asymmetry affects women *financially* as well. Our reproductive capital depreciates in value at the same time that data shows our human capital is appreciating most sharply. And our reproductive capital is an important feature on the marriage market, just as education, beauty, and other traits are. In a paper I published called "The Human Capital—Reproductive Capital Trade-off on the US Marriage Market," I show that women who make large career investments, and are therefore older at the time of marriage, tend to marry poorer spouses than less educated, but younger, women.[8] Other researchers who had observed this trend speculated that men didn't like high-earning women. But I thought the data told a different story. Up to a college degree, the more education a woman had obtained, the higher her spouse's income. Only women with graduate degrees married spouses who earned less. I postulated that marriage market matching contained two dimensions—human and reproductive capital—and educational investments increased one while decreasing the other. Luckily, in more recent data, as family sizes have fallen, we don't see women with graduate degrees at such a disadvantage any longer—the earnings benefits outweigh the reproductive costs.

But for two women who earn the same amount of money, there still remains a marriage market penalty to aging. In another study, this one called "Pricing the Biological Clock," I showed that just a year's difference in age equated to lesser prospects on dating apps. To study this, I randomly assigned ages to dating profiles, which meant that the photo and other possible corre- lates of age were held fixed. I then recruited people from dating websites to rate the profiles, rewarding them by giving them advice from a dating coach on how to attract the type of partner they were interested in based on their ratings of the profiles. (I was a grad student at the time I ran the study, which means that somewhere in my very serious French theorist adviser's NSF budget is a line for "$3,000—dating coach.") For each year older a woman was (between the ages of thirty and forty) she had to make $7,000 more in annual income to receive the same rating from potential partners.[9] This effect was driven by men who wanted children and had no children of their own currently—men who already had kids from a previous relationship had no preference over randomly assigned age. This study showed that fertility has a market value.

In fact, studies show that gay male couples are much less likely to have children, not necessarily because they don't want kids but because it's so much more difficult for a couple without an "in-house" uterus to create life.[10] Surrogacy and adoption are both prohibitively expensive, and in the latter case, difficult. To replace a man in the childbearing equation requires a few thousand dollars for sperm donation. To replace a (cis) woman requires $20,000–50,000 or so for egg donation, and $70,000–250,000 for surrogacy, which is illegal in many countries and in many US states. Only the richest gay male couples can afford the privilege of biological children. Lesbians are in a considerably more fortunate position, only requiring the cost of sperm donation, which is relatively cheap on the market due to that biological dimorphism: it requires much less reproductive labor to provide, without a substantial opportunity cost or physical risk.

If you happen to have ovaries and a uterus, hopefully this makes you realize what a tremendous source of *value* children are and that you therefore bring to the table in a relationship and your own life. At the same time, though, it certainly complicates career planning.

Women wait to have kids because having a child involves substantial dedication of time, thus interfering with our own human capital (read: career) investments. This reproductive constraint shapes our investments across the life cycle—career investments now pay off in income later, but could decrease our reproductive capital, something women—if they want to have children—cannot afford to fail to account for. But there are ways to lessen the economic impact of the reproductive constraint on yourself—such as freezing your eggs in your early thirties to give yourself more space to find the right partner later. Egg freezing is essentially like *saving*, but of reproductive rather than financial capital (we will discuss it in more detail in chapter 8).

Fundamental Barriers

Reproductive realities are an important part of the calculus of women's lives, and they're part of the constraints that impact our optimization. While we need more support from society in terms of funding for assisted reproduction technologies, and more support from corporations in terms of creating career flexibility across the life cycle (we will explore this in detail in the afterword), if we take those external factors as given, for now, we face an internal optimization: how to best time our careers and families in light of biological realities and societal shortcomings?

Similarly, when it comes to starting a household with someone else or starting a career, we encounter other constraints that come from the way society, and patriarchy in particular, has failed to evolve with the new reality of women's position as equals in the workplace. While knowing what we want is one challenge— hampered by evolutionary and social forces—*getting* what we want is still another. We can't just go shopping for the life we want to have.

Leaving aside biology, there are two basic constraints we all share: time and money. You can only spend as much money as you make, and you can only put as much time into all the many things you need to do as there are hours in the day. Let's talk about money first. The items you buy with money enter into your utility function in various ways. You eat them, you live in them, you wear them, you give them to people you love. And to buy things, you have to make money, which you get typically by working.

Simple economics models often break time down into two categories: leisure (time spent doing something that directly enters our utility function) and work (time spent making money that can be used to buy things that enter our utility

55

function). But we can also *invest* our time in creating other things of value. This includes home production, investments in our children, and investments in our own career possibilities, or "human capital".

Sometimes, our ability to make those smart investments is limited by the constraints we face right now. We might want a career in the arts but not be able to afford to make $20,000 a year while living in a major city. We might know that investing in college is the right thing to do but have family caretaking responsibilities that interfere with our studies. We have to chart our paths to optimize utility subject to these constraints.

And in doing so, I want you to write down one thing from this chapter. Just as we can't compare ourselves to people who don't have the same utility function we do, *you must not compare yourself to people who don't face the same constraints you do.*

Those who have been the first in their family to accomplish something—go to college, finish grad school, become a doctor, and so on—may recognize this story. When I was working as a first-year analyst in Chicago, I lived a twenty-minute L (train) ride north of the office, in a shared apartment furnished with used odds and ends. I was shocked to visit a new colleague's place and find it in the Chicago loop, on the twentieth floor, filled with showroom furniture. "How do you afford this place?" I exclaimed. "Oh, my parents wanted me to live somewhere safe, so they're paying my rent while I get started." It was one of many moments I experienced in those early years that highlighted that the constraints I faced might differ from others around me. When I teach my students about this idea, I write down the fundamental equation that what we want to buy has to equal the hours we work multiplied by our pay rate—and then circle the empty space next to it on the board: "Unless, of course, you have generational wealth *here* to fill this gap," I say.

In comparing ourselves to others, we must remember that just like our utility functions are unique to us, so are our constraints. Usually, if we do an honest accounting, we'll find a mix of privilege and paucity in comparison to others. I benefited from my grandfather providing a small college fund, that, combined with financial aid and working multiple jobs, enabled me to finish undergrad mostly debt-free. Yet once I graduated high school, I never received financial support from my parents, who were struggling to make their own ends meet. I've watched, with some envy, how friends benefit from a tremendous amount of free childcare from family members, take lavish vacations funded by their parents, or even just turn toward their parents for strategic advice and support. If you are a trailblazer, one of your constraints is a lack of anyone to ease your path, soften shocks, or hold your hand. Make those extra constraints you face visible to yourself. And don't be afraid to mention them to others, too. We may all be in the same game, but some of us have more protective equipment.

The Consumerism Trap

It's also incredibly important to keep these differing constraints in mind, because a huge portion of the American GDP is built upon convincing us that we need to *buy more things*. But the financial decisions that we make simply because we see that our friends or neighbors or enemies have things that we'd like to have, too (or because we see a lifestyle on TV or Instagram that looks effortless and breezy, and so unlike our current struggles), can often end up trapping us in an impossible grind. As constrained as we already are, the economy is set up to actually make us *more* constrained. Because people who need to buy more and more things also need to work more and more, even if the wages aren't so great. Consumerism not only fuels capitalism on the demand side, it keeps a ready workforce so supply can keep humming along, too.

One of the ways this trap manifests is accruing debt. Access to easy cash—called *liquidity*—through borrowing can ease constraints in a period of hardship. For example, the ability to take out student loans can allow educational investments that will pay off in the long term. But that access to easing constraints *now* at the cost of something *later* can also be our downfall when evolutionary instincts and social pressure are at odds with our deeper needs and values.

Sendhil Mullainathan, an economist who has increasingly veered into psychology and other fields to understand human behavior, talks about how our brains have evolved to solve short-term problems, sometimes at the expense of our long-term interests. The human brain is very good at marshaling all necessary resources to address the *Scarcity* we're facing in the moment, the title of Sendhil's book. If I don't protect myself right now, there is no tomorrow, our brains are constantly chattering, and more so when we're under stress.[11] Unfortunately, thousands of years and the development of complex financial systems later, tomorrow is very real, and financial decisions you make today to relieve some of the immediate pressure can come back to bite you.

Understanding where you are in the squeeze can help you make these decisions optimally. If you chart out your life cycle, in terms of the money squeeze of making investments that haven't yet paid off, the time squeeze of your job asking you to "prove yourself," and the time squeeze of parenting or other caregiving obligations, where do you land? The height of the squeeze is when the most external factors are making it hard for you to optimize. Again, these things will line up differently for different people. Squeezes can hit throughout the life cycle—when our parents age and need care, when our middle school kid starts having a rough time, or when we lose an important support we rely on. But the reproductive capital constraint and a career timeline built for men tends to conspire to create one pain point when we have young kids and also a fledgling career. If you're in a time squeeze and can see relief from the money squeeze on the horizon, "spending money to make time," as we'll discuss in chapter 9, may help. Whereas if you feel like you're in a money squeeze, but not yet in a time squeeze—possibly in your twenties—being careful with spending can help keep too many debts from stacking up later on and squeezing your future self. There are things you might need to finance during this period, like your education. Student loans typically can be had at low interest rates and so won't put too much of a squeeze on future you in your thirties. But you want to avoid like the plague anything that will involve carrying high-interest debt into your thirties (because you want to be moving resources *into* that period, not taking away from it). This means thinking really critically about credit card debt.

This is not a personal finance book, but I will offer one bit of economics-driven advice. For anything you plan on doing with debt, use a simple online calculator to find out how much that decision will cost you over the long run.[12] For credit cards, which often have 20 percent APRs (which means you pay 20 percent in interest over a year's time), you have to think about how long it will take to pay off a purchase. Often, when doing this calculation, you'll end up paying 50 percent over the sticker value for a new item in interest by the time you pay it off. If you already have substantial credit card debt, adding to the balance will increase the total time it will take you to reduce *all* the debt, and you may end up paying for an item two to four times when all is said and done. This is how credit card companies make loads of delicious cash. Often making that long-term total price salient in the short term—asking *Do I want this if it costs twice the sticker price? Is it worth that to me?*—can dissuade our instincts to purchase now and ignore the future (which are in turn sometimes driven by other evolutionary instincts to keep up with the Joneses).

This highlights a key feature about constraints: what you do now affects the possibilities you're facing in the next period, and the avenues that will feel closed off to you. So, staying in this little detour into personal finance, let's talk a little bit about the things you can't plan for: getting laid off from a job, becoming ill, or even coming to a realization that something—a job, a city, a marriage—wasn't what you hoped it would be. There are things you can do right now to make it a little easier for yourself if you end up in that situation. In other words, *today's decisions are tomorrow's constraints.* Part of why I felt so trapped and miserable when my ex stopped working was because we had made a number of "locked-in" financial decisions based on two salaries: we bought an apartment in New York and chose a private school and pricey day care. These decisions weren't irresponsible at the time we made them: they still left us room for flexibility and savings on our two salaries. But they weren't decisions that allowed for things to go very, very wrong.

It reminds me of a conversation I had with a manager at McKinsey, who was in his thirties when I was in my early twenties. I shared that I wanted to go to grad school to study development economics. His response? "I used to have dreams. Now I have a mortgage." It was an unusually frank distillation of a pattern that I've seen play out countless times among friends, relatives, colleagues, and acquaintances. Maxing out their lifestyles according to their current financial means becomes a set of chains that tethers them to decisions that feel increasingly unsustainable, but also critical to continue feeding the rotating stack of bills. When I talk to women who feel trapped, often I see the invisible pull of financial decisions they've made in the past: "I can't leave my job because of the house, the bills, the kids' schools!"

Having credit card debt or an expensive car loan will create a squeeze on your decision-making and even just your enjoyment of simple things down the line. I have a friend who constantly fought with her partner over her discount-store shopping trips to get herself a few fun things. When they sat down to take a look at their finances, it was clear that her love of retail therapy was a drop in the bucket compared to their budget-straining mortgage, luxury car loan, and private kindergarten. We're going to get creative in figuring out how to relieve constraints you face to allow you greater freedom in your utility-maximization problem.

But you can also provide this space to *future you* through being careful with your spending, and spending commitments, now. In fact, the years I had spent living frugally—working through college as everything from a Pilates instructor to cosmetics counter salesperson, saving money while I was making a good salary—helped me weather the financial storm of two-income decisions meeting only one salary, and later divorce. I was able to start over knowing that I still had a savings account, and so if things were hard in the short term on my own, I could get through it. I'm not sure I needed to put as much stress on myself as I did during those rough years in between, and so like many things, there's a balance. What are the things you *can* cut back on, and what are the things that are essential for your mental health?

Many of these same considerations apply to time. I am a passionate defender of the value of spending time on leisure and home production, which we'll discuss in depth throughout the book. However, time decisions we make today affect not just our utility today but—just like with money—the constraints on our utility in the metaphorical tomorrow. So it is crucial to also think about your time as the valuable resource it is. To ask: *Are my time investments now either creating utility or making space for future utility?*

Finally, as a last note about time—it is also worth considering how the way you spend one type of time affects the quality of your other time. For example, how does burnout from work impact the time we spend with our friends or kids? After all, biological constraints aren't just about reproduction. Investments that you make in your sleep, physical health, and mental health pay off in higher utility in quality of time spent doing other things. There, too, the inter-temporal nature of optimization rears its head: flossing is a bummer, but root canals in five years are way worse (and more expensive). Something a lot of us learn in college is that there's only so much "borrowing" against future sleep that you can do before your sleep bank is overdrawn: *If I burn the candle at both ends, I* will *get sick* is your body's way of letting you know that some constraints aren't as flexible as caffeine can make them seem.

*

And of course, as we started with at the beginning of the chapter, being a woman in a society where men still hold the lion's share of power forms its own set of constraints: what's expected of you, what support you have, and what kind of partner you can count on. All these things form the walls of a maze that you have to navigate to find your best "in spite of it all" life. Some people might find ruminating on those walls—their exact placement, height, and contours—to be a depressing exercise. But I think it's a very necessary one to start the process of cutting yourself some goddamn slack for how hard everything feels. You are not making this up! The walls are real, and high! But we're going to navigate around them, anyway.

So take a minute to make a list of some of the constraints you face in maximizing your utility. In doing so, I want you to really push yourself to find the true limitations that are imposed on you externally, versus preferences that are a result of choices you make. Finding the true external barrier is clarifying, because *then* you can figure out what choices you want to make to accommodate it—seeing those choices as constrained, but not predetermined or out of your hands. "I need my daughter to be in three different after-school activities" isn't a constraint, it's a preference. The constraints are: "I can only be one place at a time" and "This soccer class we like is a thirty-minute drive and only meets on Tuesdays at 4:00." Things we need from other people in order to function optimally may be part of these constraints, too. For instance, "My partner travels a lot for work, leaving me with a greater portion of childcare" is a constraint, as is "I have to rely on only my own earnings to make financial ends meet, because I do not have intergenerational wealth."

Some things might feel like constraints until you push a little deeper. For instance, "I can only pay my mortgage if I stay at this job" could be flipped to be "If I choose to retain my current living situation, I need at least $XYZ a month to pay my bills." There may be more than one way to afford that home.

Remember to think about how constraints interact across your life as well, such as: "The career decisions I make now will affect my earnings in ten years when I want to have children [or when I retire]."

Other constraints to help get your brainstorming going:

—The best-paying job in my field is a forty-five-minute commute from my home, but housing is more expensive closer.
—My kid needs one-on-one time with a caregiver to be regulated.
—At my current company, my manager seems to regularly overlook the contributions of women, and my career is growing slower than I'd hoped.

Don't worry if these ideas are rough now; you can continue revisiting them and refining them as the book goes on.

In the next chapter, we're going to look more closely at one of the largest constraints that women face: the realities of the modern workplace compared to the realities of women's lives, and the many ways our effort is "taxed" when doing the same work as men.

Chapter 5

What's (Still) Stopping Women from Making as Much Money as Men?

EVERY TIME WE hear the statistic that women earn approximately eighty cents on men's dollar (it hasn't budged much for twenty years), we hear in the same breath the endless reasons why that gap isn't really what it seems: women work in different fields. They want jobs with more flexible hours. They take maternity leave. The gist of all these comments being, the wage disparity is a result of women's *choices*, so it doesn't really count. I would argue *that's exactly the point*.

The wage gap reflects just how much women have to give up to make their lives work. It is a reflection of choices, yes, but choices subject to constraints that have been imposed on women by outside economic forces. *And* it reflects very real unfair penalties and taxes applied to women that limit their earning power even for those who make identical choices and investments as men. In other words, *leaning in* by individual women will not equalize the gender wage gap. We need a *systemic* overhaul. Thus, this chapter will contain little in the way of individual strategies to improve your earning power (though we will get to that in the next couple of chapters). Instead, I want to focus on giving you *permission* to stop blaming yourself for forces outside your control.

My heart broke for an MBA student who recently asked in my office, "If I decide I really want to have three kids, does that mean I only have myself to blame when my career slows down?" "Listen," I said, "having three kids might be your *choice*, but letting that be an automatic career derailer is a choice made by bosses, firms, and policymakers. Why does Mark Zuckerberg get to have three kids and no one thinks it's a 'choice' to invest less in his career?"

This chapter carries one very important message: it's not your fault. There's no amount of "wanting it" that will resolve structural problems in the American economy. And there's no amount of self-sacrifice or giving up things that make you a full and complete person that will make the rest of the world magically treat you like an equal—like a man. So instead, let's recognize the forces I'm about to outline for what they are: as constraints. As limits on your utility maximization. Limits to be dodged, ducked, and avoided in any way you can, while we work on the systemic change that is *actually* needed to bring them down.

There's an amazing chart from Claudia Goldin together with Marianne Bertrand and Larry Katz that I like to show my class to really drive home just how "not enough" really, really wanting it is. They charted the earnings of elite MBA graduates (from Chicago Booth—almost as good as Wharton, where I teach. Kidding! Kidding!!) from the time they graduated until thirteen years after earning their degrees. And while men and women have a slight wage gap when they graduate, by the end of the chart, thirteen years out, the women's ninetieth percentile in earnings is identical to the men's mean.[1] I cannot emphasize enough how truly wild this is. The ninetieth percentile of women—the most intense, career-oriented, leaning-in, full-of-grit, spectacular women—are earning the same as the *average* man thirteen years after an MBA. So what happened in between? First, husbands. Second, kids. Third, discrimination. Fourth, sexual harassment.

The Marriage Trap

So let's start with the first life event that women often encounter shortly after leaving MBAs and other educational programs: wedding bells. The development researcher in me has to point out that getting married to someone who is able to pay a large chunk of the bills is an enormous aspiration for so many women worldwide. At one point post divorce, I was dating a woman who worked in health care. Hanging out with her friends, there was often talk of their desire to marry a doctor or someone sufficiently high earning such that they would never have to work a shift again. A job was less the sparkly aspiration and measure of your self-worth that the "lean in" class so often framed it as, and more a tedious chore that one does because they enjoy buying things, having a roof over their head, and eating. But let's also remember the lesson of the "divorce revolution"—part of the reason why women entered the workforce to begin with was to protect themselves as they lost the promised economic security of marriage.

From that perspective, the problem with marriage is that it tends to make someone else's career the priority. We've talked about that golden economic concept of specialization, which used to mean one person *just* doing labor-market work while one person *just* did home production but now seems to manifest as one person leaning in more to their career while the other picks up more of the tasks at home. The idea, never spoken out loud, is that it's more efficient to have one person work eighty hours a week and make partner than to have both people work fifty and end up at lower-paying firms. I've seen it play out countless times: so many women met their spouses in school, studying *for the same career*, and yet somehow when you check back in on them ten to twenty years later, only *he* has the thriving career they both prepared for, and she's working for a nonprofit or reentering the workforce after a pause. Think about couples like Barack and Michelle Obama, who met both working at a law firm, where she was slightly more senior than he was. She built a thriving career in public service, rising to vice president at University of Chicago Medical Center, and yet she was the one whose career took a back seat when he ran for president, reducing her work duties by 80 percent to campaign for him and care for their daughters.[2]

Claudia Goldin calls the phenomenon of sixty-plus-hour jobs the "greedy" workplace. It's driven by something called "convex returns to hours"—where suddenly you earn *a lot* more money by working *a lot* more hours. Where it's not enough to show up and do the work in the job description; instead, one must be available at all hours to placate managers, prep for meetings with a team, hold clients' hands, and put out imaginary fires. And that is so, so hard to do if one is also solely responsible for firefighting at home.

You can see evidence of the prioritization of men's careers in another way: when couples move for someone's job, it tends to be the man's. Data shows his earnings go up after a move while hers fall, indicating his job was more likely to be the determining factor in choosing a location.[3]

Studies of cohabiting lesbian women suggests that they earn more relative to their heterosexual counterparts despite likely facing more discrimination.[4] Thinking about all the ways men's careers get prioritized in heterosexual relationships, and my data on the unequal split of home production, it's not hard to understand why. And so what's one of the biggest constraints preventing women from receiving equal pay in the workplace? That, on average, they're married to or partnered with men.

Bundles of Joy—and Work

A few years after that first milestone often comes the next: baby in the baby carriage. And with it, a host of gender asymmetries that enter your hypothetically equal relationship. Pregnancy, birth, and breastfeeding are all *inherently* done by whichever partner has the uterus and mammary glands. So even if a couple has managed to preserve equality in their relationship despite all opposing social forces until this moment, suddenly, inequalities are likely to emerge. This is partly mathematical: let's say two spouses start out earning equally, but then one spouse, usually the woman in a heterosexual marriage, takes maternity leave, and maybe some additional time working-but-not-leaning-in in the infant's first year of life. During that time, the other spouse, usually the man, is likely to continue his career advancement, so by the time that period is over, he's become the higher earner. Now, the issue is that if the once-equal couple were to rationally look at a division of labor, and there are now bigger returns for one person working seventy to eighty hours a week at a job, they would decide the lower-earning wife should pick up extra duties around the house, ensuring the husband has more time to focus on his work.

And something subtler and more insidious happened in the household during that time at home—the wife became the child-care *expert*. Now, not only does her husband have the slightly more promising career, but she is just *better* at soothing the crying baby, at knowing what needs to be packed for day care, which clothes the little angel has grown out of, what constitutes a developmental milestone, and when to call the pediatrician.

While women have a biological advantage in the early days of producing children—the actual technological machinery to *make* and feed them—this biological advantage often snowballs into more broad-based specialization in tasks that have absolutely nothing to do with biological sex differences. Research shows that women also do substantially more staying home when a kid is sick, managing children's schedules, and even household chores,[5] even though, as I like to joke when I present this data, I don't sweep the floor with my uterus.

When I was pregnant with my son, three male colleagues' wives were also pregnant, and I bitterly clocked the ways in which our investments in this miracle of creation diverged. Whereas I was exhausted all the time and often bent over a toilet with morning sickness, they were merrily skipping (so it seemed to me) down the office halls. When I was home recovering physically from childbirth and feeding another human with my body 24-7, they returned to the office within a couple of weeks, "grateful for the peace and quiet," and resumed sending emails. And when I was dashing to pump between classes and, yes, crying while doing so in the Amtrak bathroom, they were relieved that the start of a new semester gave them an "excuse" to let their wives handle nighttime wake-ups.

Perhaps this is the reason research shows that when universities started giving a gender-neutral tenure clock extension (an extra year to publish enough to be granted tenure) upon the birth of a child, women's tenure rates plummeted. Economists Heather Antecol, Kelly Bedard, and Jenna Stearns showed that men used the extra time to publish more papers, implicitly raising the bar for everyone, while women used the time to actually care for their new children.[6]

And of course, this issue is present in industries beyond academia. Using data from Denmark, economists have found that women in a wide variety of jobs experience a substantial decrease in their wages immediately after childbirth, and that they never fully gain this ground back—terming this the "child penalty."[7] The same authors then assembled an "atlas" of these child penalties around the world, finding that they grow larger as countries become more developed—it's not a problem that goes away on its own or one that can be solved by "family-friendly" policies like in some northern European countries.[8]

Often, when people hear me talk about how the disparity around childbirth opens up other disparities, they reflexively reach for the idea that we need more paid family leave. But we now have mountains of evidence that paid family leave is far from a panacea when it comes to closing the gender wage gap, even though it may be an excellent policy for supporting maternal and child health, as well as reducing socioeconomic inequality right now (since many wealthier women in the US do have access to paid family leave, while poorer women often risk losing their livelihood by missing a shift). And that brings us to the third force women encounter in trying to earn as much as men: discrimination.

The Unlevel Playing Field

One reason that policies mandating paid family leave don't always help women's wages is that these policies are often unfunded by the government requiring them, with costs being born by individual employers. So when companies are forced to supply paid leave, it creates a financial incentive to discriminate. Employers know they have to pay for leave for female, but not male, employees, and they compensate for the cost of this requirement by hiring fewer women of child-bearing age, and paying them less, as evidence from Colombia's maternity leave mandate shows.[9]

But there is evidence of this discrimination even in countries where the government covers the cost of parental leave. Economists Mary Ann Bronson and Peter Thoursie suggest that this has to do with promotions: as you get promoted, your team size (the number of people who rely on you at work) grows. As it does, so does the "disruption cost" if you're suddenly absent for six months, or even twelve, as is the case for parental leave in Sweden, where their data comes from, and where the paid leave policy is very generous.[10]

In anticipation of this cost, firms avoid giving women as many promotions as men, so that they won't experience as many frictions if and when women end up taking leave. The idea that this is truly discrimination is really solidified when Bronson and Thoursie looked at the data for women who didn't have children. These women experience the *same* gender penalty in promotions as women who go on to have children. And then, past the age of forty, when it becomes unlikely they will have kids, the promotion gap between these women and men disappears. In fact, these women, who have proved themselves to be reliably tethered to their jobs, start getting promoted measurably more than their male colleagues. Firms were failing to promote these women just because they *might* have children. This is irrefutable proof that our own choices are not enough to bring about equality. It truly is a system that is stacked against us.

Of course, before they can be discriminated against in promotions, women *still* face discrimination in getting hired based on assumptions about their skills and capabilities, though today, many people think this isn't true. A few years back, with the push toward corporate diversity initiatives and DEI (diversity, equity, and inclusion) officers, I started to hear the refrain that the people who really have it hard nowadays in the labor market are white men. I had a hard time believing this but wanted to find out if it could be true. Had corporate DEI initiatives made discrimination a thing of the past, at least for large, prestigious firms? The experience of women and people of color I spoke to— and my own experience as a woman of color—told a different story. But I'm a researcher, and so I could do better than collecting anecdotes; I could collect *data*.

Unfortunately, one of the best tools researchers have to study discrimination by employers—a résumé audit study— wouldn't work here. Résumé audit studies involve sending identical résumés to different companies, with the name on the résumé changed to signal the candidates' gender and race. The original study of this type, by Marianne Bertrand and Sendhil Mullainathan, had found significant discrimination against applicants with Black-sounding names.[11] But résumé audit studies, including that one, often didn't find any discrimination against women. I speculated that result was partly a product of the fact that the types of jobs you could "audit" by sending or submitting cold résumés were often administrative or lower-level positions at small companies. You couldn't use a résumé audit study for a Google software engineering position or a McKinsey consulting position. Yet these were exactly the types of firms people claimed had not only stopped discriminating but had actually gone the other direction and were giving advantages to female and minority candidates.

So, together with my colleague Judd Kessler and our student at the time, Colin Sullivan (now a professor at University of Pittsburgh), we designed a study that could be used with these prestigious firms. Instead of tricking them with fake résumés, we *asked* them to review hypothetical résumés for a very specific purpose: to be matched with real candidates that would be chosen using a machine-learning algorithm trained on their ratings of the hypothetical candidates. We called this Incentivized Résumé Rating, because employers were incentivized to rate résumés by the real matches they received—and incentives are considered super important in economics experiments.

Our findings pushed back on the conventional wisdom. On average, we found no preference for female or minority candidates, versus the "diversity bonus" we'd been told to expect. We did find these candidates were given less credit for having a prestigious internship and that they were rated as less likely to accept a job if offered, which we thought was consistent with employers thinking that *other* employers preferred female and minority candidates, even though there was no evidence they actually did! Then, when we zeroed in on firms looking to hire STEM candidates, the news got worse. We found in fact a stark penalty to being female or a minority, which was the equivalent of 0.25 GPA points. A firm rated a female or minority candidate with a 4.0 the same as a white male candidate with a 3.75.[12] So not only were female and minority candidates actually being discriminated against, they also had to contend with the persistent belief that discrimination was in their favor, which led to firms discounting their actual experience.

On top of the toll of discrimination itself, the false assumption that certain populations "have it easier" because of diversity pushes is one form of microaggression that women and minorities experience in the modern workplace. Anyone who has been on the receiving end of such comments knows how dispiriting and undermining they can be. And sadly, these attitudes can be oppressive enough to cause many qualified candidates to look for work in other industries.

Micro- and Macro-Aggressions

And that brings us to the fourth force obstructing women even when they want to lean *all* the way in to their careers: harassment. Sexual harassment might sound like an anachronistic problem of the past, but it's shockingly common: economists Johanna Rickne and Olle Folke have documented that in Sweden—a society many regard as on the progressive end of gender equality—13 percent of female employees report sexual harassment (defined as unwanted sexual attention, sexual hostility, sexist hostility, and sexual coercion) in a year's time. For women who work in male-dominated industries, that number is 25 percent—a quarter of all female employees. Sexual harassment comes with more than a personal cost to women. Rickne and Folke's data shows that women avoid workplaces where there might be sexual harassment and will leave a workplace if they experience it.[13] But those male-dominated fields where sexual harassment is more common also tend to be higher paying, on average, than female-dominated fields. That means leaving a job over sexual harassment all too often means taking a pay cut. If this harassment happens at the start of a career path—well, you can imagine the lifetime wages lost by leaving a lucrative field out of self-preservation. (And I'm not just talking about corporate jobs here—not being able to be a firefighter or union plumber *also* hurts women's earnings, by constraining them to lower-earning, noncollege careers like the service industry.)

A definition of sexual harassment that I like comes from journalist and author Rebecca Traister, who has described it as an "economic crime, committed against women as a class."[14] When women are sexually harassed, they may experience emotional pain and trauma. But they also lose *money*. Which is why it's so disingenuous, in conversations about the gender wage gap, to ascribe differences in career fields as simply "women's choices," and not systemic forces, well, forcing those choices.

It's important to note that not all harassment is the stuff of lawsuits and headlines. Many women can remember a point in their careers when they had a dispiriting interaction with an older male colleague (or more likely, several), which they probably have since analyzed repeatedly to ask whether their internal negative response was an over-reaction. I will never forget the time when, as a grad student, I met a male professor I admired from another school. We were at a conference, and I excitedly shared information about my work, feeling what I thought was genuine intellectual interest. Then he asked if I wanted to go to up to his hotel room. In that moment, I was transformed from a potential scientist, a fellow researcher, a *colleague,* to "just" a woman. An *outsider.*

Microaggressions are very real and very damaging, adding up and extracting a serious toll. Xiaoyue Shan, an economist at National University of Singapore whom I was lucky enough to mentor when she was a postdoc at Wharton, tested in her dissertation whether being a minority *itself* had the effect of discouraging women from certain high-paying fields. She randomly assigned women to study groups in an economics course and found those that happened to end up in groups where they were the only woman were twice as likely to drop the course.[15] Now add to this all the subtle lack of encouragement, lack of advancement, lack of mentorship, and lack of inclusion that women experience, and you see why I get so mad when people claim the gender wage gap isn't that big, if we hold firm and job title constant. Different employers and different job titles are *exactly* how the multiple taxes on women's effort manifest. It's the two male college professors who sat me down to tell me, "You know there's a lot of math in an economics PhD," rather than help me think through how to apply. It's the way Katalin Karikó was denied a tenure track position while working on the life-changing mRNA discovery that would one day win a Nobel

Prize. It's the STEM employers who were willing to take a man with a 3.75 over a woman with a 4.0, translating to fewer women in STEM (and less qualified men leading the field). Women's field choices and career advancement are systematically shaped by outside forces that lead to them putting the same effort into their work but getting less back in their paycheck.

And I think female students themselves have adopted a defensive posture to this potential unequal treatment. During the pandemic, many colleges altered their grading policies to allow students to take classes pass/fail. For my research team, this setting provided a natural experiment. We found that women were substantially more likely than men to keep grades on their transcript that were below their GPA, rather than replace them with the ambiguous "pass", which meant that these policies actually lowered women's GPAs relative to men's.[16] One possible reason? We experimented with how employers viewed male versus female résumés that were missing GPA. Female résumés missing GPA were treated as though they were close to the bottom of the GPA distribution. This might make sense, if men were treated the same way. But instead, when men's résumés were missing GPA, they were scored as though they had GPAs near the *top* of the distribution. This was even starker in STEM fields, where male résumés missing GPA were scored as though they had a 4.0 GPA! Without complete information, men were given the benefit of the doubt and treated as high achievers, anyway, whereas when women's résumés were missing this information, employers made negative inferences. And in a survey of undergraduates, we showed that they anticipated they would be treated differently and expected employers to be less likely to interview women with missing grade information than men. Which might mean not just changing which grades they listed, but avoiding certain fields to begin with.

*

This all means that not only do women face structural barriers in their personal and home lives to achieving equality in the workplace—reproductive constraints and an unequal home production burden—they also face systematic exclusion and discrimination in the workplace as well. They are aware of it. They feel its impact deeply. But these problems are not getting better, because too many people are still unwilling to acknowledge the reality of the situation, believing that historical advances mean that it's now men who have a tougher time getting hired. So the first thing I want you to do is take a deep breath and acknowledge that it's not you, it's the system. It really *is* harder out there for women. And yet—that doesn't mean that you can't navigate these challenges and still carve out a joyful, fulfilled, and yes, well-compensated life for yourself. In the next chapters, we'll look at some of the variables you can directly control in charting a path around the hazards of inequality—like Frogger crossing the busy street—all in your quest to maximize your utility "score".

Chapter 6

Turning Your Time into Money (Which Can Only Buy So Much Happiness)

CLOSE YOUR EYES and imagine what a moment of bliss looks like for you. The aroma of garlic as it sizzles in a pan as you cook a special recipe with a treasured family member. Cuddling up under a fuzzy blanket and watching a great movie. Finally catching a glimpse of a beautiful waterfall after a long hike. The sensation of sand beneath your toes, or the taste of an ice-cold beer shared with a friend or partner. Your dog's wet nose on your cheek. Dressing your infant after a bath and kissing their perfect-smelling head. Witnessing your teenager's pride in achieving something they've worked hard for.

Now make visible to yourself the invisible labor behind that joy. Too often, when we think about maximizing our utility, we think about the work we do that generates income. But the time invested in crafting the moments I just described—and being able to experience them—is just as valuable to your utility as the money used to purchase the material things in those pictures.

Which is why, before diving into how to plan your career, we're going to reflect a bit on exactly what role it plays in our lives, and the limits of what money can buy. The two resources we use to create utility are time and effort. We want to maximize these precious, limited resources in a way that is going to bring us as much joy and meaning as possible over a lifetime.

A common mistake people make is investing all their resources in one form of maximization: improving their careers to make as much money as possible. But money can only pull certain levers in our utility function—those driven by material goods. And trying to make as much of it as possible decreases another key input into our utility functions: *time*, to spend with loved ones, enjoy the world around us, rest, or engage in pursuits that give us a sense of purpose.

In economic terms, your career and the income you make from it affect what economists call your *budget constraint*: the amount of money you have to buy and invest in everything that creates utility for you, such as where you live, your kids' school, restaurant meals, and nice vacations. But working also reduces your time for *leisure* and *home production*, which are two direct ways of creating utility. Time invested in leisure and home production produces real and immediate economic value. Money, on the other hand, is an indirect route to utility, in that it lets you buy things to increase your utility. Your utility function is entirely unique to you. But the belief that more money, in and of itself, will directly produce greater joy and utility is a trap for all of us living in modern capitalist societies.

I encourage you to think about maximizing your resources this way: there are trade-offs that have an exact value for you that only you will know—being able to wear nice clothes versus having a tidy home; paying for private school versus having time to play with your kids after school; helping your parents with bills versus traveling to visit them, and so on. But what we cannot lose sight of in the pursuit of these values is that your *time* is just as important as the money and security you'll achieve in your career. I want a life for you filled with special memories, learning and discovery, and *delicious* restorative sleep. And for you to make that magic for yourself, to reclaim your joy, you have to get out of the trap of comparing achievements, of only maximizing resources that lead to financial gain, and focus on *your* utility in all its quirky, individual glory.

If you are a mother, or want to become a mother, this means that part of your career planning may involve not just considerations of earning potential but also considerations about which companies have the best maternity leave or insurance policies for IVF, which jobs allow you flexibility to be the mom you want to be while earning a respectable paycheck, and which jobs reimburse for care costs or provide on-site childcare. Because mothers tend to have higher investment in their kids than fathers, my vision of female liberation is not necessarily one in which no gender wage gap exists. I see in the data that, in fact, many women want to spend time at home with their children. When women have more financial resources, they often choose to provide more of their *own* childcare. That means caregiving for our kids is what economists call a luxury good—something you buy more of when you have more money. I'll never forget the moment during the 2012 presidential race when Mitt Romney said that when he was governor in Massachusetts, it cost more money to subsidize day care for low-income moms than to provide them with cash assistance to stay home, but his administration chose the day care option so that these women could "have the dignity of work."[1] *Wait a minute*, I thought. Wasn't Anne Romney a stay-at-home mom to five boys? Oh, so only poor women needed to have "the dignity of work"—got it.

Economists normally associate labor with disutility. Not only does work time cut into leisure time, but often work itself is, well, work. So when economists create models, they typically write them in a way where people's goal is to work as little as possible. But suddenly when we're talking about women, we get weird about it. We act as though work is some kind of end in itself. As though closing the gender wage gap is the goal, rather than closing the gender *happiness* gap. I think a lot about the fact that Western feminism seems to define female empowerment as "freedom to work" but that if you asked a woman in a developing country who had to work in a backbreaking job just to buy food while leaving her child behind what female empowerment meant, she might be more likely to say, "Freedom *from* work." I want a society where women from all socioeconomic means can spend the time they want caring for their own children—or, if they don't have or want to have children, spent that time with art or leisure or volunteer work in their communities.

More broadly, I want us to recognize the value of utility produced at home. Of cooking healthful food, creating livable spaces, and completing all the godforsaken paperwork. Of ensuring the next generation of responsible, compassionate citizens. That does not mean we need to have women sweeping the floors and washing the dishes at twice the rate men do—recognizing the value of these activities means recognizing their value for the whole household, and seeing them as valid, respectable, and necessary activities for all human beings to function optimally. To recognize that value but still treat the activities themselves as "women's work" not only holds back women's careers, it also squeezes out women's leisure time, as they find themselves doing both full-time work and the "second shift" at home. It shouldn't be a radical proposition that women, too, deserve to play sports, read books, and pursue artistic fulfillment.

What I'm saying is, let's stop romanticizing work. Instead, let's see it as a tool to help us reach our ultimate goal: maximizing utility. How is it a tool? Well, work can do something amazing: it converts your time and effort into *money*, which can be exchanged for other things that other people are better at making than you are! Jobs give us an ATM that we can put time and effort into, and get money out of.

So write this down: *A job is a technology for converting time into money.* That's it. Once you consider your job through this framework, it's incredibly clarifying and freeing. I'm not suggesting you can't also love your job—we'll get there in a minute. But if we were independently wealthy and didn't need to work, I suspect that most of us would invest time and effort in some of the pursuits I referenced earlier—art, leisure, family and friends, making a difference in the world. So let's talk about how to get as much out of that time-to-money conversion as possible, while keeping your sanity *and* maximizing the other things you value, too.

The Life Cycle of Your Job

Like most machines, the moneymaking machine comes in different models. Some of them require an inordinate amount of time and effort, and only spit out a little money. Some give you joy at first because they're something that you love, but that joy turns sour when years later you have very little time for other things that you love and not enough money to show for it. Some of them are kind of boring and tedious but reward you with a handsome time-to-money conversion rate.

When thinking about your career goals, it's helpful to spend a little time in that fantasyland where you *don't* have to earn money. What would your life look like? How would you spend your time? It can be painful to consider this alternate reality, because it's so far from the day-to-day that most of us experience. But I'm going to ask you to tolerate that wistful feeling for the broader purpose of truly getting to know yourself. In economics, we often consider the *unconstrained* maximum, called the *first best*, before figuring out what the optimum is in the problem with constraints. Knowing what you would want your life to look like if you didn't need to work for money can help you figure out how to pick the best time-to-money converter for your unique situation.

Does your fantasy involve lots of travel, high fashion, and expensive toys and gadgets? A healthy salary is a key piece, then, of your time-to-money conversion machine. Or is it having *time* to yourself to write, be creative, learn new things? Having as much time as you want to slow down and be with your kids and watch them grow? Efficiency in converting your time into money without eating up all the hours in the day is key. Or are you thinking, *I just wouldn't want anyone to tell me what to do?*

This indicates that the disutility of the work environment itself is important to you. Or, freed from bills, would you dedicate yourself to volunteer work and try to have a positive impact on the world? If you care about making a difference, it's worth asking whether there's a career that has a purpose you align with that still has a decent time-to-money conversion rate, or if it might be better to try to have an impact in the time that would be left over if you found a more efficient money machine. (And don't worry, if you're already mid-career, we'll soon discuss how to make changes to get to your "constrained maximum.")

Importantly, you want to think about a career holistically over your life cycle, where some momentary pain might be justifiable if it "buys" you a better life in the future. After all, utility maximization is a lifelong project. And these machines have different trajectories over time. Most people who are working seventy to eighty hours a week at a job are doing so not for the pay they get right now but for the promise of pay they're going to get in the future—by making partner, regional manager, attending, principal, tenure—whatever that brass ring is that they hope to grab. But no one ever tells us to consider this trajectory holistically at the outset. When we consider what kind of career we want in the future, we're often told to figure out what we love or what we're good at, but rarely to think about how the job aligns with our overall life goals and how it evolves as those goals and needs change.

When I got tenure and—perhaps more importantly—got the letter reflecting my salary increase with tenure, I had a "whoa" moment. Because the thing about being an academic is that the negatives of the job actually change with that magical word: *tenure.* My primary pain point was the fear that I would be fired if I didn't get enough papers published at the hands of a mercurial and opaque system. Crying over rejections that were close calls, and that meant I might have to move to a different school (and thus city). Wondering what could have been if I were just a little bit smarter or a little bit more productive. My job itself was actually fun—teaching, doing research I thought was interesting, mentoring students? This was stuff that I could see myself doing even if I wasn't being paid (although probably at a slower pace). The thing that made the job hard was the publish-or-perish *stress* and constant busyness from needing to take on too many projects to have at least some publish well (now I just take on too many projects because I'm bad at saying no, especially to myself—more on that later).

I hadn't chosen to become an economist because I was making some kind of grand optimization, with perfect insight into the fact that I would want a family-friendly career but also end up a single mother needing to cover all expenses myself. No, I chose my career path because I thought I was good at it and it would "make a difference." Somehow, I got very, very lucky. But hopefully, I can impart some wisdom to folks stepping onto the career ladder, to consider what happens to this career over your life cycle, and thus figure out if the investments you're expected to make now are "worth it".

One question you might want to ask as you consider your options is: are there examples of what this job looks like in twenty years that are appealing to you? Can you identify somebody who has been reasonably successful at this job and has a life that you would love? Another is, how good is the "time-to-money technology" of this job, especially over the lifecycle? In other words, does it get more lucrative as you progress and eventually confer a wage that will enable you to buy the things you'll need in each phase of your life? Also: do people get to enjoy a reasonable work-life balance at later points in this career, even if there's some steep investment expected now, or do the unreasonable hours and demands continue?

I had a palpable sense of relief at having "made it" upon getting tenure because my job markedly transformed on the other side of that milestone. Now I got to do the things I loved about the job without the angst that if I didn't do it *enough*, I would lose my job. I thought about friends who had gone through similar investment periods as I had—sacrificing time with their families and friends—and now found themselves still on that never-ending treadmill, accountable to the client or whoever else's schedule and whims, and wondering when they could take a real vacation. As one friend, who is on the partner track at a law firm (sorry, lawyers), put it as she continued to burn the midnight oil the year before going up for partner: the prize for the pie-eating contest is more pie.

You're not supposed to have it all figured out when you take your first job. I often advise thinking about what the next right step is for you, the one that gives you more options for the step after that, when you'll have more information about both possible careers and yourself: your preferences, lifestyle, and abilities. So even though I doubt you'll be picking the perfect career in one fell swoop, what I want you to do is continuously ask not just whether you're *good* at a field or whether you like it but whether it is taking you where you want to go. Different jobs have different levels of wage appreciation at the beginning and different expectations of how much time you have to put in to distinguish yourself from others. But they also have different "steady states" in terms of what the end path can look like. For some jobs, to get off the eighty-hour-a-week treadmill, you have to take a big cut in compensation and career growth. For others, like my tenure track job, it was a slog to get there, but in the end my investments were rewarded. Some workplaces are better than others at valuing, championing, and promoting women, and that means more money in your pocket down the line. *You* are evaluating how good of a technology this job is for converting your time into money, not just being evaluated for how good a worker you are.

Remember, all jobs benefit from you working crazy hours because you think there's a light at the end of the tunnel. But—is there? Are you investing in creating a sustainable life for yourself, or are you just climbing a mountain you don't actually want to be on top of? Are you being asked to put your nose to the grindstone again and again without an appreciable improvement in pay? In the framework of job as a technology, the purpose of these investments is to upgrade your money machine. What you're investing in is a *better* time-to-money conversion—whether it's a big pay increase at your current job, or a career change to a field that you enjoy more, or a career that's more lucrative. Be careful about making investments over and over when the hypothetical other side is elusive or available only to a select few (or seems just as miserable with just as many hours as you're working right now, even if the pay gets a little better). And when student debt is involved, be sure to do a little back-of-the-envelope calculation—is what you can realistically expect to gain in salary over your career worth the time out of the workforce and the cost of repaying those loans, with interest?

Investments that help us make a leapfrog in our money machine, on the other hand, *are* worth leaning into. I worked my tail off the last couple of years of grad school, and again the year before I went up for tenure, because there really was a difference in how much I could expect to earn across my entire lifetime based on the rank of school at which I managed to get a job, and again based on whether I managed to keep that job or had to trade down the academic ladder. Economists call this lifetime earning your *permanent income,* and it's much more worth it to trade off temporary time and effort—miss out on a little bit of leisure— when what you're gaining is permanent higher earnings capacity.

My message is to keep the dispassionate, *transactional* piece of the relationship with your employer in mind throughout your career planning. Keep in mind how your job affects your utility function through multiple channels. It generates money that you use to buy all the things you need and want, but at the cost of your time—which could be spent on lots of things you enjoy—and effort. If you like the people you work with and you have a good boss, your job probably has a lower effort cost (what economists would call a *low disutility of labor*). But rarely does a job appeal to us so much that we would do it for free (cue Don Draper from *Mad Men*: "That's what the money is for!").

Some jobs generate their own kind of satisfaction—a sense of belonging, purpose, and importance—or can be consistent with your values and mission. But you have to be careful not to lose sight of the difference between a job and a passion project. Often, women get the worst deals in their work when those lines get blurred. Research shows that women are more likely to have a preference for meaningful work, and this preference helps explain female MBA students' choices of less lucrative fields.[2] My friend who is a nurse talks about how grateful she is that her union always makes clear that they're providing skilled labor for payment—that they care about their patients, yes, but they are *professionals* providing a service, not volunteers. Another friend who switched into the health care industry did so from a "passion career" that left her underpaid and overworked. Do not let anyone convince you that fulfillment, passion, or caring is a substitute for money.

When you're young, it's easy to be drawn to exciting fields that pay little and demand a lot, because you don't need a lot of money, and your time is generally flexible. It's worth it, in other words, to have a mediocre time-to-money conversion machine as long as it also spits out enjoyment and purpose. But often, as we get older, we find that we'd rather get our fulfillment through our families (be it kids or aging parents) or communities, and become resentful of jobs that demand our time for little compensation, no matter how much we value the work. If you started out in a career you loved but find that love souring, look at the time-to-money conversion situation and ask yourself if you'd be better off getting your fulfillment on the side. It's also important to remember that not everything you want in your career has to happen *right now*—it might be possible to prioritize money for a while and then shift gears at a later point to something more fulfilling. Your career can exist in stages, which we'll discuss next.

A Book with Many Chapters

Three years into being an assistant professor with no publications since grad school, but plenty of rejections, I took a training my friend had recommended from the National Center for Faculty Development and Diversity. The founder, Kerry Ann Rockquemore, advised that we think of our careers as a "book with many chapters" rather than feeling like everything had to happen right at this moment. In my book, I was in the chapter where everything looked like it was going badly, before the dramatic turnaround. That mantra was helpful for me to remember that the "right now" wasn't going to last forever. But it also became a broader way I looked at my career. Some things I wanted to take on might not be right for this chapter. That didn't mean they would never happen. Some parts of the book where I didn't quite know what I was doing were building up my "character's" skills and resilience to navigate challenges that lay ahead. And some of the things I wanted, like a little more financial ease and freedom to work on the parts of my job I enjoyed most, might come in the third act of the book, after some dramatic plot points like "divorce".

The idea of a book with many chapters made sense coming from Kerry Ann, who had crafted just such a third act for herself. She had been a tenured sociologist, who founded NCFDD as a solution to her desire to leave her current job and find something that was both more fulfilling and required fewer hours and less stress.

Remembering the book-with-many-chapters idea can help you say no to deals that fulfil a short-term need while getting in the way of things that maximize your long-term utility. For example, saying yes to endless mentoring, filling in, helping out, and internal volunteering might give you a sense of short-term satisfaction and purpose, but if they take precious time that you could be investing in your career, they might be improving the story in *this* chapter at the expense of a happy ending. If you're focusing mostly on career milestones, maybe you're itching to make a difference. You can tell yourself: *There will be a chapter for that.* If you see your friends enjoying some life luxuries that you can't afford yet (or you could afford at the expense of squeezing other things): *there will be a chapter for that.*

To have patience for when things are at their hardest—for when you're in the squeeze—it might help to actually write out some of the chapters, both where you've been and where you're going. Being explicit about putting some things on hold for future chapters can help you feel more in control of these decisions—not a victim of circumstance but a proactive *author* of your story.

When crafting your career story, it's important to remember some basic truths about the headwinds you're facing. Of course there are many macro changes that need to happen to make it more possible for women to control the arc of their careers. But this makes considering trade-offs between different chapters of your life even more important: you simply can't fit everything in one chapter of the book. You have to take the long view and maximize across your entire lifetime.

Getting More Than You Give at Work

As you craft your career, at every stage, I want you to think about the balance of trade between you and your employer: how much are you giving, and how much are you getting? So, in a world where harassment, discrimination, and microaggressions often stop women from earning as much as men, what can you do to ensure you're getting more than you give? Continue to think transactionally about your employer. Even if you love your job, or at least some people there, remember that your employer will never love you back. Their objective is to maximize profit. Yours is to maximize your own utility. Your interests may overlap at times, but fundamentally, they are not shared. So *you* need to make sure you are well compensated, valued, and rewarded— that you're getting a good deal from your work. And one tool you have to do this is to apply to other places: get a market price on yourself. You may not know what your accumulated talents and skills are actually worth or what other industries are paying. Go ahead and throw your hat in the ring for other jobs. Talk to your friends about where they work and what people of your qualification level make there. And sometimes, that's going to mean making shifts, both small and large, to remove the constraints holding you back.

If you find yourself the winner of a fiftieth pie that you didn't want, maybe it's time to think about other fields. Or if you're undercompensated in a job you used to love, or overworked but feeling tethered to golden handcuffs, it's worth seeing what else is out there and whether you've actually chosen the best time-to-money conversion machine for you. I have two friends who have switched into nursing from very different career paths. One that I mentioned in chapter 2 became a nurse-midwife from corporate law. The other, Lisa, whose story we'll hear more about in chapter 11, started out as an organizer working for nonprofits, working around the clock and living with tons of roommates because it was all she could afford, and later worked as a doula. After two kids and a divorce, while she still wanted to make a difference, she also wanted to be able to provide for her family, something that her permanent-PhD-student ex wasn't going to help with, *and* have time for the kids that needed her. Nursing school put a greater financial and time squeeze on her in the short run, but in the long run, she's thrilled to have found a career where she has a set number of shifts per week, and she was recently able to become a homeowner thanks to her union-negotiated salary. Thinking about career changes has a lot in common with choosing one in the first place. You need to think about how your job enters your utility function and if there are things you need from it that you're not getting. How does it stack up on what you give—time and effort—and what you get—money and fulfillment? Which is what the modern women-in-the-workplace discussion has missed: it's not just about endlessly climbing or maximizing pay and career outcomes. A job should serve as a means to maximize your utility, not an end in itself.

The great thing about investigating other fields and jobs is that you don't actually have to leave to reap the benefits of this!

Changing jobs might be one way to make a big shift in the "giving and getting" equation, but there are also lots of ways to make smaller shifts, and applying for other jobs helps with that, too. In negotiation, there's a term known as *BATNA*, which means your "best alternative to negotiated agreement." A key way to avoid taking a bad deal is to make sure your BATNA is as good as possible. So, thinking about what you would do if it *weren't* this job can often help you find the ways to make this job workable.

I often give the advice when people are torn making a decision that ambivalence can be a strength, because it reflects that whatever happens really will be fine. You want to develop a BATNA so good that you really wouldn't mind taking it, and then go in and ask for what you need in your current situation. It could be more money, it could be stricter boundaries on time, or it could be more support. The principles of negotiation are important (and I recommend everyone read the classics *Getting to Yes*[3] and *Getting Past No*[4]): figure out what's valuable for you that's possible for your employer to provide. Maybe they can't offer extra compensation, but they can offer to pay for a training program for you. Maybe they can reassess your workload and redistribute some tasks. Maybe they can help you find an internal transfer or chart a career path that is more sustainable. Find your champions at your job, and brainstorm *with* them about how to meet your needs (win for you) and retain you within the limits of feasibility (win for them). And be your *own champion.* Be your own advocate for getting your needs met by refusing to make them invisible. This doesn't mean never compromising, but it means being willing to plainly state what you need, what you're looking for, and what you hope can change.

And if your job *can't* give you what you need in the short term, and you also aren't ready to change jobs, there are also some things that you can just *take.* Specifically: setting boundaries around how much evening and weekend work you do. I know what you're screaming at me as I say that: *But I* have *to do that work! It's not a choice!* Well, it's a choice by your employer to not have enough staff that everything that needs to get done can get done without people overextending themselves. Sometimes it's important to return the consequences of mismanagement to sender rather than killing ourselves to lift someone else's burden. And again, having a BATNA gives you the confidence that if your employer really wants to fire you, you've learned that the other option *was* better, because you can't stay in this workplace with an unsustainable amount of work. So set the boundary (after sending out those job apps), and let the chips fall where they may.

"But aren't we supposed to be *leaning in?*" you ask. My question is: *For what?* If there is a tangible goal that you're aiming to achieve with a clearly designated set of requirements where you feel your effort is going to pay off in future career advancement, compensation, *and* the opportunity for increased leisure down the line, then sure, tilting the labor–leisure scales a little more in the direction of the grindstone right now might make sense. But what about when, after that milestone, there's another one? And what if being overworked is more a structural feature of a capitalist work environment that loves to squeeze as much as possible from its workers for as little pay as possible by convincing them the brass ring is always just around the next corner?

As I said, there are certainly periods in my life where I've invested and worked harder than was sustainable over the long run. And there are definitely times when doing so is rational and utility maximizing, because those payoffs will yield rewards in the next chapter. But in *every* chapter, I want you to remember: this is your life *now*. This—right here—is your life. Not what happens when you make partner or attending or manager or superintendent. What do you need to make your life sustainable, happy, and healthy? I want you to be sleeping eight hours a night, eating three meals a day, seeing your kids or elderly family members, and going to the gym (or wherever else restores you) even when you *haven't* "made it" yet. I want the days where that's not possible to be because there's a true crunch or deadline, not just someone else's mismanagement and understaffing. (One of my favorite sayings: *We're not doing heart surgery on infants here.* Unless you are, in which case, I salute you. But if not, what exactly is the emergency? Who actually lives or dies based on this report or that deadline?)

Wherever you are in your career, sit and write down your nonnegotiables that you need to be healthy and sane. These are things that can't be put off for another chapter—they're critical components of the story at every stage. Figure out what of those you can start doing right now, without anyone's permission. Then, after developing your BATNA, ask for some of the ones you do need permission for—more money, for example. And if you find that it's not changing, start to chart your way out of there, even if it takes some short-term pain and investment.

Finally, sometimes our unhappiness in our jobs stems from our own internal dissatisfaction with our performance, even when we're getting paid decently. I hope the framework for thinking of your job a bit more transactionally can help you here, too. Because another thing that actually adds to the "getting" column in your job are the opportunities for growth and learning that you're being afforded, which, believe it or not, can only happen when you're not great at everything! A piece of career advice I give my students: when you're good at everything at your job and every work product is perfect, that's when you know you've stopped learning. And in fact, your job is probably getting a great "deal" from you—extracting maximum value without putting anything in. When instead you find things challenging and find yourself making mistakes and seeing room for improvement, that's when you are receiving *investment* from a job, because you are getting an opportunity to learn and grow and screw things up. We naturally seek out comfort and praise and shy away from criticism and feelings of not being good enough. But it's when we're not good enough that we stretch, grow, and get better. If you measure your success by how much you're learning to take your skills to the next level, the fantasy day where everything was executed flawlessly would be a failure of sorts, because it would be the day your job stopped being a challenge.

This mindset can help you reframe days—even years—when you feel like you're not on top of your game in the way you would like to be. Be gentle with yourself and think: *How lucky am I to get to be in a job where I have the opportunity to do things I don't quite know how to do! Making mistakes means I'm getting paid in experience.* You're getting the chance to learn and grow, something that benefits *you*, whereas your perfect work would mostly benefit your employer. Defining your own metrics for success can be a way to help yourself through rough times. So, you can make your metric, "How much did I learn and grow today?" not, "How well did I perform?" And as one way to help myself through challenging times, I've tried to always check in on a metric that I find particularly motivating: "Did I help someone else be successful today?" So if one of the things creating disutility at work is your own internal self-criticism, luckily, that's something you can learn to turn off.

Remember, as always, that what you are maximizing is your *own* utility function. I warn my students as they head off to investment banking or consulting jobs, planning to pivot later into public interest work or go to grad school, that it's very easy to get swept up in other people's goals, rather than your own. I share how my heart sank when I got my first not-as-good-as-hoped performance review at McKinsey and felt a moment of panic for what it meant for the partner track. And then real me snapped back with, "What am I talking about? I'm going to grad school!" When everyone around you is focused on a certain set of objectives, it is so easy to internalize their values as your own. I think this, too, is evolutionary—fitting in with the crowd and earning their approval is good for survival. But we have to reach into our minds and turn down the volume on what everyone else wants, and remain doggedly in touch with what *we* actually want. We might value leisure time more than others. We might value making a difference. We might have other responsibilities or health constraints that stop us from being able to achieve at the same level as others. We might just be interested in different things. Write down what you are trying to achieve and what your metrics of that success will be, and revisit these ideas every time the chatter starts to take over.

The next chapter will dive more into the science of women at work and how to ensure the unique skills women bring to the table are valued, by which I mean rewarded with compensation and promotions.

Chapter 7

Working Like a Girl

MY FIRST DAY at McKinsey happened to fall on the day of their annual women's summit, and so I and the other female new hires were invited to join the event. They had brought in a "gender empowerment" speaker who mostly seemed focused on addressing the mistakes women made in the workplace (I am not knocking McKinsey here—this speaker was highly in demand at the time!). She went around the room critiquing body language, urging us not to sit with our legs tucked under our bodies "like little girls", and imploring us to stop phrasing everything as a question and quit apologizing so much. As she spoke about the idea of "power dressing", she singled out another new hire, Steph, whom I had just met, but with whom I already felt an instant connection. Unlike so many of the other new hires, who were trying desperately to fit in, Steph seemed comfortable being herself, and I found her to be a breath of fresh air.

The speaker asked Steph to stand up so the whole room could inspect her. She was dressed in a white button-down and pink khakis that looked J.Crew-catalog-effortless. The speaker practically gasped at the sight. "You can't wear *pink pants*! No one will take you seriously," she admonished Steph in front of hundreds of her new colleagues. "And your hair should be pulled back, off your face!" Steph, who'd previously seemed unflappable to me, was clearly shocked and embarrassed. We sat in silence as the speaker went on to describe the fundamentals of a proper business wardrobe and how women could be treated the same as men if only we changed our behavior enough.

We all got the message that day, but it wasn't one of empowerment—it was that we couldn't bring our full selves to work. I wonder how different that experience would have been if we'd been told, like I tell my students, that being yourself at work can be your superpower. And that if people won't take you seriously for wearing pink pants, they're the problem, not you.

Wait, you're wondering, *don't women* need *to change? I thought the gender wage gap was because women do more non-promotable tasks, negotiate less, are more risk averse, and aren't competitive enough!* Research indeed underscores that women show differences in multiple traits compared to men, in a variety of settings, and we'll get to that in a moment. But *none* of the literature has demonstrated that the traits women exhibit more than men are actually *bad* from a profit or productivity perspective.

When I was an eleven-year-old feminist organizing a petition to allow girls to participate in the wrestling unit in gym class alongside the boys (instead of getting stuck with step aerobics!), I would have been furious at the suggestion that girls were any different from boys. Because naturally different felt linked to *worse*. I didn't want to be treated any differently just because I was a girl, which really meant I didn't want to be treated worse: less smart, less capable, less interesting. As an adult feminist and a scientist, I think the data points to biological gender differences *on average* that are both physical *and* psychological. Of course, these average differences don't represent individuals—each person has their own gender expression and fits somewhere on a spectrum of typicality. In all research on gender differences, we generally see overlapping distributions with different means— there are many women that rate much higher on a "male-type" trait than many men, and vice versa.

But nonetheless, our brains aren't just exposed to different hormones once we go through puberty—hormones that have been shown to affect behavior—they're also exposed to different developmental signals in the womb. The same way once-identical fetuses start to diverge into male and female physically over the course of development, so, too, scientists think we diverge neurologically.[1] These differences are linked to the sexual dimorphism that we discussed in chapter 4—that the female produces biologically costly eggs, while the male produces biologically cheap sperm. Because the female of the species invests more in the earliest part of life creation—the egg—evolution will push her toward investing in each offspring's survival as well; her reproductive success depends on those costly eggs making it into adulthood. The male, meanwhile, has the imperative to fertilize as many eggs as possible, because sperm are metabolically cheap and quick to make more of. This means competing with other males, and so he must show himself to be a good provider and protector of territory.[2] He evolves to be physically stronger, but also more competitive, aggressive, and risk-taking.[3] Again, these differences are *on average*, and people exist on a spectrum of traits—*of course* there are women who are competitive and men who are natural caregivers, and these average gender differences do not determine our destinies. And of course gendered socialization plays a big role as well. But I've come to find denying these realities more regressive than acknowledging them and trying to figure out how equality of opportunity can be achieved alongside them.

I recently had lunch with a prominent male economist who was visiting Wharton, and talk turned to kids, and then the fact that having children was difficult for women on the tenure track. I commented that I thought gender-neutral policies, however well intended, ignored the reality that women invested more in children and, I said, on average, cared more about children. He immediately took umbrage. His wife was also a highly accomplished economist. "I care just as much about our kids as my wife!" he exclaimed.

I was surprised to hear this pushback. After all, he was a development economist, and there were many papers focused on developing countries that looked at the differences in preferences between men and women when it came to investing in children. Giving cash transfers to mothers, instead of fathers, for example, was found to increase child health and nutrition, because mothers were more likely to spend that extra dollar on their children instead of themselves.[4] He *was* an involved dad, so maybe I should have been celebrating that—but part of me bristled at what felt like a denial of my reality. Letting the feistiness win, I decided to challenge this assertion.

"Sure, your kids are older, and I don't doubt that many dads over time grow an equal attachment to and invest as much in their children as mothers do. But is this true at the moment of birth?" I asked. "Why wouldn't it be?" he replied. "Well, I know many women who have had miscarriages," I said, "and who have been absolutely devastated in ways their husbands failed to understand, because these women were growing a life inside of them and attached to it biochemically in a way someone not experiencing that couldn't possibly be. Do you think men experience miscarriage the same way women do?" "Of course not," he conceded. Once he acknowledged that there were probably some differences at that stage, I continued to push him—why would this change at the moment of birth, when we know women's bodies are flooded with oxytocin to create mother–child bonding and establish breastfeeding?[5] For many of us—as we obsessively research organic baby food, lovingly detangle and braid hair, throw our arms around a weeping child and kiss cheeks hot with tears—we know that it doesn't. And it's painful to pretend otherwise and force ourselves to ignore the obvious differences in front of us, because otherwise we'll be told our struggles in juggling it all are our own fault for not wanting it enough.

Of course, everyone's relationship to motherhood is equally legitimate, including wanting no part of it, ever. What I want to consider is that there is an alternate reality from the one we so often hear from Western feminism that relies on minimizing or denying gender differences: you deserve to be fully actualized, happy, and financially secure *even if* you are not the same as a man. And the institutions that won't let you show up the way you want as a mom and woman are the problem, not you. Different does *not* mean worse. Because who says men are so great, anyway? Let's take a look at the science.

What Does the Evidence Say?

One classic example of how men's and women's traits may differ in ways that impact the workplace is that women tend to be less competitive than men. I have no trouble believing this, given the documented effects of testosterone, but for a long time, there was no actual evidence linking being male to increased competition in professional settings. Two experimental economists, Muriel Niederle and Lise Vesterlund, changed this.

Niederle and Vesterlund ran an experiment in which they asked men and women to choose how they wanted to be paid for completing a task in the lab (in economics, a room with computers where people—often undergrads—do experiments for pay). For adding up a series of two-digit numbers, participants could be paid via a piece rate (a set sum for each problem they did), or a winner-takes-all competition. Naturally, if you're a high performer, the potential reward from the tournament-style payment is higher. But if you don't think of yourself as a top performer, you're likely to be better off getting paid for each problem you get right. Men and women are equally good at these simple math problems, and thus face the same trade-offs between the compensation schemes. But men are drastically more likely to select the competitive payment scheme than are women.[6] This is true even for women who are in the top group of performance, meaning they are likely to win the competition, and thus they lose out on earnings by forgoing the tournament.

A male colleague mused to me that maybe these results mean it's "efficient" for there to be fewer women in competitive industries like finance. But here's the important piece too many people are missing: this canonical paper is titled "Do Women Shy

Away from Competition? Do Men Compete Too Much?" and the authors have told me people always forget about that second part of their results. They find that the majority of men in the *bottom* performance group *also* choose the competition scheme, even when they would make way more money by simply getting paid the piece rate. In fact, among the lowest-performing men, who are certain to lose, *60 percent choose the tournament.* I might want to give the women who were the highest performers but chose the piece rate a little pep talk, sure. But if I'm a manager, they're not the people I need to be concerned about. I'm much more worried about the men who, having completely flubbed the task, still thought, *I got this.*

Why don't we spend as much time speculating that male over-competitiveness might be destroying corporate value as we do asking women to change and be more cutthroat? I think about the quote by Christine Lagarde that if it was "Lehman Sisters instead of Lehman Brothers," perhaps there wouldn't have been so much over-indexing on high-risk mortgage securities, and the financial crisis wouldn't have been as bad.[7]

My own research shows a similar phenomenon in another area where women are often taken to task for not performing as well as men: negotiation. I had heard the refrain that women's poor negotiation skills were a key part of the gender wage gap so often that I assumed there must be some evidence for it. However, when I looked at the literature, the empirical research supporting this idea was surprisingly thin. So I ran my own experiment with my grad student Jennie Huang.[8]

We paid study participants to come to our lab and participate in a scenario where they negotiated, with a random partner, over a twenty-dollar reward. The catch was that there were only two possible splits: fifteen dollars for one person and five for the other, or vice versa. If a pair couldn't agree on one of those two unequal divisions, they would both get zero. Because one's negotiating partner was random, men and women could each be paired with the same gender, or opposite.

Each pair negotiated through computer interface, and then individually entered their share of the split. Naturally, a variety of fierce and creative bargaining ensued, from ultimatums to guilt trips. In the end, we found that men and women, on average, did equally well when they negotiated against one another, poking a hole in the theory that men were naturally more skilled negotiators. But overall, women received more money on average. Why? While women also performed just fine negotiating against other women, when men faced other men, they were substantially more likely to fail to reach an agreement at all, leaving them with a payoff of zero. How much more likely? Two hundred and fifty percent!

This effect was specifically driven by men who knew they were negotiating against other men—we randomly assigned whether gender was revealed to the other player or not. A man *knowing* he was bargaining with another man seemed to trigger some unproductive . . . stick measuring. Something as basic as saying "hi" and trying to establish rapport with the other player was linked to higher payoffs, but we found men were less inclined to take this kind of friendly approach against other men. Instead, they were more likely to offer ultimatums, such as: "I'm taking the fifteen dollars, so if you don't press five dollars for yourself, you'll get nothing, and I'm not going to talk about it anymore." Unfortunately, such ultimatums to another man were often met by one right back in return—"No, *I'm* taking the fifteen dollars and not talking about it anymore!"—and subsequently mismatching. All those zero-dollar payoffs added up and meant male–male pairs earned 20 percent less than any other pair type. As long as there was a woman at the negotiation table, cooler heads seemed to prevail, and some kind of an agreement was reached in almost all cases.

Our experiment showed that women not only weren't *worse* at negotiation than men but also that they were *better* at making sure some kind of mutually beneficial deal was struck, rather than being so rigid that no one ended up with anything. In a professional setting, the cost of such negotiation breakdowns could be enormous—imagine, for example, ending a long-term contract or partnership—and possibly much larger than a failure to get slightly better terms in an agreement. But despite this evidence, I've never once heard of corporate seminars for men instructing them on how to negotiate more like women.

In situations where women do accept less at the negotiating table, the possibility remains that they're tiptoeing around other people's expectations of them. Researcher Christine Exley, with coauthors, has shown that although women do not actually show more generosity or "social preferences" (preferences toward giving to others or equal outcomes) than men, people consistently *believe* they will.[9] Perhaps for this reason, when it comes to situations where women know their outcome depends not just on their own preferences but on what others expect of them, we see women act differently. In the fifteen-dollar–five-dollar negotiation game I described, if we *don't* let subjects talk to each other first, and they just have to choose blindly whether to claim fifteen dollars for themselves or five dollars, hoping to match their partner's choice, we find that when players know the other's gender, women choose the five dollars more often against men, who choose the fifteen dollars more when playing women, leaving women with lower average payoffs. But without this gender information, there's no such difference. Players know if they don't choose the same split as their partner, they'll get nothing. So men and women are not just playing each other, they're playing each other's expectations.

Because of this, giving women the advice to "act more like men" is not helpful. Christine Exley teamed up with her mentors Muriel Niederle and Lise Vesterlund to investigate women's negotiation skills and published the results in a paper called "Knowing When to Ask."[10] They performed an experiment where participants completed a task, were offered payment by another participant, and then could choose to negotiate their pay. What the researchers found was that when women could choose whether to negotiate, they used the tool of negotiation to increase their profit—opting in to negotiation when they thought it would be profitable, and forgoing it when they thought it wouldn't be. But when women were forced to negotiate in all cases, they found women's payoffs drastically reduced. There were no cases where these forced negotiations increased payoffs the women in the "choice" setting had missed—positive negotiation outcomes occurred at exactly the same rate. Instead, all the forced negotiation did was increase the number of times the woman ended the negotiation with a lower payout than the wage she had initially been offered.

All this research offers evidence that women aren't any less skilled at negotiating than men, and when they choose not to negotiate, it might be a function of skillfully navigating difficult situations where they know they may not be treated equally. In fact, research by Andreas Leibbrandt and John List shows that when women are explicitly told that a salary is negotiable, they negotiate just as much as men.[11] What holds women back from negotiating more proactively is lacking assurance they won't be penalized for negotiating, not the skill *or* the will. So let's get out of the mindset of telling women they need to change the way they approach work, and start talking about the unique value women bring to the table, how to make sure they're recognized for it, and what systemically needs to change for us to stop preaching that "nice girls don't get the corner office," and instead start building a culture where they do.

How to Work Like a Girl and Get Paid for It

Have you ever been in a meeting where someone needs to take notes, and everyone turns to look at the youngest woman in the room (or the only woman)? Many women can relate to the experience of being asked to take on "office housework"— taking notes, organizing team outings, ordering office supplies, liaising with the caterer.

Lise Vesterlund and coauthors have shown, perhaps unsurprisingly, that women tend to do more of this type of work, which they call "non-promotable tasks", since they're much less likely to appear on your performance review than finishing a big project, pushing code, publishing a paper, or client-facing work. Using another lab game, where people earn real money based on their decisions, they found that women both volunteered to do non-promotable tasks more often and were nominated more to do them in mixed-gender teams.[12] Interestingly, when they compared teams composed of a single gender, they found that the rates of men and women doing the non-promotable tasks were the same. In other words, when there were no women around to take notes, the men found a (metaphorical) pen. One solution to this, elucidated by Lise, Linda Babcock, Brenda Peyser, and Laurie Weingart, in the book *The No Club*, from their own experience being accomplished women in male-dominated fields, is that women need to, well, say no.[13] Opt out, redirect, stay seated, keep your hands folded when asked if anyone wants to take notes. They movingly document how each one of them became overwhelmed by tasks, from planning to mentoring to editing, while their male colleagues worked on their own career goals. They formed a club, meeting over dinner and cheap wine, to review the commitments that each was being asked to take on, and learn to say no to more of them. I highly recommend this book to anyone feeling overwhelmed with workplace tasks and trying to figure out how to create a more equitable distribution.

My joke now that I have tenure but am still incredibly busy and overwhelmed is "my job isn't the issue, it's just my own poor decision-making." What I want us all to consider is that often *some* of the time and effort of our work is a *choice*, and one not really driven by monetary returns. (Emphasis on *some*! Of course there are plenty of incentives to overwork that we're responding to.) It's different to be asked to pick up an additional shift with clear hourly compensation, and say yes because the money is worth the loss of leisure time. It's another thing entirely to be asked to serve on a committee, or plan a party, or do this one prestigious thing, or help, help, help for the thousandth time. These commitments exist outside of work, too. My lovely neighbor, my age with two young kids and an academic job, who always looks a little stressed out, told me she had been asked to serve on the board of the kids' day care. *Do you want to do that?* I asked. *Will you enjoy it? Will it make your life better?* These are the questions we need to answer when being asked to take on any extra labor. Let your utility function be your guide. How exactly does saying yes to this task increase my utility? If you're worried about guilt, or disappointing someone, or chasing prestige or recognition, take a moment to remind yourself that some of these things are evolutionary instincts to want to please the group but not actually about where our deeper values lie. I say all of this from the glass house of running a nonprofit in my "free time" and seeing the pop-ups from emails RSVPing to the lunch I organized to mentor PhD students as I type.

But in my and possibly your defense, I want to note, as the authors of *The No Club* do, that so often the non-promotable tasks are not *unimportant*. In fact, in the original experiment demonstrating the phenomenon, the task in question was to push a button that meant the whole team got $2, while the person who pressed it would receive only $1.25. Tasks like mentoring and investing in the success of others and the overall office community fall into this bucket of non-promotable tasks, and I don't think I want to work someplace where no one does them. So one calculation I want you to make with your utility function is whether something truly fills your cup enough because you inherently value doing it that it's worth the time and stress of having one more task. What are the things that *decrease* your "disutility of labor" by making your job more fun and fulfilling? I would then explicitly categorize this as volunteer work, and set some boundaries with yourself about how much of that kind of work you can take on. You also have to remind yourself what you're saying no to when you say yes to taking on one more thing: are you saying no to other uses of your time that could help you make *promotable* career investments? If we classify the task as volunteer work, are you saying no to other kinds of volunteer work you might find more fulfilling? Are you saying no to being able to feel on top of your never-ending to-do list and quelling your anxiety and burnout?

And finally, if it's work-related, I want you to ask if there's any way to *make this task promotable*. How can you ensure you're being given credit for it in a way that actually helps you meet your career goals? This could mean saying to your boss, "I'd love to take this on, but I'd also really hoped to invest in some professional development around *x* and *z* areas—do you think in exchange for serving on this committee, I could get access to some professional development funds to take on this training?" Or, "I'm super excited to take this project on, but how can we make sure it's recognized on my performance review, since it might take time away from client-facing work?"

It also means documenting what you do and singing your own praises when it comes time to write a self-assessment on an annual review. "I contributed to the success of others by investing *x* hours per week in mentoring, speaking on *y* panels to promote our company's commitment to diversity, and collaboratively planning *z* key events." Be specific about not just how much time went in but what outcomes resulted and how your work increased team success or served the organization's overall goals. Because, after all, if no one thinks these tasks contribute value, *you shouldn't be asked to do them.*

And that's the thing—the problem is not with women saying yes too often; the problem is with the institutions that rely on women to do the very necessary work of "pushing the button" for everyone to receive the higher payout. If you're a manager or have any influence in your institution, the most beneficial change to make is not discouraging women from taking on non-promotable tasks—it's guaranteeing they receive recognition for these tasks, and redistributing them so men take on some of them, too. One very easy way to ensure this recognition is to add a question to employee performance reviews, such as, "How did you contribute to the success of others or to the overall team in a way that might not be immediately reflected in your individual performance?"

Employers asking questions about collective success versus only individual accomplishments is also important because research shows that women self-promote less often than men. Christine Exley and my frequent collaborator and Wharton colleague Judd Kessler have found that, when women are performing at the same level as their male colleagues, they are less likely to rate their performance as very good or excellent or describe it as strongly in qualitative terms.[14] This difference doesn't have to be innate—you can imagine women being conditioned since birth that overconfidence was akin to bragging and that they don't want to be the "tallest poppy" or brightest star—a lifetime of reinforced self-doubt, as Claire Shipman and Katty Kay write about so memorably in *The Confidence Code*.[15] But in a world where men are constantly exaggerating their qualifications and accomplishments, you can easily imagine this costing women jobs and promotions. Again, I am not suggesting we should aim to be more like men. Instead, I implore managers to change systems so that they rely less on subjective self-assessments of awesomeness and more on documented evidence of impact, individually and for the team. And to women, I would say if you aren't used to singing your praises, start objectively documenting your capabilities and outcomes relative to others in your position. You're not bragging, you're benchmarking! When you do this, you'll probably realize that some of the bravado of your male teammates is just that— posturing designed to cover up the same underlying insecurity we all face. As Christine remembers a trailblazing female academic telling her, "I didn't become more confident in myself over time. I just became less confident in others."

This is another way to get paid—do not self-select out of high-paying fields because you don't *feel* like you're doing well. If we recognize that, statistically speaking, women are less likely to rate their performance as highly as men are, you can't take seriously the chatter of your classmates or colleagues making you feel inferior. Moreover, if we understand the science of discrimination, we can reasonably assume that women who *do* make it into a coveted position are not only as talented as their male colleagues, they may be even more qualified. Research shows that women-authored scientific articles published in prestigious journals are cited more frequently than those of their male peers.[16] The articles written by women had to be *better* to clear the bar, and this shows later in their broader impact through citations. And yet too often, women opt out of potentially lucrative fields and roles. Research shows women who get a negative grade in a male-dominated STEM major are more likely to switch out of that major than men are.[17] But financially speaking, you are likely to be more successful as a B student in STEM than an A+ student in English.[18] Trying to be "the best" might be winning you a smaller prize. Data from the Current Population Survey confirms this—the median bachelor's degree holder working in STEM, the person right at the middle of the distribution, earns more than 75 percent of the bachelor's degree holders working outside of STEM.[19] This doesn't mean you have to go into STEM if it doesn't interest you—my message is broader: There will be plenty of gatekeepers who might tell you no along the way; don't be one of them to yourself!

As I've said before, not all the traits described in this chapter apply to all women. The differences between men and women are averages, and they are giant overlapping distributions. I think of these workplace traits as part of your gender expression—the same way I express my gender by wearing the occasional dress, and my wife favors jeans and baseball hats. But these traits, wherever you lie on the gender spectrum, are part of who you are, and there's *nothing wrong with that.* So your challenge is to identify your unique traits and figure out how to make them your workplace superpowers. You aren't a weak negotiator—you're someone who looks for win-win solutions. You aren't overly timid and cautious—you're someone who evaluates situations carefully and takes risk exposure seriously. There is a difference between these traits and *skills*. So, yes, there *are* tips I give my students. Say "thank you" when you want to say, "I'm sorry." So, "Thank you so much for waiting!" instead of apologizing for being late; "Thank you for helping" instead of apologizing for a problem beyond your control. Learn to take up space—look at men who ask questions in class, I tell them, and see how comfortable they are taking up other people's time to get their own needs met. We can all learn to sharpen our negotiation skills by reading up on some tips and tricks. We can improve our finance skills. We can fine-tune our communication skills. By all means, invest in your workplace skills. But I want you to separate learning new workplace skills from a need to change who you are, how you express yourself, and the way you navigate a very unfair world.

The research does not support that women's workplace differences cost companies money. So, to the extent that they contribute to the gender wage gap, it's only insofar as institutions are failing to recognize the contribution of these unique traits. If women self-promote less, then firms should work to reduce the impact of self-promotion on hiring decisions, because what matters is actual performance, not how much one toots their own horn. If you're senior, reflect on how to ensure women's contributions get recognized, especially if they're to "public goods" that make the whole team stronger but don't naturally show up on performance reviews. Think about how to change situations so that you make explicit when negotiation is invited and when it isn't, so women will know they'll be treated fairly for negotiating. And figure out how to let women lead in areas where they've been shown to perform better, such as negotiations when failure to reach an agreement is much costlier than haggling over every cent, or situations where there's more downside to overconfidence and competitiveness than a more measured approach. The unique traits that women bring into the workplace create tremendous value, and we need to focus on highlighting them and celebrating them, not trying to change women.

Rethinking Flexibility

Employers often jump to "flexibility" as a catchall fix for women. The assumption is that female workers, who may have many demands on their time outside of work, would prefer a schedule that allows them more porous boundaries. But flexibility isn't always the salve employers believe it to be. When economists Alexandre Mas and Amanda Pallais studied the effectiveness of promised "flexibility", they found that women were less enticed by this "benefit" than employers assumed.[20]

In the study, women were offered different types of jobs, with a range of different possible salaries for jobs with different features. These features included work from home, schedule flexibility, and part-time work. The participants were also asked to consider jobs where the schedule would be set at the manager's discretion. By comparing which job was chosen at different salary offers, the researchers could calculate how much participants were willing to "pay", in terms of hourly wages forgone, for different schedules. The researchers found, to their surprise, that while women were willing to give up more pay than men to be able to work from home, they were not willing to take less for a "flexible work schedule." In fact, the willingness to pay for a flexible schedule was surprisingly low—women were willing to give up just 60 cents an hour. On the other hand, women were willing to pay substantially more than men to avoid the "employer discretion" schedules, where instead of being given hours in advance, the schedule could be set on short notice by the manager. Women were on average willing to give up $4.30 an hour to avoid these schedules, double what men were willing to give up. And for women with kids under four, the amount they were willing to forego was even higher.

I think the study's authors had expected to find a larger preference for "flexibility", and especially a larger gender effect. But importantly, the comparison was a standard Monday–Friday, nine-to-five job. For many women, that was exactly what they were looking for. It's not the nine-to-five that's impossible, it's the unscheduled evening and weekend time when childcare isn't available. The data told a core truth: *Women don't want "flexibility", they want boundaries.* If I ever take up graffiti as a hobby, that's what I'll spray-paint on corporate offices.

If women need so much flexibility, why is the nursing workforce 86 percent women, when shifts are typically worked on a rigid schedule? Nursing works for women because it is predictable and time-bound. Once you clock out from your shift, you know you can be 100 percent there for your family. Having the ability to actually be off the clock after working hours is not asking for flexibility; it's asking for simple limits. A company I advised lamented that they couldn't hire female workers for logistics jobs, due to the need for overnight work. I pushed back: approximately 30 percent of nursing shifts are overnight, and again, women thrive in this field. The key is the reliability being offered.

How can you put this into practice as an employee, rather than someone who has power to change the system? When you're job searching, you're also shopping for the things you want in a role and employer. Look for opportunities where there are clear boundaries on working hours. Where people can predict their evening and weekend work, and, if you have kids, "face time"— in-person work—is limited to childcare hours. These things will help ensure that you're not penalized for wanting limits on the workplace in line with its role in contributing to your utility function: a part of the equation, but far from the entire thing.

And what about those high-powered, "greedy" jobs Claudia Goldin wrote about? Those employers that view individual workers as irreplaceable, loading up each person with seventy- or eighty-hour workweeks, instead of the shorter hours and more leisure that we saw in previous generations? Well, I think we can reimagine these, too (and you should look for firms on the forefront of that). First, let's talk about the root cause of this workplace creep. Goldin has documented that we see these structures more often in industries where there's client-facing work, larger teams, more interaction, more hierarchy—lots of factors that make a single worker's time more valuable than the next person you could have take over.[21]

But she's also written about the transformation of one field, which was known for its long, demanding working hours—until more women entered it.[22] Obstetricians were once expected to be on call at all times, including weekends, because babies rarely arrive on schedule, and patients wanted to have the doctor who had been with them on the first eight months of the journey by their side on the big day. But as female OBs started to become more common in the '80s and '90s—and patients chose practices with female doctors—this standard changed. Practices developed a "care team" approach, with multiple doctors engaged in each patient's prenatal care and with rotating shifts for deliveries. This allowed them to have regular hours, sleep, and time with their families. Today, the *majority* of OBs are women (compared to 7 percent in 1970).[23] If you're a decision-maker for your employer, I encourage you to consider what practical changes you can make that allow for these kinds of boundaries. The key mantra is that investments in making your working hours compatible with the demands of life outside of work are investments in retaining *talent*. And in the modern economy, that applies to male and female talent, since few workers have the benefit of a spouse solely focused on home production.

As Silicon Valley salaries have ballooned, we've actually seen tech firms compete on benefits packages like vacation, shorter hours, and more family time, something valued by male and female employees. While tech has fewer women in it, there's actually a *smaller* gender wage gap. Goldin speculates that this is because tech has more individual contributions and less team- or client-based work, and so they're screening for "solo geniuses", not the people most willing to burn the midnight oil. Discrimination and the minority trap might be keeping women out, but once they're in the door, the model of individual contributions doesn't lead to as much stratification in career progress by caregiving responsibilities. When you think about entering an industry, ask yourself how many of those factors of client-facing work, interaction, large teams, and hierarchy there are that tend to produce "irreplaceability" and in turn worse work-life balance, compared to industries with more modular and individual work. If you want kids, ask about opportunities to slow down without getting sidelined.

In whatever industry you're in, you can *set your own boundaries*, as we've discussed. No one is going to tell you to take a break for dinner, or not to answer your phone during certain hours. Boundaries are things you set and hold yourself. Again, this doesn't mean that you shouldn't invest during certain periods. But it does mean that if the choice is leaving this high-paying industry versus finding a way to make it work for you, I'd much rather you stay collecting the paychecks but let your team know that 6:00–8:00 p.m. on weekdays is do-not-disturb time. Find the ways to lean in that are lower cost to you, but higher impact to the team and higher visibility to your manager.

Just as the field of OB-GYN transformed, so, too, can other industries decide to reshape their destinies. Law firms could choose to always have two associates know a case file inside and out, so no one needs to be on call all the time, just as nurses take shifts. Client-facing businesses can give each client two key points of contact, and alternate "on-call" hours, like obstetricians. Managers can figure out ways to give workers what they want: boundaries, not necessarily flexibility. This means making long work hours something more predictable that a babysitter can be scheduled around, instead of letting everything constantly elevate to the level of emergency. If employers push back that this costs them more, they should remember that it also costs them to lose out on talent to industries who have these practices in place. Remember, in the Mas and Pallais study, workers were willing to take less money for the job with *boundaries.* So putting good practices in place can also save money.

Of course, making changes to institutions can be a hard pill for workplaces to swallow. I often think of a study showing that women were less likely to be interested in a computer science course when the classroom was decorated in *Star Wars* posters.[24] People will tell you that they can't possibly make changes to workplace culture or performance reviews or salary negotiations—that it's just the way this business is. But I think so many of the things we *think* are necessary in our workplaces are more like those *Star Wars* posters—remnants from a time when men dominated, functionally irrelevant to the work to be done, and tacky to boot. I tell my class, to many giggles, since it's not a time they remember, that investment bankers used to take meetings in strip clubs.[25] When sexual harassment and gender discrimination lawsuits started to pile up, they were told they had to change their ways, and proceeded to kick and scream. *If we can't go to the strip club, how will we entertain clients? How will we close deals?* I imagine them whining. But of course, today no one holds meetings in strip clubs, and guess what? Deals still get closed. The Dow Jones marches onward and upward. Employers should ask which parts of their "hard-charging," "take-no-prisoners," "work hard, play hard" cultures are truly crucial to the work they do, and which are *Star Wars* posters that it's long past time to take down.

Chapter 8

Investing in a Partner

RECENTLY, A FRIEND visiting from Zambia, who I'd first met fifteen years ago doing research as a graduate student, was sitting at my kitchen table. She had shown me around and helped me find housing when I'd first arrived in Zambia knowing no one, and we'd remained close friends since. It was our first time seeing each other in person since the pandemic, which meant we had a lot of life changes to catch each other up on. We'd both been through divorces since last we'd met, and we settled in for some dating gossip while our kids entertained each other.

She had been dating someone for almost a year. He was charming, smart, had a good job. But he never wanted to meet her kids. At first, that was okay—she was also cautious about introducing someone to her kids too early. But as the relationship grew more serious, his reluctance to meet her children became a sticking point. He said all the right things about their future, but still dropped her off outside at the end of each date while she went in to relieve the sitter. He wanted to take her on a vacation, saying he would pay for everything (he made substantially more money than she did). She asked about including the kids. He looked like he had tasted spoiled food and then said she could pay for their flight and hotel if she "insisted on bringing them." It was the final straw, but now she couldn't believe it had taken her so long. "I'm a mother," she said, shaking her head in disbelief. "I need someone who is going to love my children and understand they're a priority in my life. What was I thinking?"

Well, the truth is that when it comes to romance, often we're *not* thinking. Love is what economists call a "hot state"—one where rational thought gives way to other impulses. We've talked about the evolutionary impulses and the hormonal pathways that stem from them—oxytocin, dopamine, endorphins. But now let's talk about the *economics* of the situation. The problem is that "hot-state you" doesn't know what "cold-state you" wants. Economists actually call this an *empathy gap* because you literally don't understand what the other you—the one outside this present moment—thinks and feels.[1] But often, our wants during the hot-state moment don't actually align with our overall utility function. For example, if someone craves an addictive substance, they will marshal all their resources to relieve the aversive feelings associated with withdrawal, even if it means plunging themselves into personal or financial ruin. Love activates similar pathways as addiction: flooding our brains with feel-good chemicals, that then give way to feelings of withdrawal when the person we attach to is absent—urging us to rush back into their presence.[2]

Which is why it's so important to spend as much time with your rational self, and what *she* wants, as possible before letting the heady feelings of love take over. This chapter is going to outline some ways to stay in touch with the constant, centered version of you that defines your overall life utility, rather than those in-the-moment sparkles.

Trust me that I know that "the heart wants what it wants." But having heart (or, ahem, pants) feelings for someone is what economists call a *necessary but not sufficient condition*. As in— it's necessary for a relationship to be successful. But it isn't enough. There are multiple people out there who you can feel attraction to and love for. Your feelings are one data point, but they aren't the *only* one.

I want you to go into the process of choosing a significant other armed not just with your innate sense of who you're attracted to and who is lovable but also the savviness to think about who is going to make a good *partner* in the enterprise of running a household and the other things you need to weather. If you're in a relationship right now, or if you're trying to decide if they're "the one", or if you're just trying to figure out what you're looking for: it's not too late. If you were choosing a business partner, you would want to know what skills and talents they brought to the table that complemented your own. And you would want those skills and talents to be relevant to the industry you were going into together. Here, that industry is building and sustaining a home, creating an enjoyable life, taking care of your physical needs, nurturing and providing for children (if you so desire), and securing your financial future so you can retire (and enjoy all that love!). I encourage you to evaluate potential partners based on what they bring to the table in that domain—their demonstrated capacity to excel in the joint enterprise you are undertaking.

You Have Options

No matter where you are on this path right now, I want you to remember that you can—thankfully—make choices that go beyond the traditional scripts that society has written for you. You can choose partnership without marriage. You can choose to be single and child-free or choose to be a single parent. You can explore same-sex relationships (hey, Kinsey says we're on a spectrum)! You can choose a nontraditional relationship. What you do not have to do is settle for a relationship that does not give you what you want or need.

Because love is such an overwhelming force, I think it's critically important to *slow down* in the beginning and give yourself time and space for the conversations I'll outline below, and to truly think through your deeper needs and wants before you get too far down a path where it feels impossible to unwind a relationship. Remember: love-colored glasses filter your feelings, which can in turn influence your decisions. Absolutely relish and enjoy those heady falling-in-love days. But also remember: love is the epsilon. The sizzle of early attraction will not be the only thing that affects your long-term utility. So while I hope you find a relationship that has that magic, ultimately your utility will also be impacted by whether that future partner knows how to do laundry and find their way around wayfair.com.

If you want to have children, then just as important as easing slowly into a relationship is the ability to move on from it if things aren't lining up. After all, time is much costlier to women due to the reproductive constraints we discussed in chapter 4. Time spent with the wrong person is, according to my research, literally money in terms of potential future matches. I'm not suggesting that cutting ties with the wrong partner is easy; breaking up can be insanely painful. As we discussed, the chemical pull of love activates addiction pathways in your brain that make you want to run back to that person to replace negative feelings with a flood of positive chemicals. Even if you know a relationship is not what you want long term, it can feel heartbreaking—devastating—to walk away. I've been there.

Post-separation, I ended up in a turbulent relationship with a woman I'd started dating when I was looking for uncomplicated fun. But we quickly morphed into a too-serious-too-quick relationship that was constantly up and down, and ignored some underlying deep incompatibilities. Getting ready to break up for a third time, I chatted with a friend who I admire for her uncanny ability to laser focus on her own needs. (We were both lesbian moms back on the dating market, and while I would fret for hours about how to politely turn down someone I didn't feel a connection with, she would cancel a date ten minutes beforehand because she didn't feel like getting dressed. There's probably a middle ground, but her approach was a marvel to me.) "I feel trapped," I told her in tears. "But, Corinne, you *aren't* trapped," she responded vehemently. "You don't have kids together. You don't share a house. You are not responsible for her mental state. You can leave." Nonsensically, in the throes of heartbreak, I replied, "I feel *emotionally* trapped." And I did. I felt like I would never again feel normal without this ex-girlfriend in my life. Like I would always feel she was part of the air I needed to breathe. It was a strange feeling to have, since I had recently left a marriage after a fifteen-year relationship. But as most people know, feelings are most intense at the beginning, and so this was *different*. It was a shocking introduction to the depths of my own irrationality. Flipping through my journal, I'd see how one day I could clearly document the reasons it wasn't going to work, how she was absolutely not the right person for me to have a life with or try to raise kids with, and yet another day be caught up in *feelings* (and the chemicals that accompany them) that made those things seem completely irrelevant. Yet more often than not, I woke up in the morning with a pounding anxiety in my chest at the thought of our future, my mind racing through reasons to stay or go.

So please, please take a lesson from my hard-won life experience and the science of behavioral economics: if you're finding yourself drafting pro and con lists about whether this relationship is a good fit, you probably already know the answer. Take time to journal and write down the factual truths about what you want versus what this person offers when you're not under the influence of their chemical pull. Do the work to bridge the "empathy gap" between hot-state you, who too often gets to sit in the driver's seat, and cold-state you, who will be left picking up the pieces or paying for the years spent with the wrong person.

A young woman who listened to me present my paper on housework sharing at a conference asked me if I thought the domestic labor distribution with her fiancé would improve over time. "If he's not doing his fair share now, will he start to step up when we're married?" she asked, swallowing tears. They were both PhD students, with similar workloads and schedules, and so she didn't understand why she was expected to pick up after him. "What did you do before me?" she recalled asking him. "Didn't you do it yourself?"

I didn't know what her experience would be, but I told her what the data says, which is that differences in disproportionate housework share typically don't improve over time, and in fact as couples marry and start having children, the disparity tends to widen. Time-use surveys show that throughout their life cycle, on average, women spend more time on childcare and housework and spend less time on professional work and leisure than men do. The graph below plots the difference between women's and men's minutes per day on these four activities at different ages. The activities above the line are where this difference is positive—women do more— and those below are where the difference is negative—women do less. The differentials are greatest in women's midthirties, when they're likely to have young kids at home (again, this is an average—move this peak forward or backward depending on the timing of kids or other caregiving responsibilities). I call that middle area on the graph "peak hating-your-husband time." It's the time of life when inequality within your relationship is often at its highest.

Gender Gap in Time Use over the Life Cycle

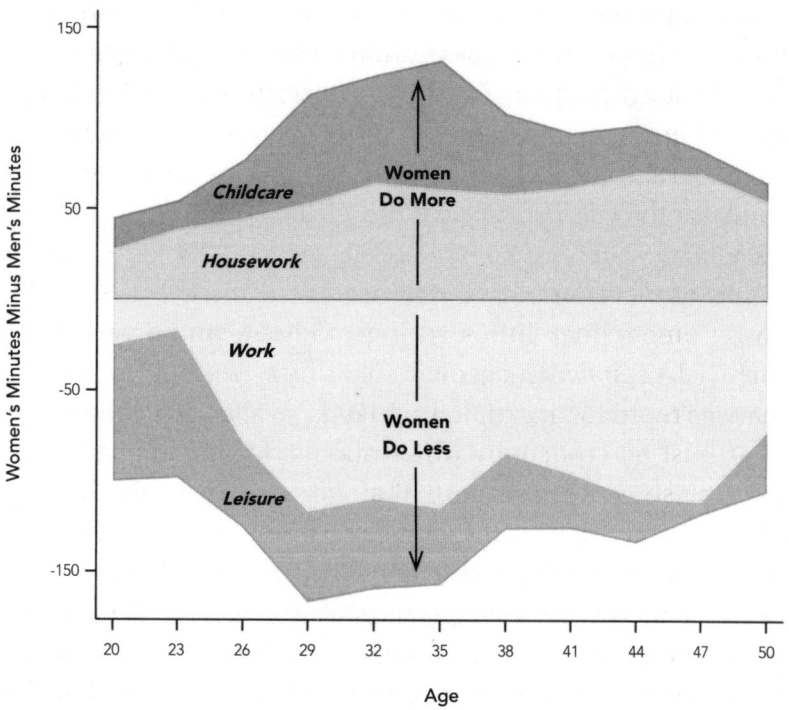

Source: American Time Use Survey (2018–2022, excluding 2020)[3]

The numbers don't lie; it's not enough to hope things will be different for you and your partner. You have to *make* them different. If you don't think you have your partner's support in achieving a different outcome, it might be time to renegotiate the terms of the deal, whatever that looks like for you.

At the same time, so many of the young women I meet worry about what will happen if they don't find their forever partner by a certain age. That's the reality of the fertility constraint; it places enormous pressures on women and sometimes forces choices that may not be in our long-term best interest. If you want to have children, it can feel like there's a ticking clock on every decision you make, from relationship to career. But as I often advise my students, having a partner or two people in the house is not a magic formula for ensuring economic success, a fair distribution of tasks, or even raising thriving children— *who* that partner is and how they shoulder the load with you are the most important considerations. Just like in career negotiations, I suggest these young women think about their BATNA (best alternative to negotiated agreement): to make their single lives as rich and fulfilling as possible, and think about what supports they'd need to have the life or even family they want *without* a partner.

One of those supports might be egg freezing. Just like tucking away some money into a savings account can be part of your financial capital management plan, egg freezing is a way to manage reproductive capital, and it helps to alleviate the squeeze of at least one constraint. Interestingly, while the image of egg freezing sometimes suggests that women make this choice out of career ambition, anthropologist Marcia Inhorn, who studies this aspect of fertility, has found that the motivation for women to freeze their eggs often has more to do with the status of their relationships than with a strategic investment in their careers.[4] The majority of the women she studied reported that they froze their eggs because they had been through breakups, were dating someone they weren't sure about, or hadn't found anyone suitable for the long term. I think it's likely a combination of both career and relationship concerns—that marriage and family have moved later in our life cycles as career investments have grown longer, stretching out periods of singlehood and dating, and then leaving us less time to pick up the pieces if things don't end up working out in a relationship we'd been hoping would last.

I'm not in favor of egg freezing as a *societal* solution to the ways we make it difficult to co-process career and family. I don't want to suggest that women endlessly put their lives on hold, subjecting themselves to more invasive medical procedures so they can work eighty hours a week, long into their thirties. What I am in favor of is giving yourself a bit of breathing room— if you have insurance coverage for it or can afford it—so that you don't compromise or commit to a sub-optimal relationship simply because you feel you're running out of time. Because choosing a life partner is not something you want to do under pressure. It is something you want to do with great care, intention—and some practical vetting.

Interviewing for the Position

Wearing my economist's hat, I often think about dating as a job interview. The tricky thing is, the "job description" for the role you're trying to fill is going to evolve over time. So even in those heady early days when all you want to do is talk about your favorite bands and movies, or moral philosophy, or whatever your jam is, I urge women to also ask tactical questions like, "Who does your laundry?" After all, when interviewing someone for a job, you wouldn't just ask about their opinions—you would ask about their experience, preparation, and demonstrated track record! We want to know: *When you were growing up, what chores did you do around the house? What about now?*

Remember that your potential partner, even if an avowed feminist, is subject to the same biases we all are. "Of course women can do everything men can do!" is an easy thing to say, but will they be willing to make sacrifices when push comes to shove to make that true? As much as many men may believe in gender equality, gender roles are a *hell* of a drug. As bell hooks writes, "I still think it's important for people to have a sharp, ongoing critique of marriage in patriarchal society—because once you marry within a society that remains patriarchal, no matter how alternative you want to be within your unit, there is still a culture outside you that will impose many, many values on you whether you want them to or not."[5]

For this reason, you want to spend some time living mentally in the hypothetical future, not just as yourself—since you know maximizing over the life cycle is one of the major themes of this book—but also with your partner. Sit down with some pizza and cold beverages and ask each other how you see yourselves "growing up" over time. What does life look like in ten years? Twenty? If you're still in the phase of bare-bones IKEA furniture, it might be worth asking: *How do you imagine your future home looking?*

There are two types of red flags to spot here: 1) men who have never thought about what they want their home to look like and are comfortable living in a generic white box (which is only a red flag if you don't want to live in a generic white box), and 2) men who *do* envision decorated walls, beautiful furniture, and a lush garden, but just imagine that it's going to somehow magically happen. So often, the fights I see over home chores aren't about the male partner thinking the female partner should do them; it's about the male partner not even realizing that it's a task that needs to be done. As in . . . tubs need to be washed out after use? The fridge needs to get organized and cleaned so it's possible to find lunch? Snacks need to be packed for school? Or bought in the first place?

Our aim in asking these questions is to identify two factors that go into the economics of marriage. First, *preferences*. If you and your partner have different preferences, it affects the gains you get from sharing a household together. If you both love eating home-cooked food, for example, then there's a huge benefit to combining into one household where one person can cook and both people get to eat. But if one person is fine with takeout every night, fights about who cooks are going to be exacerbated by the fact that only one person thinks this is actually a necessary job. So ask: *What are some of your favorite things to cook? How many nights a week do you like to cook versus eat takeout? When you get busy, what do you eat? What's important to you about food? In a future world where we're both working and have other obligations, what should our schedule be around cooking versus microwaving something versus takeout versus eating out?*

Second, you're asking about ability and willingness to do these tasks, which also play into the returns you'll get from forming a household. In my work on the division of housework, we concluded that men not being *good* at housework tasks couldn't possibly explain the data we saw, because men's time doing this work didn't increase substantially even when they were unemployed. Instead, we concluded that men received disutility—negative utility—from doing housework tasks they associated with female gender norms. Cultural norms and role models can play a huge role here—we found that the hours of home production that men versus women did in US immigrants' home countries was highly correlated with the amount of housework they did in their own households. So you want to ask whether they think there is any "proper" division of household chores and whether that division should shift if one person gets much busier at work, when the other person may need to take over tasks that aren't typically "theirs".

Every time I give a talk about that home production research, there's always a guy in the audience who asks, "But I spend more time fixing the windows and mowing the lawn—what about that?" He's not wrong—men do tend to spend more time on "exterior maintenance" than women do. The issue is that those tasks make up a much smaller percentage of the overall home production time compared to everyday chores like cooking, cleaning, and laundry (which is why being divorced didn't turn out to be as hard as I'd expected). So someone being insistent on staying in their gendered lane can create major frictions when the household needs to be nimble in reassigning tasks.

If you want to have kids, then a huge part of the enterprise you're creating is going to be centered on taking care of their needs. As I've described, most women quickly become childcare experts after having children, driven in part by evolutionary instincts to keep investing after already using a precious egg, investing nine months of incubation time, and risking their lives to give birth. And right at birth, they're often surprised by the intensity of their own attachment, driven by that biochemical process. So if you're marrying a man, you'll end up with a narrower gap between *future* you and your partner if having kids is something he's already thought about. Again, I wouldn't just ask if they "love kids"—I would look at what they've done to prepare themselves for one of the most important potential roles in their lives. For instance, does he have nieces and nephews he's actively engaged with? Did he help care for younger siblings growing up? Are any of his friends already dads, and does he spend time with those families? What thoughts does he have on how he was parented versus what he wants for his own children? When it comes to fulfilling the role of father, some level of lived experience, and a deep understanding of the job description, go a long way.

Gaining a sense of your potential partner's preferences will not only shed some light on the question of how to divide work but also on what work needs doing. A friend of mine has a prestigious career, in the same field as her husband, with the same employer. But while he's happy to have the kids in childcare 7:00 a.m. to 9:00 p.m., she wants to spend more time with her children, which comes at the cost of her working hours. "It's not my fault you don't have enough time to work," he says, "it's *your choice*," a refrain that began to sound like nails on a chalkboard to her. So you might want to make sure you're aligned on some of these expectations now: *How much do you expect we would spend time with our kids after school and in the evenings, versus rely on childcare?* You also want to find out if you have the same preferences and values around the balance of career, and thus utility bought through money, versus other sources of utility. *If you plan to go into a "high-investment" career, what hours do you think are reasonable to work? How many nights do you think we'd spend time together or with family or friends versus catching up on work?* Again, if kids are part of this plan, keep in mind that the data shows women's time use tends to change substantially post-kids. Will his?

Some of his assumptions about parenting are likely a product of how he was raised. Raquel Fernández, Alessandra Fogli, and Claudia Olivetti have found that the wives of men whose mothers worked are more likely to work, proposing that being raised under a family model in which both parents worked allows these men to form preferences more conducive to workforce participation of their wives or to be better partners for working wives.[6] Other research shows that when a husband becomes unemployed, whether a couple responds by the wife working depends on the employment decisions of both the wife's and husband's mothers.[7] So, asking about that history, too, is part of a potential partner's résumé.

In this joint-household enterprise, both careers create "revenue"—the financial resources you'll have to build utility. But often, our potential partners have only thought about one: their own. When it comes to their wives' jobs, they may have never moved past generalities like "Of course I want to support my wife's career!" Okay, what does that mean practically, when push comes to shove? If we're truly part of one household, then "all money is green" no matter who makes it. But very often, men will falter when it comes to making choices that enrich their wives', rather than their own, career prospects. And these trade-offs are very real! Remember the data from the "Winning the Bread and Baking It Too" project where we showed that men's housework time didn't move, no matter what his wife earned relative to him? Well, there seemed to be a connection between her excess housework time and the hours she had available for work. Even when she was earning two to four times what her husband earned, *she still worked fewer hours.* Some people asked whether this was because men's jobs were more rigid, whereas women were more likely to work in industries with flexible work. So we checked again, this time restricting to couples where both people worked in positions that paid hourly—for example, he might be an Uber driver and she might work in the service industry or health care. Again, when her wage was two to four times his, his housework hours stayed stuck at the same level as when the male partner was earning more—less than half hers. And her labor-market work hours were still lower than his, despite the fact that shifting time around in the household would earn the entire household more money! If he would take on some of the domestic load, and she could pick up an extra shift, the household's entire budget would increase!

This trade-off can also apply when what's on the line isn't current wages but investment in future wages. A former student recently stopped by my office on a visit back to campus and perfectly captured this dynamic. Describing having two young kids and sometimes unpredictable childcare needs, she explained, "My husband is an entrepreneur, so he feels like he can't afford to take any time off—it's 'You eat what you kill,' and so if the deal doesn't get made, the business doesn't make money. Whereas I'm salaried, so if I leave work at 4:00 one day, I make the same amount. But if I keep doing that, in five years, I won't!" Time spent picking up the slack at home can't be spent investing in our careers.

That's why I think it's worth asking *now, If one of our kids is sick and someone needs to stay home—how do we decide who?* The answers to these questions can be hard to predict, but I think it's worth *both of you* reflecting on them in very practical terms before making a lifelong commitment. A new paper called "Moving to Opportunity, Together" shows that following household moves, men's income usually goes up while women's goes down—indicating that they were likely to move to boost his career, but not hers, as I referenced earlier.[8] Confront this hypothetical before you get there: *If I got a job opportunity in a different city that would give me a 50 percent pay increase and new opportunities, but required you taking a 20 percent pay cut, how would we decide whether to move? What if you had to take a bigger pay cut? Look for new employment?*

In my class at Wharton, we discuss these issues of evaluating your partner like you would a co-CEO, right before spring break, and I joke that I'm sending them off to fight with their loved ones. When school returns, invariably there's a young woman sitting in my office asking some form of "Should I break up with my boyfriend?"

One, an MBA student from a country with more conservative gender norms, wonders if those norms will rear their head in her relationship, even as her boyfriend tells her he supports her career. She wants to have a family but also keep working, and she wonders if there will be pressure for her to take on a more traditional role in the house. I tell her that the data does show that home country norms about the ratio of men's to women's unpaid household labor are highly predictive of that division for immigrants in the American Time Use Survey—old habits die hard. That's not destiny for her relationship, but she has to ask herself what evidence she's seen that her boyfriend is willing to push against the norm, even if it comes at a cost to himself. She's been away from home for her MBA, and he wants her to move back as soon as possible. She doesn't know the right answer, but after we talk, she makes a decision that lets her gather more information: she accepts an offer for an extra year in the US, for a prestigious joint degree program she's been admitted to. "I figure if he's actually that serious about making sacrifices so I can pursue my dreams, then we'll last another year of long distance. If we don't, then I'll know I never should have gone back in the first place."

Her approach is a strategy any of us can use to evaluate whether or not a relationship is going to provide the kind of support we need. This is what in economics we call taking an *empirical approach*—which means using data to draw conclusions. If you don't have the data you need about your current relationship, is there a way to gather it? Is there an interim decision you can make that will give you more information, for when you absolutely need to make a more permanent decision?

Now that you've gathered evidence on what your current partner offers, it's time to cut to the core of what you want and need so that you can make the best decisions possible for you— all the yous.

Your Love Vision Board

After my third breakup with the same ex mentioned earlier in the chapter, a different friend, sick of hearing me cry over this woman again and again, sat me down with a box of her kids' gel pens and told me to make a list of what I wanted my life to *feel* like, now and in the future. In the midst of this relationship and as I soul-searched after divorce, I had been holding on to little moments that felt like I was *there*—at some kind of equilibrium after all the upheaval. They always tended to be while spending time with other friends with kids: cooking together, sharing a glass of wine while our kids played. "Wait . . . I could find a relationship that felt like that!" was the perhaps obvious epiphany that took me way too long to reach. So, perched on my friend's couch next to her cat, while the kids played, I wrote: "Cooking yummy, healthy food." "Time outdoors in nature." "Intentional parenting." "Feeling seen and supported by another." "Family game night." "Nesting, warm lived-in spaces." "Shared growth and progress." This became my romance vision board. Crystallizing this picture at the time felt wistful. I was about to start IVF to try to have a second child on my own. So this was a wish list for the future, I thought.

But surprisingly, after a half dozen bad dates mostly arranged to stop me from calling my ex-girlfriend, I met my future wife. And thanks to the clarity I gained from writing that list, I was able to recognize that we were aligned on the things that mattered . . . despite her dreams of building a van, living in it, and then traveling the country for three to five years (while I was hoping for that kid in the near term). She shared a vision of raising children as though they are people, a dedication to making the world a better place and an ache at its injustice, a love of nature and spirit of adventure. So then we turned to the tough problem of how to merge together our two visions for the *near* future. As she now says, "I'm still building that van. It's just going to have more seats."

The vision-board approach can help you stay in touch with your true needs and wants when romance or emotions start to take over—to remind hot-state you of the wants of cold-state you. This can be useful even if you're already in a relationship. Getting clear on what you want your life to look like can help you figure out what your true nonnegotiables are, and chart a course to get there, even if it means mapping out what your BATNA is in case things don't change. So grab your own set of gel pens or whatever art supply is closest to you, and answer some questions for yourself. Here are a few ideas to get started, although you might end up finding your own, better format.

Page 1:
What do you want your life to feel like? What are the things that bring you happiness that you want to share with a partner?

Write the phrases that come to your mind (in different colors if you like). Think about your current life and when you're happiest, and about the future and how you've imagined it.

*

Page 2:
—What do you need help with from a partner?
—What do they need to be good at?
—What shared values do they need to have?
—What do they need to know to see and understand you?

This one is more Q&A format. Write the questions out first, then write your answers to each one below them.

*

Page 3:
What do you already have? What do you want life to look like in five years, with or without a partner? What concrete steps do you need to take to get there?

This is about your BATNA—your life outside of love. What are the things in your life right now that you love that you've already created for yourself? What hidden strengths and assets do you have access to? At the same time as I was feeling romantic devastation, I had just gained more security at my job, and I realized I'd stumbled into a career with the flexibility and pay I needed to be a great mom, in a city where I could actually afford to do it. What do you envision in the future that has nothing to do with your partner? What's driving you nuts or bugging you or holding you back that you have the power to change? Being in a bad relationship, or in the state of searching for a good one, can make us feel incredibly stuck, because we're either looking for our partner to make changes with us, or we're waiting until we find a partner to start building the life that we want. I wasted too much time not going to the gym or not traveling, because my husband didn't have the same motivation to do those things. Make your life beautiful and rich and full *yourself* while you try to sort out what's not working in your love life.

And then, if you do have a partner that's falling short of being "the change you want to see" (to butcher Gandhi's words), you'll be that much better positioned to work on your relationship if you've already started being your full self, without anyone's permission.

A Performance-Improvement Plan

Now let's talk about what to do if you're already in a relationship. Just like we shouldn't settle for a partner, we shouldn't settle for a "deal" with the partner we've already chosen that leaves us exhausted and depleted. In that spirit, if you're finding that the joint load is falling on your shoulders, and love is fizzling, let's talk about how to have tough conversations and reset the terms of your relationship. I'm going to focus here mostly on an unequal division of home production, because this is so often the challenge that I see driving relationships with two reasonable people, that were once filled with love, into the ground.

I want you and your partner to go through an exercise of actually tracking the time you spend on home production (and on the mental load of home production) just like respondents to the American Time Use Survey do. And then, I want you to have an honest conversation about whether the way that work is distributed actually aligns with who is better at what and who has more time. Get two sheets of graph paper, or open up a Google spreadsheet, and write out seven days with fifteen-minute intervals from the earliest you could possibly wake up to the latest you go to bed. If you have a baby who wakes up at night, you'll need slots for the overnight, too. Then, for one week, literally fill out what you do in each of those fifteen-minute slots. You both have to do it for this to work! If you're multitasking and taking care of someone else and yourself, write that, too—"Did my hair while getting kiddo dressed." You can get granular for types of home production, and then just put "work", "leisure", and "personal care" for other times. And remember, for these purposes, even if you enjoy packing your child's lunch every day, it's childcare. If it helps you to have more shorthand, here are the high-level codes from the American Time Use Survey for home production:

02.01 Housework (cleaning, laundry)

02.02 Food & Drink Prep., Presentation, & Clean-up

02.03 Interior Maintenance, Repair, & Decoration

02.04 Exterior Maintenance, Repair, & Decoration

02.05 Lawn, Garden, and Houseplants

02.06 Animals and Pets

02.07 Vehicles

02.08 Appliances, Tools, and Toys (cleaning, repairing . . .)

02.09 Household Management

03.01 Caring For & Helping Household Children

03.02 Activities Related to Household Children's Education

03.03 Activities Related to Household Children's Health

03.04 Caring for Household Adults

03.05 Helping Household Adults

04.00 Caring For & Helping Non-Household Children and Non-Household Adults

Household management is a big one—use that category anytime you're thinking about or emailing· about or calling about or researching online about something household-related. Your partner might be shocked—and you might be, too—how little time you actually have for work. For personal care. For social connection. For exercise. For enjoying all the other things that make up parts of your utility function.

Before you share spreadsheets, ask your partner what they think would be a fair distribution of household tasks. I'd separate them into housework and household management as one category and childcare as another, because sometimes you'll find different trends across those categories. Most people will say fifty-fifty, but there might be some unique features of your jobs that make a different division more fair or practical, like one person having a long commute, or being in a more sensitive place in their career, or one partner earning a substantially larger share of the household budget, with a career that requires more time. Get these expectations out in the open before you compare notes on how you're spending your time.

Then it's time to look at the data! Who's actually spending more time on which tasks? Are there any areas that surprise you? You might find that some of the places you're overburdened are those where both people agree something needs to be done but don't agree on how much work it should require. Others might be tasks that your partner didn't even realize existed—like the fact that the kids' summer camp schedule doesn't magically materialize but rather takes hours of researching, calling, and paperwork.

Now it's time to begin reallocating the workload. But where to start? I'm partial to Eve Rodsky's *Fair Play* method of divvying up tasks wholesale—like dealing out a deck of cards (and you can actually buy the cards to do it on online).[9] The reason I think it works is that if you assign someone part of a task, you still end up with the "household management" piece of it—conceptualizing what needs to be done, managing it, monitoring progress. The women I know who are happiest in their marriages are those who say, "Oh, I don't cook at all." Men have been weaponizing incompetence for decades, and it's high time we got hip to it. "I don't even go near the fridge," one friend says, "that's *his* domain." This is capturing the benefits of specialization—developing real expertise in a specific domain. Make one person the kitchen expert and one person the cleaning, bill-paying, or organization expert.

The key consideration is that you also have to align on what "done" looks like for these tasks, or else your husband can claim bathroom duty and then clean it once a year. Similarly, you might want to know *what* your toddler is eating. That's where Rodsky's concept of "minimum standard of care" is helpful—that you both have to agree on what the bare minimum, nonnegotiables are for each task, and then totally ignore how the other chooses to execute on that. And maybe you hold on to the things that you have the strongest preferences about, or that bring you joy to execute, like my friend who delights in choosing her kids' clothes. But if you find yourself having deep, rigid preferences about *everything* around the house, you might be your own worst enemy when it comes to reclaiming your time. I want you to identify the areas that you can let go of, and then not just lightly remove yourself but wholesale abandon them. If you jointly assign your partner the task of buying clothes for the new school year, I don't even want you to know what size your kid is. If your other half is in charge of cleaning—*you don't even know where the broom is kept.* Will this need readjustment and renegotiation? Definitely. But is it better than you trying to do everything, being exhausted, and resenting your family instead of spending quality time with them? Also yes.

Keep in mind that in working to more fairly allocate household tasks, you're swimming upstream of gender norms, and so that means you need to over-correct in the places you can control. Because so much defaults to you, especially if you're "mom", it means you might need to assign a higher percentage of the explicit task list to your spouse, while you fill in the implicit gaps like "finding a new childcare provider" and being the one who your kid calls to when they're crying (or, without kids, the one who notices when things need restocking in the fridge or bathroom, sees messes and wipes them up, and envisions and creates nice home spaces).

This conversation about reallocating tasks might also be one about values and ambitions. Did you start off as equals and somehow get derailed along the way? Did you end up taking on more tasks at the same time you had kids, and then lean into those responsibilities because it "made sense" as your partner's star was rising more rapidly? Those decisions do not have to be set in stone. You may have ended up with a divergence in career paths that does not align with your goals or values. Use the language of economics: if you invested in home production and child human capital, while your partner had the privilege of investing in their own human capital, it might be time to reset that balance. How can your partner lean in to your career? Do you need more than equality—do you need time to catch up on investments that you didn't get a chance to make? It is never too late to reset the terms of your relationship or the gendered roles we've slipped into. Similarly, if your partner started out expecting to earn more, but their career didn't pan out as hoped, and you're now winning the bread and baking it too, it might be time to look at how patriarchal expectations line up against the reality of your relationship.

If taking on more tasks at home is a hard pill for your partner to swallow, they have some work to do in individual therapy, because *you* have places to be. I've heard so many friends struggling in their marriages talk about working on their partners' mental health, executive functioning, and parenting skills. It's *exhausting*, and, it isn't your job. Being a good partner is one thing, but taking on the work of raising another full-grown adult human? Who also has the capability to seek out community, resources, books, and professional assistance? That's part of the incredibly unrealistic and outrageous expectations that society places on women. And, hard as it may be, it's something we can revolutionize for ourselves by returning that work to its true owner.

If these conversations don't start to make things better for you, well, that's where chapter 11 comes in. But first, we're going to take a hard look at the time you're spending on leisure, home production, and parenting, to make sure you're optimizing *for yourself.*

Chapter 9

Converting Time into Joy and Meaning

WE KNOW THAT jobs are a technology that converts time into money. But what converts time into utility? Well, *you*. We're often told that "time is money," but no one ever says that "time is utility." And that's a reframe I want you to keep in mind, because money on its own is meaningless. We care about money because *money can be exchanged for utility*, and that's why we should care about time, too. So in this chapter, we're going to look at all the subtle deals you make in how you spend your time and how you can get more out of them. We have two goals: 1) make the time you have more *meaningful*, thus ensuring you maximize the utility you get from it, and 2) make *more* time for you to convert into utility.

There are two ways to make utility directly, rather than through the indirect route of earning money first and then spending it on things you value: through home production and through leisure time. Home production is any activity that produces something that gives you utility: cooking a meal, cleaning the house, or keeping your kids alive and thriving. As we've discussed, the term *home production* is useful because it reflects a too-often-overlooked fact that these activities create *value* in our lives. There is this cultural idea that housework is somehow not "real" work—which is strange, because as we've discussed, it used to be one partner's entire job. Or maybe not strange, given that was within a framework of patriarchy that historically devalued what women contribute, as feminist economist Nancy Folbre has observed.[1] This minimization makes it even more difficult to recognize the demand that this kind of labor places on women (and how carrying a disproportionate share of it can impact women's career advancement, stress levels, and energy). Buying new pillows for the couch helps create a place we enjoy, getting the car repaired helps ensure we can safely get where we need to go, meal planning helps us eat healthier and more enjoyable food, and spending time with our kids builds their human capital (and is cute to boot)—we'll focus on that last one in chapter 10.

The issue isn't that we are spending time doing these things but rather that the terms of the world have shifted so that now these unquestionably valuable, unquestionably important things are considered "extras" that we (meaning mostly women) have to squeeze into the margins of our lives, rather than being someone's sole job, leaving little time for leisure and enjoyment. I don't want you to ever apologize for spending time with your kids or caring about your space or your health. I do want you to identify the value you're creating and the time inputs required so that you can be strategic about when and where to invest your time.

Now, let's talk about *leisure*, the economics term for "having fun" or "relaxing". When it comes to converting your time into utility, leisure seems like the easy part. All you have to do is pick something that you enjoy doing or that adds to your well-being and do it! Which means, for example, sleep! Unfortunately, in choosing how we spend our time, we're facing that ongoing battle between our long-term utility interests and short-term impulses that might make our brains ill suited to solving the problem of "How do I make my life the happiest?"

Making Time Off Count

Leisure time creates utility because it directly benefits us in some way—physically, psychologically, emotionally, spiritually, whatever. It is additive and, in that sense, productive. But too often—and I know I'm not saying anything groundbreaking here—the way we spend time in between work and home production is on stuff that lets us "zone out" and *feel* like we're relaxing but doesn't actually *fuel* us over the long term. If you add up your metaphorical video game score at the end of your life, how much weight will Instagram videos carry on there? I'm not suggesting that we don't need to veg sometimes. We do! But I also want you to ensure you're aligning how you're spending what little free time you have with what brings you the most utility.

The scope of this problem reared its head for me when I asked my undergraduate students to recount a recent moment of joy. In addition to "taking my dog to the beach" and "cooking traditional recipes with my grandmother," three of the answers were: "taking selfies," "scrolling TikTok," and "online gambling." These answers screamed out that there may be a gap between a rational view of what uses of our scarce leisure time will maximize our utility and the practice of what actually happens.

Let's talk about the science of this gap. We know many people believe social media to be addictive. Economists have tested this by showing that if you pay people to reduce their usage, they continue to decrease use even in periods where they're not being paid—that is, once you break the addiction, their optimal level of use is lower.[2] They've also shown that social media creates what's known as a "product trap," where people want to consume something because other people are consuming it—the formalization of FOMO—rather than because it actually brings them pleasure. Using an experiment on college campuses, researchers found that while individuals would need to be paid to turn off Instagram and TikTok themselves, they were willing *to pay* to have everyone on the campus, including themselves, turn off the outlet.[3] The authors conclude that a product can create consumer surplus (what determines if we use something) while nonetheless decreasing consumer *welfare*—that is, people will keep choosing to use something, even though in the end it leaves them worse off. How is that possible? Well, because the designers of social media sites have hired neuroscientists to maximize their objective function—profit—instead of our own. Videos don't auto-play on social media because people *enjoy* it more when they do, they auto-play because we spend longer looking at them when they do, because it's hard to break away in the middle of something. Notifications activate our reward centers associated with social inclusion—pathways trodden by the need for social ties to survive throughout our genes' evolutionary lives. This is important because unlike a paid service that requires us to decide whether we want to re-up every month—where our rational, utility-maximizing brains would consider what brings joy to our life—social media companies don't need our dollars. They need our eyeballs. They make money by selling our attention to advertisers. And our decisions about attention all live in that "system one" instinctive zone where rationality gives way to impulse.

This is the reality of the economics of social media companies: you're not the customer, you're the product. They trick you into spending longer on their sites so that they have more valuable attention to sell to advertisers. They do this by delivering more dopamine hits, by capturing our passive decision-making, and ultimately by stealing our joy and meaning that we could have gotten through other sources.

There are other neurologically hardwired barriers to utility. Our brains are *present biased,* a term coined by behavioral economists, which means our brains are too focused on short-term payoffs relative to our overall utility function. To maximize utility, we need to consider our entire life cycles. For example, whether or not exercising feels good in the moment, it provides us a much higher quality of life as we age and lowers our chances of broken hips ("#$%! osteoporosis!" a friend and I shout as we lift weights together). The way we know a decision is a function of this bias, rather than just a true preference for today's utility over tomorrow's, is by comparing these trade-offs in how people make future plans versus how they think about things right now, with the temptation of immediacy. Research shows that if you ask a group of people if they would take $100 in six months over $110 in seven months, very few would say yes. But if instead you offered the $100 *right now* versus $110 in a month—the same time / money trade-off—82 percent would choose the immediate payoff.[4] Everyone discounts the future to some extent—it's less salient, we might not make it until then, and resources we have today can be used to produce returns that help us tomorrow. But that kind of discounting should be consistent—you should be able to predict how much next Tuesday is worth to you relative to next Monday. Instead, the bias of "right now" gets in the way once next week is actually here.

You can imagine this force would be especially prone to wreak havoc when dopamine-laced immediate returns compete with slow-burn benefits from activities like artistic pursuits, exercise, or reading a good book. And one of the things that too often gets short shrift has some of the slowest-burning benefits of all: *sleep*. Researchers have linked insufficient sleep to everything from dementia to heart disease.[5] And yet in the short term, neglecting sleep feels like a cheat code: I get more time to make money and utility, and can just drink extra coffee in the morning to feel like myself! However, the health, productivity, and well-being effects eventually outweigh the short-term benefits. In fact, economists have found that even college students are aware their sleep choices are not optimal for their well-being. When researchers offered to pay students to meet sleep targets of their own choosing, they found that 60 percent chose targets that provided an incentive to sleep more, even though they could easily receive the maximum payment by simply choosing the time they already slept.[6]

There are plenty of books that focus on how to give up social media or meet your goals around exercise that utilize the latest in behavioral science—one great one is *How to Change* by my Wharton colleague Katy Milkman.[7] This is not that book. I am here to simply make you aware of the economics of the problem. Of the potential gap between what maximizes your utility and the way we make decisions about how to spend our time, and the way capitalism exploits that gap. Armed with this information, I trust you to solve this problem. So let's talk about figuring out what actually gives you utility and then structuring your life around it.

Paying Yourself First, with Time

We started with the easy question of what to do with the time that you have earmarked for leisure, and unfortunately, even that wasn't so simple. So you can imagine that when you're trying to figure out *whether* to spend your time on leisure versus something else, even more variables come into play. My editor describes having a free hour and getting dressed to go for a run but then seeing the unfolded laundry on the way out and ending up pairing socks in her athletic leggings instead. And then there's the mom guilt, which we'll dive into more in the next chapter. You decide to hire a sitter and get dinner out with friends, but your kid gives you big eyes and tells you that you never spend any special time together. Or you get asked to volunteer for something and experience what the authors of *The No Club* call "the Diva Moment": when you momentarily feel loved, valued, and admired for being sought-after (named after Sally Field exclaiming, "You like me!" after winning an Oscar).

What all these moments have in common is noise—chatter from different sources that floods our brains when we try to do something for ourselves. In choosing how we want to spend our time, we have to get used to listening to a different part of ourselves—the constant, omnipresent part who will be with us through our entire lives—rather than the temporary flares of chemicals and emotions that create internal chatter. I want you to practice the exercise of turning up the volume on your inner truths about what you are seeking in life—and turning down the volume on the other forces pulling you away from that.

So thinking about the definition of utility that we started with—things that would increase your total video game score if you look back from the end of your life—I want you to consider the uses of your leisure time that enhance your utility the most. Because that's the amazing power that you have: by spending time with family and friends, you can directly turn your time into utility. You have a utility machine already built in! This realization is why protecting your time from things that *don't* bring you utility is paramount. Spend some time observing yourself and what activities you find bring you the most fulfillment. Is it being outside? Moving? Seeing a close friend? Reading? I want you to identify the things that you do with your free time that bring you the *most* long-term joy and fulfillment. If you weren't so busy or tired, what would you spend more time doing? Our mission is to figure out how to get you more of those things.

There are three ways we're going to do that. The first is by flipping the script on how our automatic choices often undermine us, by "paying yourself first" in leisure time. The second is going to be by substituting money for time or finding other creative solutions. And the third, and arguably least fun: making hard choices.

Let's talk about what it means to pay yourself in time. *Pay yourself first* is a personal finance adage that refers to putting money into savings or investments before you do the rest of your budgeting. The idea is that by taking the liquid cash out of your checking account immediately, and putting it toward long-term goals, you reel in some of the behavioral forces that sometimes cause us to make "mistakes" that run counter to our long-term interests. In developing countries, economists have studied a savings method known as ROSCAs—rotating savings and credit associations—where individuals deposit a small amount of cash each month, and a rotating member takes the entire pot. This savings method doesn't earn any interest, so it's surprising that they're so popular, versus simply stashing the money somewhere for later use. The economic answer for why they're used? Self-discipline. By paying into the rotating fund, individuals discipline themselves to save up for a larger expenditure they can make when it's their turn to collect the pot—powerful evidence that sometimes we need to protect ourselves from, well, ourselves.[8]

We can take a similar view of time. If it's not immediately removed from our budget (in this case, our calendar or schedule), it can all too easily slip through our fingers. Leisure time must be accounted for in advance and treated as a sacred obligation, just like a meeting with your boss, instead of the "treat" you're allowed to have if you got through your entire to-do list. Because the to-do list will always be there, but time will not. Proactively planning in this way results in time more meaningfully spent maximizing utility rather than simply zoning out after a day of endless work. And surprisingly, planning for this time can also make you feel like you have more time, instead of less.

In a world where we are all perfectly rational, constantly optimizing marvels of intentionality, this solution makes no sense. All the other stuff you were doing must have been important if you didn't have any time for leisure. In the *real* world, the one where I just spent an hour reading the internet before writing this sentence, setting aside some of your time for the activities you value most might just help remove some of the "clutter" that tends to expand to fill the available space. Researchers have found that students *know* they will procrastinate and end up getting less done than they want to. In an experiment, when given an opportunity to commit themselves to harder work in the future with their current, more rational brains, students would sign their future selves up for more work compared to when they made the choice in the moment, with the temptation of procrastination right there.[9] Our use of time is not meticulously budgeted and allocated with mathematical precision. Instead, both science and human perception show that time is a squishy, malleable concept. Have you ever felt yourself suddenly be able to complete something in thirty minutes that you had been working on for hours when you knew the deadline was approaching?

"Flipping your calendar" to fill in the activities you truly value first will "starve the beast" that is procrastination. When deadlines are more hard and fast—when we have to say no to someone else instead of ourselves—we very often marshal the discipline to get things done on time. But we can do this for ourselves, too, with the knowledge that leisure time actually nourishes and recharges us in a way that will make the rest of the time we have for work and everything else more effective. Flipping your calendar can also help you say no to things that guilt compels you to do but that only leave you feeling stressed and frayed. So stop running out of time for an enjoyable weekend activity and end up scrolling your phone, or even cleaning the house instead. Take your list of the leisure items that recharge you the most, and *pay yourself first*—put them on your calendar and block out the time. Again, we can use the behavioral finance analogy: we should treat our own savings and investment goals as just as important as our landlord and constrain our other decisions accordingly. Treat yourself as someone who doesn't deserve to get paid last when it comes to time.

Which Jobs Should You Hire Yourself For?

Now that we're thinking about time as something that you can either pay to yourself, to spend on utility, or spend on something else, I want to extend this idea to home production.

I recently met a woman—the one I mentioned in the intro whose husband swims every day while she hasn't taken a run for four years—who felt completely depleted in all ways. She had gotten so used to coping and trying to make things work that she didn't even know where to start in trying to improve things for herself, a fact she readily admitted. I pointed out to her that her household was investing a lot of the shared time and money budget on her husband's mental and physical well-being: those swims and leisurely walks and finished philosophy books were paid for in *time*, time that could have been spent taking something off her plate. So what can you spend from your shared budget on making *your* life easier? I asked.

She wasn't ready to think about doing yoga or getting drinks with friends—not yet. First, she needed help. So, given that they both had fairly well-paying jobs, I suggested she find the tasks in her day that didn't absolutely require *her* to do them, and find a way to outsource them. "I'm not going to tell you not to put your kids to bed or read to them—I know you value that time. But do you need to put their toys away?" I asked. "It would be harder for me to hire someone and tell them where everything goes than to just do it myself," she said. "Okay. Then do it in a way that feels ridiculously luxurious," I replied. "Hire a professional organizer for a hundred dollars an hour. Then she'll know exactly where everything goes in your house, because she'll design it." After all, in terms of each of their possible market wages, her husband's swims were costing them way more.

By continuing to do these tasks herself, she was deciding to *hire herself* for these jobs. Was that the optimal allocation of household resources? Let me explain.

Economists tend to have a unique approach to outsourcing household tasks that can definitely induce some eye rolls, as in a 2013 *New York Times* article about economist power couple Emi Nakamura and Jon Steinsson that read in part, "They even hired someone to spend hours going through thousands of old family photographs to figure out which are the 'good ones.'"[10] Because your time is a crucial resource that can be used to invest in your career or for the leisure or family activities you deeply value, economists like Nakamura and Steinsson encourage people to think about whether the marginal value of their time is worth more than the money it would take to pay someone else to do a task. This is the basic reframe that cuts to the heart of the matter: *not* hiring someone to do something that *can* be bought on the market is a choice to hire yourself for the job.

Now, there are a lot of considerations in this calculation that sometimes mean that *is* the right decision, and which make outsourcing far from a one-size-fits-all approach for female happiness. We'll tackle these in turn: the ethical considerations, economic accessibility, and the practical considerations of sourcing and managing someone to help.

First, outsourcing labor is not always economically realistic— sometimes the only wage you can afford *is* your own. In fact, a society where upper-class women are able to benefit from a lot of outsourcing tends to rely on a certain degree of income inequality. There's a paper I teach by Patricia Cortés and Jessica Pan that shows how the availability of low-cost immigrant workers helped women in Hong Kong increase their labor supply.[11] And indeed, the availability of outsourcing and of alternatives to women's time (like grandparents) has been shown consistently to be crucial to women being able to supply labor outside the home.[12]

But something my students usually catch in that paper is that the relatively wealthy women in Hong Kong are referred to as "women", while the relatively poorer immigrants working for them, also women, are referred to as "workers". People who help take labor off your plate so you can spend more time on either work or leisure, it should go without saying, are also *people*. An equitable society would be one where they, too, have the ability to pursue their own utility. One of my professors in grad school, Lena Edlund, who's Swedish, told us that in Sweden, where there is much less income inequality, people tended to cut their own hair, because paying someone to do it was so expensive. If I could solve one economic problem, I'd rather women at the bottom of the income distribution could earn a living wage rather than women at the top of the income distribution being more able to easily afford taking things off their plate. In other words, sometimes the solutions to solving gender inequality are at odds with those to address other inequities.

However, as an individual without a magic wand to solve social problems, if you *can* afford it, there are ways to harness the benefits of outsourcing while reckoning with these ethical considerations. *Who takes care of the children of the people taking care of your children?* is a worthwhile question to ask yourself when considering any outsourcing scenario. If you're privileged enough to be able to afford help cleaning, cooking, or taking care of your kids, can you do it in a way that contributes to sustainable livelihoods of other people? For example, if you cannot afford to offer sufficient pay that includes paid time off and other benefits to a nanny, it might make sense to choose a day care where they're able to harness economies of scale by having teachers care for multiple children, and thus pay workers a higher salary and offer additional benefits. When using a cleaning service, you can think about putting money away to provide sick time or injury insurance in case the person working for you temporarily cannot work, or using a professional service that provides this for their employees, even if it costs a little bit more.

In terms of economic accessibility, this is where the frame of "Would I hire myself?" is useful. Because there are plenty of things we've already decided *not* to hire ourselves for. We do not grow our own food (at least, not the bulk of it). This is because the wage we can earn working in the market pays us enough that it doesn't make sense to pursue laborious farming instead of allow other people to specialize in farming, produce food more efficiently, and us to purchase it from them. The same goes for making our own clothes. Many people, in fact, used to do this, but the global economy and new technology have made the price of clothes fall, because it is much more efficient for them to be mass-produced, and so buying them is actually far *cheaper* than producing them ourselves. The movement toward aesthetic DIY-ing is a push away from harnessing the economic gains of specialization—of benefiting from someone providing one type of labor while you provide another. Restaurants, for example, are not just luxury items; working-class people have been using "takeout" to harness specialization since the Middle Ages.[13] Because getting a hot lunch for the price of an hour's work might actually be worth it if preparing the same quality of food yourself would cost you 75 percent of the price *and* an hour of your time.

And I'd like to note how much more comfortable society is in outsourcing male-coded tasks *that could be home produced* than female-coded tasks. Hiring a landscaper to cut the grass, or a handyman to clean the gutters, or painters to touch up the house is considered a norm, because we assume that *men's* time can be valuably spent earning money on the market instead of insourcing home production. But when it comes to female-coded tasks like cooking, cleaning, and childcare, we suddenly feel like the budget to hire someone is an unaffordable luxury rather than a basic requirement.

So taking a truly comprehensive view of the cost of insourcing a task—of hiring yourself for it—which includes the time, the cost of materials, the stress of doing it—I want you to take a hard look at whether investing that time in your career or just in your sanity would have payoffs beyond the cost of something that feels a little out of reach. Again, from that *New York Times* article: "That's why Steinssón and Nakamura paid for housekeeping services even when they were penniless grad students. Outsourcing household tasks meant they had to take on more debt, but they calculated—correctly—that spending an extra hour working on a paper was better for their lifetime expected earnings than spending that same hour vacuuming." Economists call this *consumption smoothing*, and the idea is that one should think about total lifetime earnings when making decisions as to whether you can "afford" something, and use more of those earnings in the *now* when times are tough than in the later when you'll be comfortably retired. There *are* some periods in our lives where we need to invest to get through them, and we will see those investments pay off later.

In the econ world, when you borrow, you're taking money out of a future period—out of future you's pocket—and bringing it into the present period. When you save, you're doing this in reverse—taking money from this period and mailing it to the future. This "technology" comes with some costs. Everyone likes money now more than money in the future, so getting money to yourself right now costs extra, called *interest*. Similarly, when you save money, you get paid this premium for helping other people get their money right now. Whether it makes financial sense to spend right now depends on your "cost of capital." From where would those funds come, and how costly is this to your overall utility picture? For example, if you receive a retirement contribution match through your work, most financial advisers will yell at you if you're not maxing that out, because it's "free money"—money that future you can enjoy that's paid for by someone else. Another way to think of it is as 100 percent interest on the funds you put in. So cash for present-day wants or needs that comes at the expense of this type of savings is much costlier than cash that comes from other sources. If you have credit card debt, then spending now versus paying it off is also very costly, because of the compounding of interest over the period it will take to pay it off.

The same logic does not apply to taking money out of savings—here the cost is only the interest rate you're forgoing—or even to taking on additional student debt if you can reasonably anticipate a high-paying job in the future. If you are on a career path with steep growth, where you can anticipate earning much more money if you make it through the current really hard period, that is your cue to see if money from your future could solve any problems for you. This is the idea of Era 3 in "The Squeeze" graph (page 31), "the Ironic Relief"—the period where (sometimes) time constraints *and* income constraints alleviate at a similar time, because kids get older, career investments become less crucial, and those that you already made start paying off. If you are on a path that has a destination—a moment when you're going to hit a career milestone that brings with it some extra money, and less of a "do or die" mentality, then that period of upcoming relief means future you won't value that extra cash as much as present you does. It won't make such a big difference to her, because she won't be so squeezed. If, however, you're in a situation where you expect your earnings to be roughly the same in the future, maybe adjusted for inflation, then you most likely want to move things around within the present period rather than borrowing from the future—future you will value money just as much as you do now and will be mad at you for not leaving her more of it.

But there may be trade-offs you can make in the present moment—driving that old car for an extra year, or cutting back in other areas—to free up resources. Remember: the objective is utility, so you have to decide whether material purchases or services that free up your time are going to bring you more utility. Even picking up some additional work now—depending on your industry, an extra shift, a freelance project, a temporary side hustle—might make sense if it allows us to hire *someone else* instead of ourselves for some of the household jobs, and therefore relieves other forms of time stress. Sometimes, taking tasks off our plates even has immediate financial or career returns by restoring creative energy that we can pour into the marketplace that pays us for our time and skills, instead of using it for home production. And if you live with a partner, this is a joint problem. Do you as a household need to figure out some ways to increase earnings that would give you a little needed wiggle room to spend on creating time? Investing in your physical and mental health is not frivolous. It cannot be that your sanity is the thing that is negotiable while everything else is a necessity.

If paying to outsource labor truly isn't an option for you, that doesn't mean there aren't strategies you can use to reduce the burden of some of your home production tasks. Can you trade tasks with friends, create car pools, or just invest in simplifying your life so certain things don't need to happen (more on that last one later)? For some reason, I always find it easier to clean up someone else's mess than my own. Can you and a friend have your catch-ups while alternating whose kitchen you clean? This way, home production work becomes partially leisure time, and you get more utility from the same time investment. If driving your kids back and forth to activities is the killer, are there other parents you can split the drive with? Can you barter babysitting for something that you enjoy doing that produces value for other people? If you have young kids at home, it's a limited time problem, and so leaning on whatever resources you have for this period makes sense.

Making It Easier to Make Things Easier

One of the common obstacles to outsourcing is figuring out how to take things off your plate without creating a ton of management work and additional mental load (which, you will not be surprised, often falls on women!). After all, someone has to find and interview childcare (and in many areas, there is a labor shortage on that front).

This is where it's important to remember the challenges of present bias. When something is hard up front, like thinking through financial or logistical barriers to hiring someone else instead of ourselves for household tasks, our brains overweight the short-term costs relative to the long-term benefits. Imagine the math like this: let's say that having your family pictures on the walls is going to give you 1 utility point every day for a year. That's 365 points! But the cost of researching someone to do it, explaining to them what you want done, and paying them for it is 20 utility points. If we zoom out over that year time period, it's a no-brainer! But if our brains take a tighter focus, we get: *I'm giving up 20 utility points right now to only get 1 point tomorrow? No, thanks.* This is a trivial example, but we make decisions like this all the time. So, each day, we choose to do things a little bit worse rather than paying an up-front cost to make a problem better. But by doing so, we're robbing our-selves of the longer-term utility of actually using our time the way we want—and having enough of it for a change.

Once we find the resources to outsource, we have to figure out which jobs we personally don't need to do. It's easy to outsource tasks we're not very good at doing or that require a specific kind of knowledge or expertise. This is why we rarely fix our mufflers ourselves or do our own electrical work. In economics, the idea of someone with a superior labor skill set is called *absolute advantage*, and it's pretty straightforward. But there's also a concept known as *comparative advantage*, which my first economics teacher—in high school—explained as follows: Michael Jordan might be better at mowing his lawn than the kid down the street, but he still hires the kid, because Jordan's way *more* better at playing basketball.

So consider the many things you're good at doing but feel like you don't have time to do. These ones are harder to let go of, I know. Start with the areas where you don't have strong preferences about how things are done—which will help you relinquish the mental load along with the task itself. Like, I am *in theory* an organized person, but in practice, with so many things to juggle, it's a different story. My friend introduced me to a surprisingly affordable home organizer who changed my life by coming over once a month and putting in place systems and bins for spaces like under the kitchen sink, where I don't care where stuff goes—I just need it to have a place to go. You can also try a compromise position: if you love cooking but find it's taking up way too much time right now, are there shortcuts or ready-made options you could use for weeknights, while you get to cook at a slower and more enjoyable pace on weekends? Reframe "DIY" as *in*sourcing, and remember that the people who are amazing at it on social media are optimizing subject to different constraints than you (i.e., they don't have a sixty-hour-a-week job, don't have kids, or this *is* part of their job by being an income stream).

When I lived in New York, I often felt like my attempts at outsourcing created more work and friction rather than providing relief. I remember someone advising me to host an au pair, and at the time, I scoffed. The idea of affording an extra room for someone else to live in was laughable. But once I was in Philadelphia, where the cost of living was significantly lower and houses were bigger, the math changed. For a single parent, having someone who could look after my child *and* help out around the house was life-changing. I realize that this is not the right solution for everyone, but the lesson is transferable to other situations—it relies on an economics concept referred to as *complementarity*. Complementarity refers to one thing increasing the benefit of another. So ketchup and fries are complements, because having one makes having the other one much more valuable. But you can also have complementarities in production, where one task makes you better at completing another task. In this case, taking care of a child is complementary with cleaning up after a child. Complementarity is also one of the reasons women get stuck doing so much domestic labor— once you do something well, you're the person who's "good at it," and so it's just easier to be the one to do . . . well, everything.

But you can harness this force to your advantage! First, in any outsourcing situation, figure out if there is a natural way to pair together tasks that are complementary to one another. For example, can you pay your dog walker a little extra to also order and restock pet supplies? Tip your babysitter for tidying up the toys in the closet after the kids fall asleep? You could even place an ad for a roommate who can also help with babysitting! Second, remember that doing a task once is complementary with doing it again. *You* are an expert in how you want things done because you've done them over and over again, and you spend a lot of time with yourself and your own preferences. The good news in that is that outsourcing is hardest in the beginning! The more times you've outsourced a task to the same provider, the more efficient it becomes (which is why we tend to go get our hair cut at the same place, assuming we like the outcome).

So zoom out, add up the utility points that are possible over the long term by making some changes today, and find a way to solve these problems rather than letting your joy die by a thousand tiny cuts.

Throw Out Your Houseplants

We've already discussed tracking your home production time to have tough conversations with your partner. Now I want you to have some tough conversations with yourself. The next thing we need to ask is: if it's not worth hiring someone to help with it, is it worth doing at all? Our goal is to align how you spend your time with your utility function.

We've talked about the forces that make it hard for us to optimize rationally: the power of temptation, love, guilt, and all those channels of evolutionary reward that activate short-term happy chemicals but might steal away deeper joy and meaning over the long term. Evolutionary incentives to seek social inclusion for the purposes of survival make us want to say yes to things other people want us to do. But now, in your actual life, people liking you is not going to determine whether you make it through the famine. This is one type of noise we have to turn down.

So, too, is the force of social comparison. Just because other people are doing something doesn't mean that it's right for you. This lesson applies to money as much as time. I've seen over and over people buying the house at the maximum of their budget, only to be hampered by the payments and constrained in their choices (e.g., to leave a toxic job). Or to run up credit card debt keeping up with friends spending out of trust funds, then needing to make different choices to finally haul themselves out a decade later.

Economics research supports these psychological tendencies. While our actual utility should be affected by the purchasing power of our own salaries, Haas School of Business economist Ricardo Perez-Truglia has found that people are deeply influenced by how much *other people* are making. He uses evidence from a natural experiment where Norwegian tax records became accessible online, allowing people to easily discover what their friends and neighbors were earning. The result? The subjective well-being and life satisfaction of people who earned less than their peers plummeted. Their salaries hadn't budged at all, but learning that other people were outearning them made them feel badly about their own status.[14]

These "less-than" feelings—which I would argue should not be part of our true utility—can cause us to make suboptimal decisions. In another experiment, Perez-Truglia, with coauthor Nicolas Bottan, studied how doctors made decisions about location when entering the residency match program—where they'll be assigned to a hospital in one of many different locations. They found that people valued relative income rank almost equivalently to cost of living in making these decisions—that is, they would be willing to accept a higher cost of living—and therefore being able to purchase fewer goods and services with their salary—as long as they moved up the relative income distribution, and therefore could potentially afford relatively more than their neighbor.[15] In other words, humans have a tendency to seek out being "king of the hill" on a small foothill rather than a mere duke on a bigger mountain.

All these factors can drive us to make a suboptimal trade between our time and money. If we need to keep up with the Joneses, we may push ourselves to work more to make purchases other people have or to do things that make us feel important. The authors of the book *Your Money or Your Life* describe my adage of converting your time into money in more visceral terms: *You're trading your life force for material possessions.*[16] Rethinking how much of your life force you want to allocate to different uses is a crucial piece of optimizing your utility.

Sit down with the list you made of how you spend your time (or make a new one if you've managed to shift some things around with your partner). Color-code the activities you feel really good about, that you're sure you want to be doing, and the ones you feel iffy about. I want you to pay attention to how you feel when you do something with your time that you end up regretting. Sometimes flattered? That's the diva moment. Sometimes guilty? That's social pressure or comparison. Write down some adjectives you associate with the parts of your day you feel are only so-so uses of your time.

Now write some adjectives down for the parts of your day you're more certain of—the ones where you know you're doing the right thing. Calm? Relaxed? Happy? Settled? Fulfilled? Don't worry, I'm a realist—I do *not* think that every moment of your day can be like that. But I do think that differentiating for yourself how different parts of your day make you feel can help you tune in to which uses of time are really creating utility for you (and which you should therefore try to replicate) and which uses are working against you and that you should try to scale back on.

To really map this out, you should also pay attention to tough or not-so-fun moments that are part of the "production process" of something that does bring you substantial utility. For example, I don't always feel happy and relaxed when I'm rushing to get dinner on the table, but I do bask in the utility of family meals, going around the table and sharing the best and worst parts of our day, connecting with the people I love over nourishing food. These are places where we can ask whether there's a more efficient way to produce the same end result in terms of utility—maybe some of those family meals could rely on takeout on especially busy days—but at least we know there's a clear link between our time spent and the production of utility. The same goes for investments that will pay off later, like studying for a certificate that will enhance our careers. Other activities, like volunteering for a committee a friend guilted us into serving on, are much less clear.

As we discussed earlier, unpaid jobs that are not career investments *and* are not the top of your list of chosen leisure time need to get recoded as *volunteer work*. Which, more specifically, is a donation of your time. Do you want to and can you afford to donate that much of your time right now? Sometimes we might realize that our volunteer work is actually a form of leisure—we enjoy it and want to do it. Other times, we might realize that it leaves us feeling depleted rather than restored in the way that leisure time should make us feel.

During the pandemic, I got deeply involved in local organizing to benefit people living in homeless shelters (who had temporarily been moved to hotels throughout NYC). I found my skills as a former consultant who loved a spreadsheet were incredibly useful in the social justice space, where people tended to lead with feelings instead of GANTT charts. I charged ahead with such enthusiasm that I was soon spending countless hours a week on this work that was decidedly not my job—squeezing other things, including my academic work, into the margins. The group I was working with was doing a lot of good, and it was hard not to give it my all when it felt like we could really make a difference. But if I'm being honest, my passion for this work was partly about meeting my emotional needs. I was in a difficult moment in my career (and my marriage), and whereas I felt like a failure as an academic, I felt effective and needed as an organizer. I was at the center of something important. This didn't mean I needed to give up the work I was doing, but being honest about what was driving me to do it meant finding ways to have an impact while having better boundaries about my time that also made the work sustainable. And after all, movements that empower multiple people are going to be longer lasting than those that are driven by a very burned-out team of one. My work ended up becoming a nonprofit organization that I still choose to run as a volunteer. I make it clear to myself that this is something I'm doing because I find it personally rewarding and fulfilling, and I remind myself when the work feels hard that this is a *choice* of how to spend my time on utility. And that means setting some tougher boundaries on other donations of my time, like being asked to speak to student groups or do other campus service.

If you find yourself burning out on altruism, try to re-tap into your reasons for doing it in the first place—the impact it has on people's lives—instead of on the interpersonal dynamic of feeling pulled by someone's request of us, or the emotional rewards of feeling important. *Yes, this thing might need to get done, but am I the only one who can do it? Will it genuinely* not *happen if I say no and let someone else volunteer?* Setting boundaries can be especially hard when the problems really are enormous, and we feel like perhaps our extra work really would make a difference. Here I think the key is just to keep our efforts in proportion to what is actually possible for us to do, without throwing off the entire utility-maximization equation. If we get overwhelmed and burned out, we won't be around to help the next time. Making our good works sustainable helps us show up consistently and for the long haul. And tapping into the part of your utility that thrives on others doing well also has the added benefit of helping to alleviate the envy that can often cause us to overextend ourselves at work. Tell yourself, *I care about the good thing getting done—not me being the one to do it*—and celebrate someone else's accomplishments or good work.

I'm sure all your choices make sense on the surface. But there's a hidden economics concept I also want you to consider: opportunity cost. For every use of your time that has some benefit, you're *giving something up* to have it. The cost for any use of your time is what you could have had instead. Peace? Relaxation? Time with your family? Better mental health? The question isn't whether you're doing something worthwhile with your time—of course you are. The question is, is this the *best* way to use that time?

My colleague drives her kid across town thirty minutes each way to get to school, taking a total of two hours out of her possible work, sleep, or enjoyment time. "She *has* to go to that school," she'd tell me if I asked, but I would push back. How much is her going to this school, versus the one in your neighborhood, contributing to your total utility, versus you investing that extra time in your work and getting tenure and therefore having higher income *and* more time for the rest of your life?

You need to be *ruthless* in protecting your time from things that are not investments in your future and do not bring you joy. I think of it as Marie Kondo, but for your time. Part of that process means accepting that you're not supposed to be perfect. Hold on to things that give you pleasure, both to do and to have done. Cook if you enjoy cooking, and use shortcuts if you need everyone to eat but you don't enjoy it. Garden and keep houseplants if you enjoy taking care of them. If the sight of their decaying leaves just makes you feel guilty? Toss 'em.

A lot of us have tapes in our heads that our worth is based on our external presentation. Looking put together. Getting good grades. Cooking well. Making crafts. Whatever we were praised for. We rarely got the message that our inner lives were important—our thoughts, feelings, and processes. Or that we had inherent worth totally separate from anything we ever produced or accomplished. But you don't have to keep using this old and unhelpful definition of success. Success is you enjoying your life and filling it with the things you value. So if watering your metaphorical houseplants, fertilizing them, and trimming their brown leaves isn't part of how you produce utility? Throw them away. And anything else that is draining your time and energy and not giving you utility in exchange.

Accepting imperfection also means setting some limits on how crazy we make ourselves to be green and sustainable, as important as I think these values are. But I've seen over and over the burden of these adaptations fall on individual women, instead of being broad policy changes we all share the load for. The recycling, the compost, the natural cleaning products. By all means, live a life that is green and sustainable. But also do not hold yourself to a standard of perfection. My wife put it well when I fretted about throwing away some (very old, destroyed) things we didn't need instead of finding someone who could possibly use them—"I just try to be thoughtful about how much waste I create!" I implored. "You are being thoughtful about it," she said firmly, opening the trash can. "You thought about it, and the best thing to do right now is to throw this out." Sometimes the best thing to do with a time suck is to toss it, whether physically (like a plant) or metaphorically (like a commitment we regret making), and read a good book instead.

The next chapter will tackle how we make these trade-offs with the cutest time eaters of all: our precious kids.

Chapter 10

Raising Utility

MY BEST FRIEND in college, Miriam, was the first person in her family to have access to higher education. As the daughter of blue-collar workers from a small town, she was laser-focused on making her family proud. By the time she was thirty, she had achieved her goal: she was a successful corporate lawyer on the partner track.

For as long as I'd known her, Miriam was pretty sure she didn't want to have children; she'd never felt the call, and she worried that motherhood would be at odds with her professional goals. But then, as so often happens, she met someone who made her rethink everything. He was a great guy that she knew would be a great dad. He wanted kids, and she wanted to want them, but she was terrified that having children would signal the end of her career, and more. One night, she called me on the brink of tears as she wrestled with the decision: if she got pregnant, would she come to resent her husband? Would she even, potentially, resent her future child? "Corinne, what if I don't love them?" she asked. Well, five years later, she's just welcomed her third. She took six months of parental leave with each one. And despite emphatically insisting that she planned to breastfeed for three months and not a minute more, she nursed each of her babies for a full year.

If I were writing an economic model of parenthood, I would model our utility functions as transforming once we have a child, and in ways that we cannot actually predict. To understand this, we have to revisit evolutionary biology a bit.

The so-called *selfish gene theory* states that evolution will select for traits that allow our genes to make copies of themselves. This means before we have children, the best way to ensure our genes can one day live on is to keep ourselves alive—to be focused on our own well-being. Selfish genes will also want our brains to care about people related to us, who we share some DNA with, and anyone in our communities who can help us survive.

But once we have a child, the whole structure of the optimization problem that has heretofore driven our lives is upended: now, the best way to ensure the survival of our genes is through the survival of our *offspring in addition to* ourselves. *We* still matter in this evolutionary calculation because we're the vessel for producing other offspring that can help our genes survive in the future, but there's a constant tension between that potential and the living, breathing embodiment of "passing on our genes" that now exists in the real world, rather than as a hypothetical. Then you add to this bundle of joy-slash-genes another evolutionary force: that its own selfish genes want to do everything possible to promote *its* survival, and so it is laser-targeted at triggering sympathetic responses within its parent, as effectively as social media spars for the attention that it needs to survive.

So is it any wonder that our own decisions after having a child tend to surprise us? I've seen so many friends who were convinced they would be rational, cool, unworried parents morph into the very anxious, fretting, gear-lugging stereotype they'd once mocked. When it comes to breastfeeding, for instance, many women pre-motherhood shrug and say, *If it works, I'll do it. If it doesn't, I won't.* But when the baby arrives, the combination of biological and social pressures often becomes almost impossible to circumvent. When kids reach school years, we swear we won't let our schedules revolve around theirs and yet soon find ourselves planning our meetings and commutes around soccer games and dance classes. "My kids have a love of variety," a colleague tells me, using an economic term for consumers' tendency to prefer a bundle of different items over more of the same. "So I find myself cobbling together eight different summer camps, each with different hours, snack rules, and locations."

Meanwhile, an older generation tut-tuts at us for being too anxious, for spoiling our children, citing how much simpler parenting once was, and suggesting that we're simply making things too hard for ourselves. This advice is rarely helpful and instead makes us question our choices and ourselves. We start to think, *Are we crazy? Are we making this harder than it needs to be?*

The answer is no. The science on child-rearing has changed remarkably over the last fifty years, and our expectations for our ability to manage "work-life balance" haven't kept up.

A Brief History of Parenting

The parenting advice that dominated the '50s through the '70s in America was of the Dr. Spock variety (his book *The Common Sense Book of Baby and Child Care* hit bookshelves in 1946).[1] While Dr. Spock made some adjustments from earlier, rigid parenting models, his book reassured parents that there was nothing to worry about—having a baby didn't need to be a fuss! Parents could take a laissez-faire approach. When it came to sleep, kids were expected to snooze through the night at an early age: "The cure is simple: put the baby to bed at a reasonable hour, say good night affectionately but firmly, walk out of the room, and don't go back."[2] The easy availability of shelf-stable infant formula, introduced in the 1950s, was making the early days of motherhood less time-intensive, too. By 1970, less than 10 percent of moms were breastfeeding at six months.[3]

Time use on childcare in the historical data is U-shaped—it's higher in the 1960s, when many women are providing full-time supervision to children, instead of working and relying on childcare, then it falls sharply by 1970, when women begin to enter the workforce at greater rates, before rising again in the late 1990s.

But during this time, child psychology was rapidly advancing. Scientists started to understand how babies learned, and the ways in which touch, responsiveness, and verbal interaction were important for their development.[4] Parenting styles didn't change much at first, though. While Dr. Ferber's *Solve Your Child's Sleep Problems*, published in 1985, advocated a kinder, gentler approach to sleep training—one that gradually removed parental supports—the basics were still the same: the baby needs to sleep, so mom can go back to work.[5]

Looking at a graph that depicts time spent on childcare over decades, with the deep valley between 1970 and 1990 (see chapter 1), my research coauthor Jeanne laughed. "Corinne and I were that forgotten generation," she explained to our younger research assistants. "Dinner was whatever our moms could fit in the microwave." "It's true," I added. "I spent a lot of time in the basement reading the encyclopedia."

My mother, who trained as a psychologist after going back to school following her divorce, was, relatively speaking, on the cutting edge of the movement that advocated for investing in young children's cognitive development. She breastfed, she read to us, and she bought Montessori-style toys designed to teach rather than distract. Nonetheless, when she went to school, we were carted along with her—left in the car while she ran errands and waiting in the break room at her college when she was in class. My siblings and I played along the creek with whatever we could find (sometimes—no exaggeration here— rusty scrap metal and old tires). We rode bikes freely around the neighborhood, getting into trouble with other kids, and irritating the adults. We transported ourselves to our activities by biking or walking. I cannot remember a single time being "tucked into bed," versus simply told to go there and complying. If we wanted to hang out with her, it meant doing what she was doing—watching her shows on TV, helping to cook or clean, going to some boring lecture or club meetup. Times were changing, but time use wasn't—yet.

Then came the '90s. On the graph, we see childcare time start to increase in 1995. It coincides remarkably well with a moment widely perceived as a sea change in parenting: the publication of Dr. Sears's *The Baby Book* in 1993. *The Baby Book* replaced Dr. Spock's no-fuss advice with responsive, attentive, and of course *attached* parenting.[6] Breastfeeding rates, which had blipped up in the '70s before declining again, started to rise once more. Attachment theory—science that had started as niche academic work—was becoming a mainstream understanding of how kids develop. The upshot: attentive caregiving mattered. Too much TV was bad. The words you say to your child affect their speech development.[7] Touch is crucial to babies thriving.[8] Playpens, once a ubiquitous place to stash a child while you did other things, vanished.[9]

Economists described this moment as a changed model of human capital—their word for human intelligence and potential—development. Before, we had focused on educational investments like high school and college. But now, increasing data suggested that early childhood, infancy, and even the period in utero were crucial for later life outcomes:[10] research showed that mothers who fasted for religious holidays or who were exposed to the Spanish flu while pregnant had children who earned less money as adults.[11] High-quality early childhood education increased later life outcomes.[12] Group day cares where dozens of kids watched cartoons and ate graham crackers might keep your child safe, but they wouldn't foster healthy *development*. They wouldn't help them compete in "The Rug Rat Race," a phenomenon economists Valerie Ramey and Garey Ramey cited as the source of the enormous shift in parental time use, in 2010.

And so while some elements of home production have gotten cheaper over time, making the next generation of humans has gotten far more expensive. These expenses came in both time and money: as quality standards for childcare got higher, the financial cost of parenting also rose. It's much less expensive to have one staff person for twenty children and a TV than a 1:6 ratio, or 1:4 ratio, for infants. The rate of childcare inflation has outpaced other essentials like housing, transportation, and groceries since 1990.[13] And, post-COVID, while the inflation rate of other items has fallen, the rate for childcare has continued to climb, with shortages of workers and pandemic-era subsidies expiring.[14]

These rising standards of childcare impacted both parents' bank accounts and their *time*. And this time burden is disproportionately shouldered by women. For this variable, however, there are no charts evidencing how expensive it is for the economy. Reading Dr. Sears's book when I had a newborn, I couldn't help but notice the constant intonations that women really shouldn't focus on professional work, that mothering was more important. Dads were expected to chip in, sure, but breastfeeding, babywearing, co-sleeping—this advice was all reallyabouthowtobethebestpossible*mom*.Itwasnot"attachment parenting," but "intensive mothering," as sociologist Sharon Hays aptly renamed the phenomenon in her 1998 book *The Cultural Contradictions of Motherhood*.[15]

Take, for example, the imperative to breastfeed. Breastfeeding not only typically requires a larger investment of a mother's time,[16] but because babies don't stay as full on breast milk as they do on formula, they need to be fed more frequently and wake up more often at night. Compared to formula-fed babies, breastfed babies are less likely to sleep through the night by three months.[17] This is where the idea that "breastfeeding is free" becomes problematic—it is only "free" because women's time—their unpaid labor—is all too easily dismissed as something of no economic value. Parenting blogger Ruth Wong has noted that even the recommendation to put babies to sleep on their backs means lost parental—and really, maternal—sleep. Back-sleeping works to prevent SIDS because babies sleep less deeply. And, well, that means they also . . . sleep less deeply. An engineer by trade, Wong set out to estimate exactly how many hours of parental sleep were lost for each life saved by the recommendations—her answer: 42,500 hours.[18]

I see this huge shift in how we spend our time as a silent epidemic. Women blame themselves for not being able to keep up, when really, they don't have the same hours in a day as the working moms from a generation before. And nothing has changed to offset this new intensive investment—we've maxed out on time-saving technologies for housework, and men aren't helping: their minutes on housework haven't budged since the 1970s. So we're left with an equation that just doesn't add up— trying to be equals to men in the office, and equals to the women who came before us, while also parenting as a full-time job.

So if you have children and a career, and life feels impossibly hard, please understand that no, you are not crazy, and no, it is not your fault. In this time and place, being a mother and a worker *is* impossibly hard. It's wonderful that, thanks to science, we have better information than we did fifty years ago about what keeps kids healthy and promotes optimal brain develop-ment and social and emotional well-being. But along with this knowledge has come a fundamental shift to our understanding of the child production function and the role our time plays in it. In short: the math has changed.

This understanding of how our time affects child development is a Pandora's box of knowledge that we cannot close again. Now that we know babies are safer when we put them to sleep on their backs, *what kind of monster* would put them on their stomachs and let them sleep soundly instead? And similarly, if there's an iota of research showing that breastfeeding has enduring health benefits, who would give their kids *formula* instead? And if you can contribute more to your child's development by taking three months of maternity leave, what kind of a heartless "raven mother" (the term in Germany for mothers of young children who return to work) would rush back to the office? So why not six months? Or a year? After all, there's no better caregiver than *a child's own mother.*

Of course, any mother of an older child can tell you that these pressures don't evaporate after preschool. Knowing that too much screen time is bad for brain development, how could you let your kids watch a show on their iPad while you squeeze in a little extra work or maybe a nap? Or, fully aware that smartphones pose a threat to teen mental health, how can you not supervise your teen's every waking moment?

I don't want to draw a parallel between putting babies to sleep on their backs—which is a strongly evidence-based safety precaution—and the rest of these examples. But I do want to make the point that just because we know something is helpful does not mean that there aren't costs and that a rationally optimizing individual doesn't need to make *trade-offs*. After all, avoiding contact with the outside world would probably protect our children from viruses and accidents but isn't a practical or reasonable approach to parenting. And one important factor that allows children to thrive is the income we're able to earn— which buys essential goods like housing and clothing—as well as our own self-actualization, which lets us be better parents as well as good role models.

We make trade-offs in every other domain. For example, we know that lower highway speed limits would save lives, but we choose lower commute times instead. Chemicals in the atmosphere and water are regulated according to how many cancer cases they'll cause per million. Not whether they cause cancer but whether they cause *too much*, because of course those same chemicals also produce products that people value, and in turn corporate profits. And, in fact, public policy is more than willing to make trade-offs when it comes to children's health and well-being that individuals would be culturally shamed for considering. Using the passage of the Clean Air Act, economists Adam Isen, Maya Rossin-Slater, and Reed Walker show that reducing pollution in the year babies are born leads to higher workforce participation and earnings—and yet particulate matter remains dangerously high, especially in poorer communities.[19] Regulating it more—reducing particulate matter to safe levels that wouldn't affect fetal and infant development— costs money and slows down business growth. And so the government makes *choices*. We as parents are expected to do *everything possible* to protect our little bundles of joy, but when data shows something else is putting them at risk, society largely shrugs. Recent evidence showed that when the bat population collapsed in some US states due to a fungus, farmers increased their use of pesticides to compensate for the now uncontrolled insects. This led to an *8 percent increase in infant mortality* in affected counties. Importantly, the paper points out, this use of pesticides was fully within regulatory limits.[20] Other people, it seems, are allowed to risk your child's health, especially if it makes money.

So if we can acknowledge that women's time is valuable and costly, too, then we can start to think more strategically about how we want to invest it. Every parent will chart their own course based on the needs of their families, but I hope that having some context for how we arrived at this moment leaves you feeling a little more empowered to make decisions that are right for *you*. Caring about your child's development is not trivial, nor is it a self-created anxiety the way generations of yore might suggest. The way time shifts after having kids makes perfect sense—children introduce a novel technology for making utility with your time. Not only can you directly enjoy being with them, but the time you put in to nurturing them has incredible returns for their future abilities. And, of course, parents value their children's future outcomes. Is it any wonder that parents choose to invest resources in home production and caretaking? It is also not your *only* imperative in life. You can identify which inputs have the highest return, what is possible, and what trade-offs you're willing to make for your unique human capital-in-progress.

Family Values

When it comes to our kids, guilt and fear are powerful forces shaping our decisions. We worry they aren't signed up for enough activities, that their friends are doing more, that our vacations aren't as much fun, their grades aren't good enough, that we're buying too much plastic, that they don't have enough playdates, that we don't spend enough time outside . . . the list goes on. Listen: someone else's child is always going to have more of something. And just like you can't compare yourself to people with different utility functions, you can't compare yourself to people with different children. Their optimization problem is totally different from yours! You have to define your values and priorities when it comes to parenting just as you do in other areas of home production.

Sometimes, an assessment of the parts of the tasks that you find most important will lead to other insights. I ran into an academic friend at a conference two years after giving her an impassioned speech about how dashing out of work to pick her son up from day care and then driving him home to the baby-sitter before coming back to teach her evening class absolutely was not the best use of her pre-tenure time. *There has to be someone else who can do this*, I'd said.

"That conversation was so helpful," she shared, updating me that she had decided not to go up for tenure and instead take a lower-pressure job within her university. "I realized that your excellent advice genuinely wasn't possible for me. And then I thought about why, and I realized other moms were having a different experience. Absolutely, for other kids, the babysitter could have done the pickup. But my kid's needs are different, and he needed more of me. So I decided to change my vision for myself—the same things weren't possible for me as for someone else, and that's okay!"

I gave her an enormous hug and told her I was proud of her. Because she looked happy. Because she was making a decision that was truly, deeply connected to her inner values and needs, instead of the messages of achievement that we're constantly fed. She shared that her son was thriving now that she was spending more time with him and that she'd advocated for him to receive extra services at school. She felt good about her choice, because it was clearly the right one for her family's needs.

This is why I balk at the depiction of women's earnings decreasing after having children as "child penalties." Sometimes women step back to make deliberate, strategic child investments. Just like money, time is a finite resource. If I see a couple spending less money on restaurant meals, alcohol, and travel after they have kids, I wouldn't call it a "child penalty" in spending but rather a change in priorities. Similarly, when we see women's earnings drop after having children, some of that gap represents choices that are being made to reduce labor supply—to shift their time from market work to time with their kids. Child penalties are really *child investments*.

What concerns me is what can happen to women's careers after that point and how difficult it often is to continue on a high-investment track after temporarily taking some time away. But I think the data tells a story that when women have more financial privilege, they use some of it to reallocate their time away from moneymaking and toward direct utility-making once they have children. We see it in the fact that "child penalties" are larger for more privileged women, and smaller or absent for Black women, who may have the least access to substitute financial security.[21] And we see it in the fact that women with higher earnings do not spend less time with their children.[22] The more educated a woman is, the higher her opportunity cost of time is—the costlier it is for her to spend time outside the workforce. But also, the more valuable the time that she'll invest in her children, and the less replaceable she is through conventional outsourced solutions.

Remember, economists who study women's labor supply decisions over the last thirty years have reached the conclusion that "own childcare"—taking care of our children ourselves—is a luxury good. This doesn't mean luxury as in designer handbags—it just means something that isn't feasible in our budget set when we're very strapped for cash, but that we make space for as our financial possibilities expand. This is why I advocate for childcare subsidies that are "provider neutral"—that is, they should pay the same whether the mother is the one providing the care versus if it's being purchased on the market (more in the afterword). If you're lucky enough to have paid leave, or another salary that can cover the bills while you take a step back, maybe it's a little bit freeing to see the time you're spending with your children as something you're making a conscious choice to *purchase* instead of something you're trapped in.

This was a hard-won realization for my friend Summer, who decided to take a break from her career for the sake of her and her family's well-being. Summer was raised by a Black single mother whose five children all earned college degrees—achievement was a second-nature instinct to her. But living with an autoimmune disorder that often left her hospitalized when she pushed her body too far, the increasing demands of motherhood and a full-time job were putting her health in peril. She reevaluated her priorities and decided to downsize her lifestyle and focus on being a mom and keeping herself healthy. "I used to think all I had to do is survive. But why am I pushing myself to the limit and then having to save my life all the time?" She said it had been a big adjustment to her identity. That she struggled with what to say when other parents asked her what she did for a living on the playground or at school drop-off. But ultimately, she shared, "I don't owe anyone anything. My life is mine to live."

You don't owe anyone anything, either. Just as we've embraced the feminist message that we don't owe patriarchy to fit into traditional beauty standards, we do not owe it to the world to meet expectations that don't serve us, be it home production ex-cellence—Instagrammable décor! Bento box lunches!—*or* career achievement. You are not failing anyone by choosing yourself, and your best life, over the roles that have been written for you.

If, however, you find that you want to invest in your children *and* your career, let's discuss the economics of *creating literal life* without "leaning out."

Leveling Up Your Leave

The first year of parenthood upends our worlds in myriad ways, and it's when so many of the life choices we've made are brought to the forefront. The dissonance between the person we thought we were, the path we thought we were on—and our sudden new (adorable, needy) reality—can be disorienting. The data is clear on one point: women who have children tend to earn less in the workplace than women who don't have children. We've already discussed how this may be the result of a rational "purchase" of own childcare, rather than an externally imposed penalty. Nonetheless, there are economic forces that fuel this earning loss, and our goal is to rewire these mechanics in our favor.

I have observed (and experienced) women agonizing over the "right" timing to start having children relative to career milestones. And while it's understandable to want to hack this impossible matrix of decisions, I'm not sure the "when" of kids makes much of a difference. First of all, control over the timing of pregnancy is imperfect at best. No matter how much technology has improved, we still do not have the full ability to "save" or "borrow" our reproductive capital. Second, there's never a perfect time. It is capitalism's job to make you feel totally, completely irreplaceable, and amid constant crises, it's your job to recognize that if you're not there to catch the ball, someone else will. If you want to become a mother, doing it at the time that works best from a holistic and biological perspective is more important for your utility than doing it at the perfect time career-wise.

What we often spend less time considering—and what we do have some real control over—is the "pre-leave" penalty women pay in anticipation that they *might* take leave. This is what Mary Ann Bronson, who researches the discrimination women face prior to forty, calls the "gender penalty" rather than the "child penalty." And this is something I want you to minimize for yourself as much as possible.

Communicate strategically: Your employer will be transactional with you if it affects their bottom line, so you get to choose how much information you share with them, and when. If you want to pretend to be Marissa Maier, who famously had a nursery built next to her office so she didn't have to miss a beat at work, that's between you and whatever god you worship. But then when the time actually comes, if you do want to take leave, here are some ideas on how to navigate it.

Wait for whatever point you think is most strategic to bring up the fact that you're expecting, or your plan to take leave. When you do, use talking points to convey how your plan to take parental leave will actually be beneficial to your employer. The goal is not to be dropped from opportunities or promotions. Note that demonstrating to younger employees that someone can be in your position and have a family is important for attracting the best female talent, and in turn the innovation, ideas, and competitive edge they bring to the table. If you're a manager, you can explain that you will think of your leave as a career development opportunity for your team, and describe how you'll proactively work to prepare other team members to replace you and give them opportunities to develop new skills and capacities while you're gone. If you're an employee, you can jointly brainstorm with your manager, who you can begin working side by side with now to ensure a seamless transition while you are on leave. Lay it on thick: your goal is the success of the organization, and you are totally dedicated to ensuring that success. If you're in a profession with a union, like teaching or nursing, talk to your union rep about what your rights and options are before the time comes, and get their advice on when to disclose information to your manager.

Choose your "out of office" setting: A coauthor and friend who is pre-tenure recently welcomed her third baby, and she felt confident she could juggle breastfeeding and work. She was at a sensitive enough point in her career that after a month fully off, she wanted to tune back in. But she fretted, "If I join the weekly team call, am I setting a terrible example for our graduate students by working over leave?" Which is interesting because a generation before, the worry was over the perception of not "being serious" about work. One of my mentors at Wharton relayed rushing back into the classroom a few days after giving birth thirty years ago to prove that she didn't need to be treated differently from her male colleagues.

You get to decide how you want to use your leave based on what makes sense for you and your family's life—based on your utility function. Not what anyone says you should do or thinks of you.

If you want to tune out entirely and enjoy those tiny toes and new baby smell, not to mention feeding a human whose stomach is the size of a marble around the clock and recovering from the equivalent of major surgery (or literal surgery, in the case of a C-section), I salute you. You might find yourself consumed by bonding and physical recovery and domestic labor for the entirety of your leave—and there is nothing wrong with that. This is an enormously valid way to create utility. While any parental leave you take will likely have a cost, due to the time outside the workforce, where others are accumulating human capital and promotions, you can think of this as the outcome of optimization, to put that time into "purchasing" own childcare, and all the utility that comes with it. That time is not wasted or lost.

If you're at a very sensitive point in your career, you might find that unplugging entirely doesn't feel like an option. Or maybe you're on a second or third kid, or just feel like you've hit a stride with childcare and you miss engaging with your professional work. In any case, I want you to use the principle of marginal return to your actions—where can you put in the smallest effort and get the biggest payoff? Staying in touch with a client, solving a problem for a colleague—is there anything you can do that's highly visible while also not creating too much effort, nor creating a huge boomerang effect where suddenly more work comes back to you?

If you're able to afford it, securing some childcare for just a couple of hours a day probably has zero negative impact on your child's development, and a lot of positive impact on your mental well-being. If it feels like you can't afford a professional care-giver, consider whether you might ask for some support from a trusted family member or friend. Leaving work aside, shower-ing alone, taking a walk, going to a store just to be around other adults—whatever makes you feel human—is worth a couple of hours away from your baby.

If a bit of career-investment time is on the agenda, another option to consider is making *general* human capital investments, instead of company-specific ones. Worried you'll get passed over for a promotion when you get back? Can you learn a skill or get a certificate that both makes you more eligible for promotion *and* more competitive on the outside market so you can drive a tough bargain upon your return? Do you want to take some time to invest in a creative project or side hustle you've always wanted to get going but never had mental space for until now? When we're actually *working*-working, so much of our day is unproductive email answering, meetings, and back-and-forth. I found that if I wrote my research papers for just two hours a day on maternity leave, literally setting a timer for thirty minutes at a time, I actually got a ton done. Looking back, that was too much—I wish I hadn't felt like I needed to put myself through so much work while caring for my son. But if you do decide to dedicate something like one hour, three times a week, to a professional activity while you're on leave, I think you'll be amazed by your own capacity.

Those human capital investments also need not be in your specific field. Another way to use these moments—and the huge shift in perspective that accompanies parenthood—is to consider alternate paths. If you find yourself dreading returning to your job, or realizing you are not set up for success as a working parent under the structure of your current employer, leave gives you the opportunity to shop around a little bit. Importantly, I want you to remember that the tremendous stress you feel right now, and even the emotional turmoil of a mom considering returning to work, is *temporary.* So take the long view, thinking about the entire life cycle of your career, and remembering that all too often there aren't as many "on-ramps" for career paths as there are exits. Are there ways to plan your career that both accommodate the moment you're in right now *and* plan for the future when the squeeze passes? At the same time, does this career path offer any kind of destination that you're interested in reaching? Return to the book-with-many-chapters idea and reflect if the current milestones you're striving toward are leading to the ending you want to have . . . or if it's time for a plot twist.

Invest in dynamic complementarity . . . for your spouse: Economists and moms Laura Gee and Olga Stoddard remembered venting to each other about how no matter what they did, how busy they were, or how available their husbands were, their kids' schools usually contacted them first. Olga's husband was listed as the primary contact at her kids' school and handled about 50 percent of the pickups and drop-offs. At one of those drop-offs, the teacher handed him the sign-up for a parent-teacher conference and said, "I know this isn't your responsibility, but could you check when your wife would want to meet with us?" Laura reflected that as experimental economists, they had the skill set to find out if they were the only ones trapped in this private hell or if it was a broader phenomenon. Together with theorist Kristy Buzard, whom they brought aboard to help them narrow down the reasons schools and other external actors might behave this way, they wrote a bunch of fake inquiry emails to school principals, offering contact information for both the father and the mother. Although they sent 50 percent of the emails from the mother and 50 percent from the father, consistent with their experience, they found that the mother still received 60 percent of the calls. Perhaps more galling, even when the email explicitly stated that the mother had "limited availability to chat," she still received half the calls! By contrast, if Dad said he had limited availability, he only received 10 percent of the calls.[23]

This experiment shows the real-life impact of the cultural idea of mothers as the default parent. This assumption of Mom being the one "who's got it" can all too easily set in, especially if Mom is the one doing the acclimation and day care adjustment when she goes back to work. This is why I think paternity leave is so crucial.

While you might not be able to set national paternity leave policy, you do hopefully have some influence over the paternity leave policy for your household. If you are married to a man, I encourage you to explore if it's financially feasible for him to take three full months of leave. What you are investing in is the lifelong equality of your parenting relationship, instead of being the "baby person" who turns into the "toddler person." This is the curse of complementarity—time investments down the road are always going to be complementary to those already made. So the more you can increase those early investments, the better your chances of creating a more equitable household later on.

Paternity leave isn't just good for your baby, it's good for you. Research shows paternity leave substantially improves *maternal* health.[24] With a first child, there's lots to do even if you're not the one who can feed a baby with your body, like all the laundry, cooking, and cleaning so the person who's physically recovering doesn't have to do it. (Bonus: later on, he can't claim he doesn't know where the detergent is.) With a second or later baby, there's a lot of parenting to do for those other small people who will feel suddenly displaced and extra needy.

And because I believe paternity leave is so important for establishing parental equity, I think it's worth men taking time off even when they don't have access to paid leave. I do not want to sound out of touch here: I know that there are many households that simply cannot miss a paycheck, which is why what we really need is national paid parental leave. If that's you, you're not "marginal" for this decision—the economic term for someone on the border between a yes and a no—it truly is not an option. But I also think a lot of people say, "We could never afford that!" reflexively, without considering what other investments they make of comparable size.

Ideally, when you start planning to have a baby, you can also begin saving for any amount of your and your spouse's leave that will be unpaid. Think of those three months of leave as an investment in eighteen years of more equitable parenting and domestic labor with your spouse, and thus also a direct investment in *your career*. Research backs this up—promising new evidence from Spain, by Libertad González and coauthors, showed just two weeks of dedicated paternity leave policy resulted in moms who were more likely to be employed for the two years after the birth of their child, and earn more money, compared to moms whose spouses took no leave.[25] It's hard to measure the total utility impact of decisions that subtly shift something across our entire lives, but a better and more equal partnership is pretty darn close to priceless, and investing in paternity leave is one way you get there.

To make this investment in complementarity work, dads must embrace that they are not "helpers" but *also* the baby's parent. He, too, can scour the internet for the latest safe baby gear recommendations, subscribe to the parenting newsletter, go to baby swim class, and make pediatrician appointments. You can also consider delaying some of his leave so that he can take a few weeks off when you go back to work—maybe you both take four weeks together at the beginning, then you finish your leave while he goes back to work, and he takes the second half of his when you're back in the office—so that he will not just experience being a parent but experience being the *only* parent. If he's the one orienting the baby at day care, maybe they'll call him instead of you in an emergency.

Remember utility: My final note about maternity leave is again an appeal to not just see it as a potential "trap" in your career climb but rather part of the unified purpose of your life. You are here on earth not to achieve but to live. If you've decided having a child is part of your purpose, then there is nothing that could be more important for your utility than to spend time with that child—both to invest, yes, and also just to *enjoy*.

The principle of making utility can also help you decide which parenting investments are "worth it." Many moms find breastfeeding *nice*. It's bonding time with your baby, it releases endorphins, and if you're at home and going to be feeding them, anyway, why not use your body's own capacity to do so? Pumping while at work is a different story entirely: it takes time that is not time spent holding your cute baby, it's messy and inconvenient, and you still have to pay someone to actually give your baby the milk. There's no wrong answer on whether to breastfeed and whether to pump at work, but the principle of utility maximization tells us we can have different answers to these two things, rationally. The added utility value of breastfeeding might make it "worth it" even though evidence on physiological benefits is sparse (and weighted toward the first three months), while the economics of pumping are completely different.

So when you're home with your baby, I urge you to keep your eye on the prize: your total lifetime utility, of which your baby's human capital is a part, of which career accomplishments can be a piece, but where everything has its own place. It bears repeating here again: *your job is a technology to convert your time into money.* It helps me sometimes to remember the absurdity: all the career stuff, all the jobs, all the glass skyscrapers, all were built from our evolutionary drive as a species to accumulate resources in order to procreate. And now, sometimes we're so busy accumulating those resources that those of us who become parents feel like we're doing something wrong by fulfilling these evolutionary desires. If you experience a panicky feeling rising inside about how you're not doing enough, or what other people are achieving while you're on leave, hold your child close, breathe deeply, and say, "This *is* life."

Chapter 11

When It Doesn't Work

NOW THAT WE'VE talked about many forms of optimization in your life, it's time to revisit one of the most important "deals" you're in, see if it's working for you, and discuss what to do if it falls apart. Soon after my marriage ended, I was on the phone with a reporter discussing hiring discrimination when somehow the topic of divorce came up. I disclosed that my husband and I were in the process of separating, and she responded by sharing that she was newly divorced. Suddenly bonded in that way that serendipitously happens when two women recognize shared experiences, I confided that I was worried about how everything was going to work on my own. I was huddled in the bedroom working, making the most out of sharing a tiny New York apartment while I prepared to move to Philadelphia. Things felt bleak.

"Corinne," she said, "you think it's going to be harder, but it's actually going to be easier." She told me that every woman she's known who's gotten divorced has found themselves with more time, not less, even as solo parents. "When you're married," she went on, "you might have put in effort to make a big family dinner every night. But when you're divorced, you give the kids an apple and a cheese stick and then you eat whatever you wanted to eat, anyway."

I was reassured, but not entirely convinced—and yet the data would later show that her assessment was spot-on. Women's investment of time in home production—cooking and cleaning—goes down, not up, after divorce. Of course, no one gets divorced to spend less time cleaning. No one plans to or wants to leave a marriage. But I'm sharing this information with you in the same spirit it was shared with me: to remove a bit of fear from the equation as you weigh your options.

Of course, contemplating the end of a relationship doesn't mean the relationship *has* to end. As in all situations, however, your bargaining power comes from your BATNA—best alternative to negotiated agreement. Being convinced that you have no possible options is exactly how you get locked into a bad deal. It's also possible that you don't plan for divorce, but it arrives at your door uninvited: the other person filing, infidelity, or a sudden insurmountable difference. So for anyone who's married or considering marriage, I think it's helpful to understand the empirical impacts of divorce. (And even if you never want to get married, please keep reading, because there's plenty of universally helpful advice in this chapter!)

Schrödinger's Divorce

In previous chapters, we've covered some of the pitfalls of the "divorce revolution"—that unilateral divorce laws made marriages less secure and negatively impacted women who had invested in home production (and thus their husbands' careers) to the detriment of their own earning power. I think marriage with someone who wants to be an *equal* partner is transformative—it creates the commitment needed to sacrifice personal interest for overall family well-being, and in doing so creates more utility for everyone involved. It also can have the benefits of returns to scale—cooking one meal for two, sharing a house—and specialization—whether that means the traditional focus on one person doing more home production and one person doing more market production, or just one person being really good at electronics while the other takes care of the car. But when we're talking about divorce, we're not talking about a good marriage; we're talking about a marriage that's gone wrong. And what the data tells me is that women in *these* marriages weren't really getting to benefit from these forces.

To study what happened to women's time after divorce, my coauthors on the "Winning the Bread" paper and I used a data set called the Panel Study of Income Dynamics (PSID), which repeatedly surveys American households every one to two years. This type of data, which tracks the behavior of the same people over time, allows us to create something called an *event study*, where we align the data not by calendar year but by the year of an event, like a divorce, and then graph an outcome before and after an event. The PSID asks respondents how much time they spend on housework, which includes cooking and cleaning, but not childcare.

We looked specifically at survey results during two life events: marriage and divorce. It's perhaps not surprising, given that the PSID covers a period since 1968 and given that the more common specialization pattern even today is for men to focus more on labor-market work and women more on home production, that upon marriage, women's time on housework goes up and men's goes down. The fact that men's time on home production decreases upon entering a marriage tells us that, generally speaking, men like having that housework done, and know how to do it themselves but just prefer someone else take it on. The fact that women's time spent on home production increases, even if we keep the number of kids constant, reflects her taking on this work for both members of the household—specialization.

But what really shocked me was the data showing that women's time on housework decreases upon divorce—even women with kids. We're not counting childcare time itself, but children generate an enormous amount of additional domestic labor in the form of cooking, cleaning, laundry, and so on. In my mind, getting divorced meant losing an adult with whom to divide this workload—going from two pairs of hands to one. And yet, despite women on average being the primary custodial parent, their time spent on domestic work drops. Men's time spent cooking and cleaning, on the other hand, goes up—suddenly, without a woman around to do it for him, he learns how to use a broom. He also spends more money on meals outside the household, outsourcing the production of the goods he used to receive from his spouse's labor.

Divorced women, though, spend less time cooking and don't spend any more money on outsourced meals—they're not getting less, they're *doing* less. Rather than losing efficiency with fewer hands to help, women gain time by having less domestic labor to do. Because as it turns out, their husbands were *creators* of work to be done more than they were *doers* of that work.

Of course, it's not all upside. Women typically experience a loss of income when they leave a marriage, and thus a lower level of consumption (spending) for themselves and their children, as a host of research by economists like Raquel Fernández (using data from the US) and more recently Hanno Foerster (using data from Denmark) has shown.[1] The reason for this is the still-substantial gender wage gap—in every country in the world, men are higher earners, on average, than women. And, in fact, this gap is larger than the gender wage gap suggests, since the gender wage gap compares full-time employment. Women also are more likely than men to work part-time or to not be employed at all. So, overall, women tend to earn a lot less money than men. The underlying reason for this is of course the investments that women make in home production, child human capital investments, and everything else we've discussed throughout this book. Those investments cut into women's possible earnings even when she is the higher earner—how much more could she have done if she had gotten the same time investments from her partner as a man in her position would have? And current divorce laws do not fully make up for this gap through child support and alimony upon divorce. These are all reasons why women tend to lose some financial resources when they get divorced and often work more to make up for it.

This is why I urge women to start planning for divorce well before they need to—ideally as soon as they get married (I know, so romantic), but, more realistically, as soon as things start to feel rocky. Economists model divorce as coming from shocks that change the terms of the relationship, amusingly referred to as "love shocks." And the whole idea of shocks is that we can't see them coming. We predict the future based on the path we're on and what's likely to come next. But what if we find out information that changes the trajectory of that path? What if our relationship changes? What if our partner changes? What if we change? In the here and now, we hope things will work out. But we need to account for a possible realization in the multiverse. A world different from today, where you *can't* count on your spouse anymore, or don't want to.

So set yourself up for Schrödinger's divorce—you don't know if it will happen, but you need to plan for it just in case. Working to make yourself financially independent, or have the potential of increasing your earnings if you need to, will give you the most options down the line. Invest in your kids and bask in spending time with them, yes. But insist that your family also invests in you. If you're taking time off work, insist some of the household budget is allocated toward certifications or continuing education that would keep your skills current. Keep in mind that today's decisions are tomorrow's constraints, and think about how you can set yourself up in case you need to support yourself and your kids (which could happen even without divorce)—keep your toe in the working world, keep contacts active, create a small business or passive income stream on the side, and so on.

If you have debt, focus on paying it off while you're still married. Even if you're working less or earning less, marriage law views you as a single economic unit of production, because of all the other ways you're contributing to the household. His paycheck is a joint asset in the eyes of the law, but your assets or debt when you came into the marriage aren't. So using joint household assets to shore up your financial situation in the worst-case scenario is a smart move. It's also smart to consider not just the letter of the law but possible out-of-court settlements—a common default position in settlements is whatever you have in the bank account, something that could be detrimental if his larger paycheck is getting deposited into his separate account, despite the shared nature of the economic production required to earn it. How do you make sure that your contributions outside labor-market work are being recognized in the financial structure of your household? For example, if you earn less but contribute more to home production, can you make sure his greater financial resources are going into shared accounts and assets?

Also remember that working time creates a retirement account and social security credits. Pay attention to how much of what you're investing in are *public goods* that both people in the marriage benefit from versus private goods that you would take with you in the case of divorce. Your spouse's human capital and the career milestones that they accumulate while you're taking on the lion's share of the housework and kid-work are *private* goods, and worse, they're assets that are invisible to the court and won't be divided. In a world where your marriage certainly stays together, those investments continue to benefit you and your children over the long term. Which, as we've discussed, is exactly one of the core purposes of the marriage contract—putting aside individual interests for something that creates joint value, the same way a business contract allows the sharing of proprietary materials one wouldn't share with an unaffiliated firm. But we don't live in that world anymore, where a marriage is for sure forever no matter what. So do some mental accounting on how much of the joint work of your marriage is going into something that you can take with you in case the marriage dissolves. And if the answer is very little, it's time to do some rebalancing. Again, when a relationship is solid, no one wants to think about this.

But if things go really wrong, you will be in a much safer position—and a more empowered one—if you don't need to solely rely on your spouse for financial support.

Cost-Benefit Analysis

Relationships can break down for a multitude of reasons, and men initiate divorce as well as women. This was the reality for far too many women in the 1970s, who had entered what they thought were "till death do us part" contracts, only to find out that they could be pushed to the side for someone younger, often losing the financial stability they'd relied on. But if *you're* in the position of thinking about divorce, and deciding if it's what you want, let's take a brief moment to take stock of what that means economically.

If marriage is a contract, then divorce is dissolving that contract. It means splitting one household into two, but also splitting two lives mutually dedicated to a shared purpose into two. (If you have kids, or the court awards spousal support, a portion of the contract will be replaced with a new written, rather than implicit, one). In addition to (what's left of) this commitment to each other, you are going to lose three key benefits: 1) income pooling, 2) returns to scale, 3) time pooling / specialization. To understand if this is what you want, let's break down each of these factors so that you can assess if they really are benefiting you.

Income pooling is the economic term for sharing financial resources in the household. This happens to varying degrees, from having a single bank account into which all resources go, to keeping separate accounts and sharing expenses. If more of the things that you consume are paid for by your spouse's earnings than your own, then your financial resources are likely to decrease upon divorce. Now, if your spouse is the higher earner, that doesn't always mean that you're getting the long end of the deal in marriage. You have to ask yourself how much of the shared household "pot" is actually used to your benefit. Often, in a marriage gone awry, financial control and decision-making might already be skewed in a way that doesn't work for you, and having a court-ordered structure could be an improvement.

And if you're the higher-earning partner, you may lose control of some resources, in that the court will mandate a certain amount of sharing, rather than you "bargaining" within marriage over how these resources are shared. However, again, you need to realistically assess the status quo—is hassle or guilt currently giving you less control in practice than you'd get through a court agreement?

Returns to scale in a household refers to the benefits of sharing housing and all else that comes along with cohabitation. These benefits are real and should certainly be considered in the equation. Here, too, the benefits you're giving up depend on the current terms of the relationship. If your current preferences or needs are very different from one another, then the benefits might be more limited—as they were with my long commute. For example, different preferences around budget and location might limit the benefits of shared housing. So will different preferences either for consuming or making home-produced goods—the idea of one person making a lovely dinner for two *sounds* great, but if the reality is actually a fight, or one person always doing the work, you might already be missing out on some of this efficiency.

Which brings us to the last household benefit, *time pooling*, and the possibility for specialization that comes with it. If you were to become your own household, there might be some *income* sharing that remains, through child support and / or alimony. But there will no longer be time sharing. You can only consume a home-produced item if you produce it with your own time. You also lose access to the ability to specialize, by one person using more time for converting to money, and the other using it more to make utility for the household through home production. In other words, while you can still use your own time for either money or direct utility, you lose the ability to use someone *else's* time for those things, or at least influence the use of that time.

Here, too, the state of the relationship determines the relative significance of this loss. Is the current specialization arrangement serving you? Recall also that effective specialization requires commitment—you each have to *believe* that you'll be around to reap the long-term benefits of separate investments. The less stable the relationship, the less it feels like a good "deal" to invest in home production while someone else gains human capital. So, the question is, how much do you stand to gain compared to what you have to lose?

If you're the lower-earning partner, and will have fewer financial resources after divorce, you will be better off if you can proactively plan for that reality. Sit down and figure out your costs of operation—how much you will need to spend on housing, how much on childcare, how much support you expect to receive, and so on. Make a budget. Then I would encourage you to think creatively about ways to minimize your immediate financial burden. Would moving somewhere with a cheaper cost of living help? Is there an investment you could cash out? Can you ask for a raise at work, or start applying to other jobs now, to quietly improve your financial position before you need it?

Sometimes, when a marriage isn't working, the drain it places on your energy outweighs any help it might provide in paying the bills. When you end a bad marriage, you are going to reclaim mental resources, energy, and time. And remember, time is the building block of utility. It can be converted into money or turned directly into happiness. The extra time you have from disengaging in a losing battle can go into strengthening your own human capital and growing your earning power. That said, you can't do it *all* on your own, so it's imperative that you ask for the necessary resources you need—and deserve. The next section will discuss how to do this without losing your sanity.

Keep Your Eye on the Objective (Function)

Despite the emotional strife of divorce, there is tremendous power in knowing the cooperative phase of your relationship is over. As economists say, your objective function—what you're maximizing—changes once a marriage ends. Before, the priority was getting your spouse's buy-in and feeling seen and respected by them. Now, what's important is achieving mutual agreement on the terms you want, with as little drama as possible. The goal is no longer to win the point but rather to win the day.

I urge you to sit down and, with the help of a lawyer, write what you ideally want—child support, custody, asset division—and then what you can live with. Understand that divorce law is fundamentally flawed in many ways, but it does give you some core rights. In the US, all property that was acquired during the marriage, including the increase in value of preexisting property, is marital property. This is part of the core understanding in US law of a married household being a single economic unit of production. That means that even if he made every single mortgage payment, the house is still a joint marital asset to be divided by the courts (with the exact percentages varying by state and judge). Through the joint marital property provision, US courts recognize that homemaking is a contribution to the joint economic production of the household. (If you're reading this book in another country, you should familiarize yourself with local laws in this regard—many other countries do recognize joint property in marriage, although some offer the option to separate by default when entering the marriage.) My grandmother was awarded half of my grandfather's assets by arguing that she had supported him in law school and then done 100 percent of the home production during his lucrative career as a lawyer, and so the spoils of that career were as much hers as his. In addition to asset division, if you are the low earner, you will be entitled to both child support and possibly some amount of alimony or "spousal support." Again, it is unlikely to make up for the income sharing you had in place in marriage, but it also may come with many fewer strings attached. (One note, if you are in a relationship but not married, you do not have the protection of asset division—but if you have children, you are still entitled to child support.)

If you are the high earner, here's where things get tricky. Unfortunately, although the law was indeed written to protect women who were not on paper the income earners or property owners, despite contributing equally through their labor, it is not actually written as gendered. So I have seen plenty of men use it to claim spousal support or assets from their higher-earning wives when they were in reality busy being a "guitar hero" or chasing a pipe dream business, not doing home production labor that contributed to the household's overall economic production. This absolutely infuriates me, because the laws are gender symmetric, whereas the investments we make are *not* gender symmetric. But what the courts will grant you is only the worst-case scenario if you cannot reach an agreement yourselves. So in addition to understanding the legal framework, you need to be thinking about the *psychological one.*

You will use all your hard-won knowledge from the marriage you tried to make work to achieve the outcome you need, somewhere in the middle of what you want and what you can live with. Remember, you don't have to be in a relationship with or live with your ex anymore! So if they say, "You're such a @#$%!," you say, "Okay, if you think so. Anyway, can we talk about the schedule for next month?" Getting a drama-free settlement where you have the time with your kids and resources that you need is the way you maximize your utility function. So vent to your friends or therapist, put your ego to the side, and stay laser-focused on that objective, treating your ex like a difficult but important client.

I also strongly encourage you to do everything you can to avoid going to court, while heavily researching (and consulting with a lawyer about) likely outcomes in your state or country if you were to go to court. Why? That's your BATNA in a divorce:

what a judge will give you. But it will be expensive to get there. Internally, you have to factor in the cost of legal representation through a trial and the fact that judges recently have been more prone to granting shared custody schedules that may not align with the reality of childcare in your household and tend to be an excuse to avoid child support.[2] Because fifty-fifty schedules are often a gambit to reduce child support responsibilities, if your number one priority is more custody, you can often get it by agreeing to meet your ex halfway on child support obligation.

Even if you draft your own agreement or use a mediator, you should get a lawyer. You need someone advising you on your rights, what a judge is likely to decide, and what the process looks like. That's keeping your BATNA firmly in place to increase your bargaining power. But the more you can make the process with your ex collaborative, and give them a feeling of control and being heard, the more likely you are to get what you want. Figure out ways to give concessions on things that aren't important to you. Draft an initial agreement with the help of a lawyer, and then say, "This is just a draft; happy to adjust the holiday schedule or the language wherever you think it's important." Let your ex make adjustments in places you really don't value that much (but don't say that—say, "Hmmm, that's hard for me, but if it's important to you, I'm willing to change it") and remain steadfast on the core things you need. Again, you don't have to *feel* like you're on the same page anymore! That chapter is done! Keep your eyes on the objective function of your new life: you and (if applicable) your kids, period.

Letters from Your Future

One beautiful fall weekend last year, K and I hosted friends from New York: one of K's former preschool classmates and his mom. She was at a crossroads. She had been in an unfulfilling marriage for too long and felt stuck, unhappy, and a bit hopeless. She and I had last shared deep conversations while I was still in New York, in a similar situation, and expressing frustration at how everything felt *impossible* and I didn't see that changing. But spending time with K and me in our house free from marital tension and someone else's messes, and walking around our neighborhood bumping into friends and basking in the easy community of being right where you're supposed to be, she remarked, "You're like a letter from my future." I knew exactly what she meant. I, too, had a letter from the future: my friend Lisa, who had left a bad marriage and found hope and happiness, about two years ahead of my schedule. I was there when things felt hopeless for her, right after leaving and embroiled in a messy custody fight, and then had seen as things suddenly got easier—the clouds parted and revealed a beautiful life that was everything she wanted, and more importantly, all hers.

Lisa was a birth doula, which was how we met—she had been mine. Her husband was a perma-PhD student who had never contributed in a financially significant way to their household. Just before giving birth to their second son, Lisa—always prepared—had cooked a tray of homemade mac and cheese. She tucked away a portion for herself in the back of the fridge, knowing that she would welcome the comfort of a cozy meal in the bleary-eyed postpartum days to come. When she returned home from the hospital and was in the ravenous fog of breast-feeding, she asked her husband to heat it up for her. "It's not there anymore," he replied. It wasn't there anymore because he had eaten it, citing the fact that "there was no other food in the house."

It wasn't long after this incident that Lisa filed for divorce. Of course, the mac and cheese incident was the final of many straws, emblematic of her ex's inability to consider anyone other than himself—of how she wasn't just alone in this relationship, she was worse than that. Not only was he not actively adding—taking care of her and the baby—he was actually *subtracting*. After splitting up, Lisa realized she would need to make changes to ensure the financial security of her family, and she decided to go back to school for nursing. In the short term, everything got harder. Less money, less time, more stress. I remember taking a walk with her when she was in the thick of it—deep in never-ending mediation, taking endless classes, watching debt pile up.

Then I watched as slowly but surely, her life fell into place. Our kids loved each other, so K and I spent many weekends at her apartment uptown, which morphed from sparsely furnished to decorated and homey. The custody agreement and divorce were finalized. She finished nursing school and got the job she'd wanted. She started dating, then found a great boyfriend. Eventually, she and her boyfriend, now husband, bought a house in the Hudson Valley, where her kids could play outside in the backyard unsupervised. Seeing her life blossom brought me so much joy and gave me the confidence that I, too, could move toward some big changes.

Charting a new path for yourself and being fully responsible for your own choices is scary. Sometimes when things aren't going well in a marriage, a feeling of hopelessness sets in that can morph into a self-righteousness that we nurture in place of happiness. When something turns out badly, you have the little thrill of being right, instead of whatever actual benefit you would have gotten from something turning out well. In fact, being mad at our spouses or partners can even become a useful crutch to avoid being mad at ourselves. We can't keep the house clean, because they always leave it messy. We can't achieve our goals at work, because they won't look after the kids so we have enough time. We can't be healthy, because they keep too much junk food in the house. These barriers are probably real. *And* having a place to externalize the blame short-circuits holding ourselves accountable for the way we want to change our lives.

Being in charge of your own happiness is one of the hardest things about extracting yourself from a relationship. Giving up our martyr complex means losing the dark solace of being right for the deeper joy of actually having what we need. So if you are trying to make it work, I want you to see what you can do to get the things you need right now. It's up to you to make your life happy, in this relationship or out of it. That's why I will be forever grateful for the advice my therapist gave me during one of my many "breaking points" in my marriage, about two years before I actually asked for a separation. She said, "I want you to take all this energy that you're putting into your relationship right now and put it into yourself. What would happen if you made yourself the project, instead of the relationship?" As I told her about how unhappy I'd become, she pushed me further: "When were you happy? When have you felt most like yourself? What's stopping you from being that person right now?" It was my job to go to yoga, right the listing ship of my career, and spend time with my friends, even if I wasn't getting what I needed from my marriage.

After getting divorced, I learned which of the stories I'd told myself were true and which ones weren't. While it was true, for example, that I wanted to feed my kid healthy meals and spend more time outside and was able to more effectively hold boundaries on screen time and bedtime alone, it was unfortunately false that my ex was the reason the house was always a mess. It turns out keeping a house clean was really just that hard, and entropy was a natural and incredibly frustrating force. Now, I didn't have anyone to be mad at about the dishes in the sink or the suitcase that hadn't been unpacked yet on my bedroom floor.

But the beautiful piece was really learning to listen to my *own* preferences again. I hadn't realized how much I was compromising to make things work, and the insidious ways my life was being transformed by it. It reminded me of a scene from a Julia Roberts movie, *Runaway Bride*, where, after interrogating her pattern of getting into intense relationships and then leaving them, she has to sample various preparations of eggs to figure out which one she actually likes, instead of just ordering whatever her current boyfriend did. Your fury, your sadness, they were your preferences submerged. And as much as divorce is a process of finding your footing financially and physically, it's also a process of rediscovering yourself.

What my friend saw on that fall weekend was the life that was all mine, and the glimmer of what could be hers, too. I think sometimes one reason we're scared to end a marriage is because we want to fit into a recognizable story. "Everyone" has kids who are close in age. I always wanted a two-parent family. Or even, all my friends are putting up with their lackluster husbands, so why can't I? But if these stories lack *happiness,* they aren't the right ones for our lives. You don't have to follow anyone else's story—you can write your own. And I want it to have a happy ending.

The next chapter will address other shifts you might want to consider, in case there's a different kind of bad deal holding you back.

Chapter 12

The Big Shift

I THINK MANY of us have had the experience of entering adulthood and thinking that at some point we would have everything figured out, then being shocked to discover we often feel as unprepared to navigate life's challenges as when we were teenagers. I laughed out loud recently when I read a tweet from sociologist Tressie McMillan Cottom that read, "Starting to question if putting myself in charge of myself was a good idea." You might feel that way now. I do not want this book to be another piece of gaslighting, suggesting the problems in our lives can be solved by one simple trick or life hack. These problems are *hard*. But I also want you to consider the real payoff of confronting them. Being in the driver's seat of your own life is a tremendous opportunity to seek out joy, passion, and fulfillment—all the things you deserve.

Part of the reason these decisions are so hard is because of the external forces that have created, and perpetuate, our constraints. There are still enormous structural changes needed to make the world a place where women operate on a level playing field (we'll discuss those in the afterword). But even if we can't create the perfect conditions for ourselves now, we can create something *better*. Economists refer to this notion as *second best*. The idea is that there are constraints that stop us from being in an "ideal" world, but we can maximize subject to these constraints and achieve the optimum conditional on things . . . being kinda messed up? That's the philosophy of this book—I want you to find your "constrained optimum." I call it "having it *almost*"—the new version of "having it all" that can support us finding what we need rather than crushing us under the weight of a million expectations.

In sharing the history of households transitioning from a specialization model to a dual-breadwinner model, with longer periods of being single and living independently, I wanted to underscore the fact that it simply is not possible to manage home production with the same level of excellence we may have been conditioned to expect. We also have to remember that careers have become more consuming, precisely for the same reasons that we've become richer over time. We're doing more complex tasks, enabled by more sophisticated technology, that produce value in ways that intersect with more people. But what makes us command a higher salary at work also makes us less replaceable, which leads to more demands on our time. So, just as supporting structures like multigenerational families and household specialization have broken down and parenting time has skyrocketed, careers have become more intense. This is what creates a perfect storm of *How am I supposed to do it all?* The reason it feels like there just isn't enough of us to go around is because there's not.

A few days ago, I realized in a panic that my car had a mysterious shudder that I'd left unaddressed before a planned road trip. My thoughts quickly escalated from *How am I going to get this fixed in time?* to *I'm never going to be on top of everything, no matter how hard I try—I'm such a failure!*

We've all been there. *You are doing your best in an impossible situation,* I say to myself, and to you when you have these moments. We built our images of what it means to be "on top of" our personal lives by watching role models who were living out a completely different economic reality. But listen to me: in this day and age, no one, absolutely *no one* is having it all in all ways all the time. People who seem like they have it completely together are either *presenting* a version of themselves that may not match the internal reality or benefiting from hidden advantages just outside the metaphorical or literal camera's lens.

If we want to find happiness and joy and use our time to make meaning, we have to acknowledge the realities of constrained optimization: structurally, the American economy does not support women's needs. And we are trying to do too much. That means we have to shift our expectations of what is ideal and find true contentment in things being imperfect in some areas of our lives. In some things being late, or messy, or good enough. So let's talk about how to take stock and find those last levers to pull to *realistically* get what you need out of life.

Renegotiating the Bad Deals

We all make choices that we think are the best possible ones at the time we make them. We don't deliberately choose a job that leaves us exhausted or a marriage that leaves us crying in the bathroom with the water running. And yet, sometimes we end up in situations that we can feel in every fiber of our bodies just can't go on like this, at least without us shattering into a million pieces. I remember teaching three classes when I was just back from maternity leave, commuting back and forth to New York, missing bedtime more times than not, and resolving to myself that I could not do it anymore. I was either going to find a different job or something else was going to change. The first thing I did was find a visiting position for one year where I could teach less and commute less. Then the pandemic struck, I didn't commute at all, and I instead taught online. During that visiting year, I only had to teach one class and was able to offer a class based on my research on gender economics, instead of the broad intro microeconomics class I was teaching to MBAs at Wharton. With the amount of burnout I'd previously been experiencing, every piece of my job had felt like a chore. But in this new model, I rediscovered my love of teaching, connecting with brilliant twenty-year-olds over Zoom who wanted nothing more than to talk about the economics of being a woman.

I asked my department chair at Wharton if I could teach a class more centered on my research when I returned. To fit it in with the needs of MBAs, I suggested Economics of Diversity and Discrimination, which would cover the economics of both race and gender, and the way in which investments in equity could create a competitive edge for firms. While my department chair cautioned a new course was a lot of work to take on pre-tenure, I needed to teach something I felt passionately about. I was convinced the short-term pain to prep a new class would be worth it to reclaim my love of teaching and let it become something that fueled me again. Even though I didn't have everything figured out when I resolved that things needed to change, I look back on that conversation as the moment I started to try to create a better deal for myself. And now after a few years of teaching a class I *love* to students who *want* to be taught by me—a queer woman of color at Wharton business school—I'm so grateful I gave myself the gift of investing in this class so that future me could have something better. Teaching a class I cared about made work, well, less work. Or, to put it in economist terms, that part of my job had lower *disutility of labor*.

I want you to picture your utility as a curved line on a graph. Often, when we talk about making changes, we're talking about moving along the line to get to the highest point—inching this way or that way by readjusting something small to try to squeeze a little more utility juice out of our current life choices and structure. But now picture that there are a number of curves on the graph, stacked on top of one another like Pringles. The deeper, structural choices you make in your life determine *which* curve you're on. Looking for bigger shifts in your life is about looking for whether there are any deals you could renegotiate to leapfrog you to a higher curve, where you wouldn't be constrained to just move left and right in tiny increments. In economics, we call this the difference between *local* versus *global* maximization—local maximization is trying to find the highest point holding all the parameters of the problem fixed. Global allows you to change more facets of the problem to find the overall highest possibility.

These choices that affect *which* curve you're on, rather than just where you are on a curve, usually fall into one of the following categories:

—Where you live (what city, how close it is to your job, the cost of living, your community) and how you live (who you live with, owning versus renting, cost)
—Major expenses (schooling, car, credit card debt)
—Your job (field, employer), and the terms of your employment (how much you're paid, how many hours you work)
—Your partner and your partnership "contract"
—Childcare arrangement, kids' schools, and other support

Each of these factors carries with it a set of constraints that shape your optimization problem. If your job requires night and weekend work and pays *x* dollars a month, that forms the constraints for how much time you can spend with your family versus sleep, and where you can afford to live and what kind of outsourcing is financially feasible. On the flip side, where you live shapes your commute time to work, your cost of living, local supports like friends and family, and how much time is required to get to different activities. Whether considering job changes, moves (closer to family, away from the city, closer to work), or breakups—you must be relentless in seeking what you need *structurally* to enable you to create a happy life.

A great example of this comes from an amazingly successful woman in the publishing industry who followed what she thought was her bliss from Manhattan to a house in Connecticut.

More space! A yard! Lower cost of living! What she found was that her time was suddenly consumed with driving her kids everywhere. And commuting to her job, which was still in Manhattan. And then spending her weekends repairing things in a house where suddenly nothing worked. Her husband, an academic, was supposed to be the one repairing things, as her high-powered job mostly paid the mortgage. But that meant her having to plan, schedule, and follow up. She kept trying to change things to make her new life work better. Finding the kids a car pool to camp; ordering groceries so she wouldn't have to shop after her long commute. But those were local moves on a curve that wasn't working for her. "I've realized that having a building superintendent is actually feminist," she told me, after deciding to move back to Manhattan. Sometimes to get out of a bad deal, we have to let go of our expectation of what's *supposed to work*—a bad deal wrapped up in a bow of what would be a great deal for someone else. We think we *are* maximizing, we just haven't quite factored in everything that truly determines our utility. The house in Connecticut was *someone's* dream, but it turned out it wasn't hers. It seemed like success to her to get her family a bigger home, but then it came with bigger headaches. She's back in a Manhattan apartment with a twenty-minute train commute, the super fixing her plumbing, and her kids thriving in a great school—within walking distance.

Moving, changing where your kids' school or day care is, finding a new job, or even leaving yours: these are all examples of making *global* changes in things that affect our happiness, rather than making small adjustments in a structure that just isn't working. But doing this isn't just about waving a magic wand—it often means swallowing a tough pill of the constraints we face and figuring out how to maximize around them.

I saw an inspiring example of this with a friend of my wife, Faith. Faith is college-educated but, like far too many Black women with college degrees in America, underpaid—working in education. Her husband's income is higher than hers, but inconsistent, frequently leaving her bouncing between qualifying for public benefits and not, and scrambling to figure out where the next mortgage payment will come from. And . . . he doesn't do anything to help around the house. Like, zero. She's a page out of Jessica Calarco's book—holding it together all on her own, and yet somehow managing to make magic for her family with homemade meals, seasonal décor, and coordinated outfits. But when she welcomed her third under five (along with a teenager) this summer, Faith felt underwater. There were now three kids to get dressed, feed breakfast, drive to day care, pick up, feed dinner, give baths, while meeting the emotional needs of a teen—how was it going to add up when she went back to work? She couldn't afford the outsourced solutions that are too often tossed off as advice to working women—"Get a nanny to do the pickups!" "Get someone to watch the baby and start dinner!" Moreover, Faith had been in a feud with her sister who lived nearby for almost a year, cutting her off from a vital source of familial support when she needed it most. Faith was sure she was in the right and the one who was owed an apology (and I tend to agree). But other people's feelings are outside of our control—an external constraint.

Facing this impossible constellation of constraints, Faith made a decision that left me in awe. She threw the three kids in the car and drove to her sister's, calling her from the driveway. "Hi, I'm here—thought you'd want to see the baby. This has gone on long enough." Of course this wasn't the most important reason to make up with her sister, but pretty soon, the two were back to carpooling, or helping to pick up each other's kids if they got sick at day care. In this example, swallowing her pride was a key step for Faith to reclaim her own agency. Was it better to be right or happy?

Now, I won't suggest that this is a straight or obvious path. Even when you know *something* has to change, it can be incredibly difficult, emotionally and practically, to identify that something and then to actually change it. As I recently shared with a friend who was deeply unhappy, but also felt trapped in her current situation, sometimes in our lives we build a tower of blocks on top of a lumpy, misshapen, crooked foundation. If we remove that foundation, it seems like everything would come crashing down. And so we persist with our wobbly, barely balancing tower. But the reality is, if we removed that block, we might be able to rebuild the tower on firmer footing. The misshapen block seems necessary because of all the other pressures in life—with everything weighing down on that one point, it seems impossible to change it. And sometimes, trying to make a change *will* result in the tower crashing down, before we rebuild it once more. But, I think it's just as important to spend time with the *must* of change as it is with the *can't*. What we're giving up by relying on that lumpy misshapen block, and constantly contorting our tower (the rest of our lives) to balance on it is the possibility of the *balanced, strong,* and *functional* tower we could build with a better foundation. We are losing *so much* by avoiding the short-term pain of making hard change.

So if you're still struggling to make change (or if it's not obvious for you what isn't working right now, or what the steps are to fix it), one approach is to start from the other direction. Instead of starting with the first step on this journey, start with the end point: imagine yourself in five years, in a version of the future where things *are* working. Imagine the hard part is over. You've addressed what has been holding you back. You've started over after a toxic job, paid off your debt, found a new home. What would future you say about what your life is like on the other side? Spend the same care reflecting on this as you did your partner vision board in chapter 8. Be your *own* letter from the future. Literally write a letter from your future self, like an elaborate description of a vacation. Let future you tell you all about what life looks and feels like in this forthcoming reality you've created for yourself. What do your days feel like? How do you spend your time? What emotions do you feel? What kind of home do you live in? What supports do you have in place? *That* is what you can have if you start to do some hard, and even painful, things today.

Things won't magically shift toward the vision you have for five or ten years out, but having that vision will allow you to work backward and figure out what choices you can make now that push you in that direction. Think about the concrete steps you can make, whether financial planning, career planning, relationship overhauling, or just adjusting how you spend your time to start bringing you toward your vision right now. If you need to make a big change, sometimes starting with small, manageable steps is the way to ease into it. Advice blogger Captain Awkward calls this "making the job smaller." Like, I'm intimidated by folding the whole basket of laundry, so I'll just fold a few pieces and make the job smaller for tomorrow. For major life shifts, here's a list of "make the job smaller" first steps:

"I need a new job." → Let people in my network know I'm looking, update my résumé, and start applying for positions. In the meantime, schedule an informational chat with someone who has the experience to help me navigate this change.

"I need a shorter commute." → Make a list of neighborhoods that are closer to work, and research the school ratings in those areas. Look at housing prices and property taxes and consider if renting might be a solution if buying isn't an option. In the meantime, ask my boss if I can work from home a few days a week.

"I need a divorce." → Call my friend who got divorced last year and ask for a referral to an attorney or mediator for a consultation. In the meantime, plan a week away with my kids and friends, and feel what it's like to be in a different space.

"I need to get out of debt." → Create a one-month spending freeze where I only buy absolute essentials, and use points, gift cards, trades, or free resources for everything else. In the meantime, put some of my savings toward my highest interest card.

Write down the small steps you can take *right now*. These small changes create a sense of self-efficacy and momentum that can ease the path toward the bigger ones. When you're ready, map out a timeline for the bigger change. When do you want to have a new job? When do you want to be out of debt, or make the move, or have your divorce finalized? What are the things that need to happen first to enable those changes?

You do not need to settle for the deals you've already made. The terms of every relationship and contract can be renegotiated. You are the architect of your own life, and it is time to reimagine it in a way that both maximizes your long-term utility and leaves space for joy. *You only get one life*, a friend said to me, affirming my choice to, well, change mine completely. Remember, today's decisions are tomorrow's constraints. Start doing right by future you today so that the letter from the future is one saying *thank you.*

Having the Big Conversation

If what you need to change is in your workplace or relies on someone else's buy-in, then, armed with the facts in this book, it's time for some big conversations. Remember, a critical part of asking for what you need is also developing your BATNA in case you don't get it, and setting boundaries about how much you'll do in the meantime.

After doing your homework, ask for a time to talk. Critical to the success of these conversations is to enlist your boss, colleague, partner, or whoever you're negotiating with in shared problem-solving, without falling into the myth of a fixed pie where what's better for you takes away from them or others. As we've discussed, the idea that women are worse at negotiation is a myth, and typically "feminine" traits like a greater aversion to risk-taking can in fact be a superpower. I want you to use your unique superpowers, rather than trying to be someone else.

Take a page from the girls in Zambia that Nava Ashraf, Natalie Bau, Kathleen McGinn, and I taught to negotiate with their parents for more schooling.[1] When we found out that girls were dropping out of school at much higher rates than boys, we held focus groups to ask them why. They said that while their parents were willing to spend resources to send their brothers to school, they weren't willing to spend the money to educate girls. It felt hollow to us to deliver a traditional "empowerment" program to address the lack of schooling for girls in Zambia— "You can do anything!" would ring false in a world where these girls were facing very real constraints. The reality was that they couldn't just be independent, self-sufficient, girl-power-driven go-getters. They were deeply dependent on and intertwined with others, and the institutions and norms they were facing were stacked against them. Any pathway to change had to recognize those ties, honor them, and yet still push the margins of what was possible. Luckily, the classic negotiation texts taught in business schools already contained the tools that we thought might genuinely make a difference in this situation: if you can propose solutions that create value for other people as well as yourself, you'll find yourself with bargaining power you didn't know you had.

Instead of teaching girls to argue with their parents, we focused on finding a respectful approach and emphasizing shared values. "You don't care about me!" became "I know we both care deeply about education." An outside observer might be surprised that an empowerment program included brainstorming ways to show deference to parents. But our curriculum emphasized the difference between trying to "win" by taking a position and arguing for it, versus collaboratively trying to meet everyone's interests. The focus was on finding out more about the barriers and roadblocks that stood in the way of the other person being able to say yes. This flips the discussion from an adversarial one across the table from each other to one where you're on the same side, examining a problem and looking for solutions together. Girls not only learned to identify the barriers and challenges their parents were facing but also find their own agency in lessening those burdens or contributing to the shared aims of the household. Our approach worked: girls who were randomly assigned to receive our training ended up staying in school for longer and being more likely to complete twelfth grade. What's more, their parents actually rated them as more respectful and helpful around the house after the training—far from the backlash you might expect from a program empowering teen girls.

The girls ended up with more of what they wanted—education—without the parents feeling that they got the short end of the stick. When you advocate for a change you need someone else's buy-in on, this is the energy you need to bring.

For example, if advocating for more equitable policies at work, think about what your manager or CEO's incentives are and how supporting women serves their goals. I think the business case is clear: we're missing out on incredible talent by continuing to systematically exclude 50 percent of the population that could be producing the next big idea. Remember, by failing to make spaces equitable, they are actually hiring worse people, investing in worse leaders. Transforming our work and home spaces so they work for women makes everyone better off, and it's time for you to make that case so you can get what you need.

More Than Surviving

One of the most important considerations I hope you'll take away from this book is the permission to pursue a goal that is a way more radical proposition than it should be: *happiness*. No one questions whether men should be able to pursue happiness and self-fulfillment, but when we talk about women pursuing pleasure, happiness, contentment—it's akin to scandal. So let me state it plainly: your utility function includes your own well-being and happiness. I want you to *enjoy* your one "wild and precious life".[2]

Prioritizing happiness doesn't make you a monster, even though it can feel deeply uncomfortable in a world where we've been socialized to believe caring for ourselves is selfish, and selfish is the worst thing a woman can be. But this narrative is untrue. Of course we try to take care of other people. Of course we want our kids' lives to be as happy and enriching as possible. But these priorities shouldn't just be about sacrifice; they are also goals that maximize our own utility. Our happiness comes from, in part, giving to and taking care of others. Our loved ones' happiness is often our own. And . . . our own happiness is our own, too.

A friend who works in finance, Jia, one of two women at the senior director level in a large firm, is exhausted every time I see her. Recently, she reflected on how her goal of supporting her family had morphed into something unsustainable, for her and them. She climbed the career ladder at first because she needed to—to pay off student debt, to take care of her family back home in Asia, to provide for her kids. But now there was no end in sight to the late nights, weekend crises, and feeling of being constantly behind. "I'm so burned out, I can't keep going like this," Jia would tell me, before repeating the same thing to me the next time we managed to grab lunch months later. What she started to recognize, though, was the deeper toll her work was taking. That she was impatient with her children. That she couldn't actually be present and enjoy a cute moment with them, because she was thinking about the endless to-do list. And that she was experiencing back pain and migraines. It took losing a close family member for her to experience a wake-up call. "Life is too short," she told me, resolving to make a change. "All of the men at my level have stay-at-home wives. Every single one. I can't keep trying to keep up with them, and being miserable, and watching my kids grow up while I miss all the best parts." Jia plans to ask her employer for a sabbatical, and then for exactly what she needs to make the job sustainable, or to look for something else with less pay, yes, but potentially with a whole lot more utility.

If I cannot convince you that the pursuit of personal fulfillment is one reason why you are on this earth, perhaps I can sway you with evidence underscoring that the well-being of those you care for also depends on your happiness: research shows that parental mental health affects children's well-being.[3] That old saying of "You can't pour from an empty cup" is true. After I made major changes in my life, I watched my son thrive. I was able to be the patient, loving, happy parent that he needed, instead of a constantly angry, exhausted shell of myself just trying to survive until bedtime. What he needed, I realized, wasn't a "two-parent home" or some other idea of normalcy that I'd envisioned in the grand plan for my life. He needed me, his primary caretaker, to be okay. Because then he could be okay. *We* could be okay. He needed his mom to put on her own oxygen mask first.

Letting yourself become worn down into a pile of resentment and exhaustion in the name of your family is not actually good parenting. Would I jump into a literal lake of fire for my kids? Absolutely. But should you subject yourself to a *metaphorical* lake of fire that makes you miserable, grumpy, and short-fused because it might make their life a single iota better, in theory? Absolutely not.

We are so used to looking at everyone else's needs that we've lost sight of not only what we need or want but even the fact that we have our own experiences separate from those we love, care for, and work for. This is why being explicit about our utility function can be useful, because it allows you to see that it includes what's best for those you love as well as your own health, happiness, and well-being. If it helps, keep a "joy journal." Every night, write down the things that day that brought you joy and pleasure. This can range from the sensual pleasure of biting into a fresh summer peach to the deeper satisfaction of mentoring someone junior to you. Clock the moments where you just feel able to *be*. Happy, relaxed, content. Because although utility is not the same thing as "happiness", you cannot maximize your utility if you are never having fun. You cannot optimize if you're just barely able to survive. The present matters. And yes, good times ebb and flow. Some chapters of our lives are harder than others. Sometimes loved ones get sick, sometimes we get sick. Sometimes our kids go through nightmare phases (I'm sorry, "disequilibrium" or "periods of less regulation"), sometimes we have an insane week at work, or sometimes we find ourselves out of work. But if your "joy journal" is mostly blank pages and life more often than not feels *impossible*, I want you to understand this as an imperative rather than an option: something has to change.

Taking care of your own needs doesn't mean abandoning your family to go on a yoga retreat every weekend or tossing your responsibilities to the wind. It's as simple as making yourself coffee every morning just the way you like it, and sitting and drinking it before anyone is allowed to ask you for things. Or making yourself a sandwich for lunch the good way, the way you usually only make them for a picnic or when you're making them for someone else. There's a headline from *The Onion* that has always stayed with me as being way too on point: "Mom Hasn't Ordered Favorite Pizza Topping in Over a Decade." If you are married to a man, and especially if you have children with one, I want you to ask yourself very honestly how often he goes without his preferences for dinner being met, versus how often you do. It's time to rediscover what you like on your pizza.

And I know some of you might be thinking—*I'm drowning here and you want me to make a fancy sandwich?* And I hear you, I promise. But the thing is, you *already do it.* You do it for our kids and loved ones all the time. We throw together the spirit day outfit at the last minute or take the time to make lunch a little extra special. We use all our energy reserves making sure holidays are picture-perfect for friends and family. We make magic for other people all the time. Why don't we do it for ourselves? You are your one constant companion in life. You are your partner, best friend, parent, therapist, and sometimes heckler. And you deserve *joy*. As you learn to put on your own oxygen mask first, you may also discover the mental space and fortitude to think about those bigger structural changes we discussed earlier in the chapter. Read and refine your letter from the future. *You* are your own hero. You are going to start building that future. Today.

Crafting Your Own Vision

In 2013, Sheryl Sandberg, then the COO of Facebook, published *Lean In.* This book, which sold millions of copies, became a part of the zeitgeist and a shorthand for talking about women's careers, as you've seen me use it. But for me, while surely the book hit on some core truths about being a woman in the corporate workplace, it also rang hollow about so many women's experiences. Sandberg offered women a specific vision of success: climbing the corporate ladder, being treated as equal to a man, having everything, but no time to enjoy it. While she acknowledged the systemic constraints facing women, her advice mostly ignored them. It sounds like it was written by your boss—*Work harder, give me more. You can overcome the structural problems if you just buckle down!*

With this book, I wanted to offer a different perspective on "success". This one, aimed at serving your interests, and not those of your boss or capitalism more generally. In this alternative world, women define what success looks like for them in the context of the many constraints they must navigate just to get through the day, let alone their careers. You'll know you've "made it" not when you have the corner office but when you, simply put, feel happy. When you're not constantly depleted. When you have the time to connect with friends or the energy to exercise. When your shoulders soften. When you don't snap at your partner or your kids. When you feel fulfilled and satisfied in your life.

That's why some of the stories in this book involved women finding ways to eliminate constraints standing in the way of their careers, and others were about women stepping back and rebalancing their careers with other sources of utility. The path to "it all" looks different for everyone. For some, it might involve recommitting to a flawed marriage and figuring out how to rebalance the scales of time to create a more equal partnership. For others, it might entail thinking more critically about future life choices, such as where to live; if or when to get married; whether or not to have children. For still others, it could mean making hard decisions to change careers, end relationships, or rethink commitments that drain their time and energy. For me, it was getting a divorce, moving to be closer to my job, and settling down with a woman who does my laundry while I travel for work, coaches my kid's soccer team, and never asks me what to make when it's her night for dinner.

Throughout the book, I have shared real stories of women who confronted the deals that were making their lives untenable and made changes that allowed them to fully maximize their utility. I promise you these changes were not easy. I promise you there was self-doubt and probably a tearful moment or two or several along the way. There is also, in every life decision, some sense of ambivalence or even grief about the road untaken. As I struggled with whether to pursue IVF solo on the cusp of forty, I couldn't help lamenting what could have been. *Why couldn't my marriage have worked out, so I could have had two kids close in age like "everyone else"?* But after making it through those dark days, I see how much I have gained by making enormous changes, including the wisdom to craft things for myself differently this time around. I had to embrace that my "happily ever after" would be different from anyone else's. I could have everything I needed, but not everything everyone else had.

As women, we will always face unique constraints, and there are no easy solutions to compensate for the external factors contributing to our pain points. There are always trade-offs. But that doesn't mean you can't use the framework we've worked through to help you get the best deal possible with the cards on the table.

The traditional notion of "having it all" might be a myth, but that doesn't mean it's not possible to find our constrained optimum, our having it *almost*. And to carve out satisfaction, fulfillment, and, yes, joy. The key is letting go of the things we can't have and finding out what we need to be happy with what *is* possible. Sometimes getting through the heartache to the other side means recognizing that this is *your* story. It is going to be as unique and complicated as you are. And there are no wrong answers, except settling for less than you deserve.

This is a lesson I had to learn the hard way. After I finally made the difficult decisions and got through the painful aftermath, I had to confront why I had allowed myself to persist in a life that left me exhausted and miserable for so many years. I felt a deep grief unfurl inside me. My heart broke that I hadn't thought I deserved more. I silently resolved not to ever let my own well-being become the very last priority in my life.

As I worked to build a new life in Philadelphia, I also had to get reacquainted with myself. I had ceased to exist as a solo protagonist of my life and somehow become someone who existed only in relation to others. Mom; wife; friend. In every relationship, I seemed to find myself in the role of caretaker, rushing to ensure everyone else's needs were met, making it all too easy to lose sight of my own experience. At one point, I took a good friend visiting Philadelphia to my favorite museum. I eagerly watched her face for signs of the awe I felt in this place, and found none. To be honest, maybe she was just tired. But I fretted over her apparent indifference and hurried through the visit so we could move on to the next thing. This was a place I loved. The paintings were hanging there before me, as breathtaking as ever. But somehow, my lens of experience had become *how other people were feeling*. How did that happen? When had I lost touch with whether I enjoyed something and started evaluating everything only in terms of whether everyone else was happy and satisfied?

I used to love traveling on my own. When I did my graduate work in Zambia, I thrived in an environment where I was constantly improvising, exploring, out of my depth. Where did that person go, who so totally, completely belonged to herself? Now, the idea of going places alone made me feel anxious, unmoored.

I had gotten accustomed to having someone to do things with and for. Even with an every-other-weekend custody schedule that allowed for some time to myself, I rushed to make social plans to ensure I had something to do.

When I was invited to a conference in Paris, I accepted, with the plan that I could piggyback a fun getaway with my now wife onto a work trip. As it turned out, the timing didn't work for her, so I would have to go solo, at which I felt intense disappointment. But as the date drew near, the anxiety about traveling alone morphed into a sense of possibility. This was a chance to reclaim a lost part of myself. To spend some time living in my own experience.

I started to view the trip as a challenge. I was going to arrive before the conference and spend an entire day doing *whatever I wanted*. Gardens! Food! Museums! I stopped by a farmers' market and bought and immediately ate ripe apricots. At a clothing stall, I grabbed a twenty-euro dress that spoke to me. I went to Musée de l'Orangerie and sat quietly with Monet's large water lilies. I went to a café and ordered what looked best to me—an orange tart—and was rewarded with the magic of something so simple and yet so astonishingly good that you turn it over in your mouth before swallowing and stare at your fork in disbelief. And then I decided to trek to the Eiffel Tower.

You see, I had been to Paris once before, also alone, right after college on a shoestring budget. I had just started dating my future ex-husband, and I remember spending lots of time using phone cards to call him, or writing emails back and forth at the internet café (it was a long time ago). During one of these calls, he asked me not to go to the top of the Eiffel Tower; he wanted us to experience that moment together one day. At the time, I thought it was a romantic gesture. (I know, I know.) But we never went to Paris.

It felt poetic to me: I was first here when my relationship was just starting, and now I was back as my divorce was being finalized. And I was going to go up to the top of the Eiffel Tower.

I walked the mile or so from the museum along the Seine, taking pictures as the tower grew closer with each block I covered. It was a beautiful, bright day—it could not have been more perfect for this project of reclamation. I reached the tower, went through security, and was delighted to find they still had tickets available for the ride to the top. After a long wait in line, I stepped into the first of two elevators, to the second floor. And . . . the sky suddenly opened up. An almost comical torrential downfall was released from the heavens. I managed to get one picture of Paris from the still-sunny side of the tower before the blackness spread. Then, the announcement: the elevators to the top would be closed, we could get refunds at the ticket office.

I went to the gift shop to buy an "I heart Paris" umbrella and then made a cold, wet, and miserable climb down the stairs. Yet I nestled this comically ill-fated mission deep in my heart. Because this experience—this interrupted, soggy, far-from-scenic experience—was mine. I was here with myself, and I had done exactly what I wanted to do all day, and existed within my experience of it, for better or worse.

There's another lesson there, which is that should you find yourself in Paris on a sunny day, you should absolutely go to the top of the Eiffel Tower, because you may never get that chance again. Or more generally, that it's hard to reclaim time lost, experiences missed, and a lifetime ignoring our own needs. Though I missed out on my opportunity to experience that iconic view, I did manage to reclaim my perspective. I became reacquainted with my tastes, my desires, my passions. I found that there was a person who still lived inside of me that deserved joy and fulfillment and to taste piping-hot street food and look at art all by herself. Whether or not you are ready to make a big change—in a relationship, a job, or something else—I am demanding that you make a big change within yourself. To start seeing the mission of your life as maximizing your utility function and remembering that that utility function includes you.

I know that you are *doing it all*, and then some; I know that you can't try *harder*. Instead, I want you to try *differently*. I want you to pursue what matters most for your utility, and to jettison the things that require your time and energy but do not serve your values. I want you to know you deserve a different lived experience. You deserve to feel whole, rested, and complete. You deserve to *have it all*—not the perfectionistic, unattainable version of "balance" defined by society, but the version that feels right for you.

Take a deep breath. Pick up a metaphorical pen. It's time to rewrite your story, with you as the heroine, who overcomes constraints to find your best life amid a deeply broken system. I'll be rooting for you.

Afterword
Making the World Work for Women

Over the years, I've witnessed the men in my life strive linearly toward their professional goals, while female colleagues and friends carefully plot a career path that also takes into account so many additional factors—finding time to support family members, raise children, create healthy home environments, and serve their communities. Men have the freedom to embrace an opportunity without considering the downstream impact on those around them. Before a woman says yes to a new challenge—one that might require more time, effort, a longer commitment, more travel—you can bet she has planned for every possible contingency. And when the squeeze of "balancing" all these responsibilities becomes too much for her to bear, she makes the kinds of tough choices that we have been discussing.

My primary goal in writing this book was to help women understand what they are up against and to empower them with data that allows them to make informed choices and negotiate deals that will lead to greater long-term joy for themselves. But any discussion of individual change must also include a discussion of the structural changes needed to remove constraints on a social level, for everyone, especially those with less access to the financial and other supports that that have helped some of us bob and weave around those limitations. Because even as we continue to make better deals for ourselves at every turn, so many of the challenges we face just simply do not have individual solutions. So let's take a look at the *collective* changes that could benefit everyone. Some of these changes have to be enacted on a government level, while others are needed in the private sector. I want to challenge all readers of this book to imagine a world where instead of women continuously needing to lean in to make things work, society leans into women.

Parental Leave

Parental leave is an example of how powerfully government agendas can help or hurt women's daily lived realities—and the unexpected backlash that can come with well-intentioned but poorly executed policies. When parental leave isn't implemented correctly, it creates an incentive for employers to discriminate against women, as we discussed in chapter 5. But even when it is implemented in the right ways, it carries the possibility of increasing statistical discrimination against women and the gender wage gap. But to focus only on the gender wage gap is to miss the true objective of paid family leave. The point of guaranteed, legally protected parental leave is to ensure *all* women have the opportunity to care for their children, not only financially privileged ones. The evidence is unequivocal that maternity leave increases maternal and child health and well-being.[1] So the question is, are there ways to implement paid leave that could make it less likely to create more discrimination?

First, because of the research showing employers are less likely to hire women when they'll be on the hook for paying maternity leave,[2] any prudent parental leave policy needs to be underwritten centrally—by the government—rather than a cost directly absorbed by employers *when they hire women*. That is, the requirements for firms to provide parental leave need to match the funds raised centrally by the government. This could be achieved without an actual *cost* to the government budget by implementing a payroll tax that all businesses pay, not just those with female employees or those with employees on leave, that creates a pool that funds leave pay, which is the case in many countries and 12 US states. However, just this on its own does not prevent discrimination, as the research from many countries with generous state-funded paid leave policies shows. Firms discriminate not just because they will need to *pay* for leave, but also because they will have to suffer the inconvenience of *having an employee on leave.* Perhaps for this reason, the literature actually shows better outcomes in terms of discrimination with shorter periods of state-guaranteed leave—eight to twelve weeks guaranteed paid, rather than six to twelve months (this doesn't mean individual employers can't offer more; it just means that for the universal standard, a shorter period is less likely to lead to increases in discrimination against women who might not even want to take that much leave, or have children at all!).[3] In deciding whether to lengthen the term of leave, governments need to consider the likely impacts on gender equity, and if there are any ways to counter them, in addition to the social welfare and socioeconomic equality impacts.

However, I think there's hope here, too, for governments and organizations willing to get creative. If employers are really serious about preventing statistical discrimination in hiring and promotion against women, they should compensate managers for the disruption of workers on leave, so that managers know they'll be "made whole" if they promote a woman who later takes maternity leave.

For example, automatically building in a "1.5 FTE (full-time equivalent) replacement" policy when an employee goes on leave gives managers more resources to work with. Another option would be to create an additional bonus pool for teams with a worker on leave, to compensate everyone for taking on a bit more of the work. I haven't yet seen an employer put a policy like this into action, but it reminds me of the steps firms had to take to stop business units from overly competing with one another. If they just rewarded managers for their individual business unit's profits, then the manager of one soda brand, for example, would have an incentive to try to undercut the price of the other soda brand, which might be under the same corporate umbrella. Companies figured out they needed to reward the managers for overall business success or find other ways to take these incentives for undercutting away.[4] Similarly, employers that really want to ensure women are promoted in a manner consistent with their merit could figure out a way to lessen the individual "pain" this creates to managers not seeing the full picture of how it will benefit the organization later on to develop these talented leaders. (More advanced governments can encourage these kinds of policies by providing subsidies to employers or even adding funds for this to the existing payroll taxes, rather than just focusing on funding the leave itself.)

I also think it's crucial that employers create a norm around male employees taking leave. I would like to see organizations encourage high-ranking male employees to take paternity leave and communicate to their teams that they are (and truly be) offline. Doing this sets a standard and intentionally creates a culture where *not* taking paternity leave is viewed as unusual . . . "Oh, your wife is home alone with an infant? Huh" and long stare. Even better, employers can create incentives for men to take leave: teams with men out on paternity leave get the same +1.5 FTE replacement, or that increase in the team's overall bonus target, which will make other team members encourage men to take it. Heck, consider making three weeks of leave mandatory for men!

Evidence from around the world now shows that dedicated *paternity* leave is important to get men to take their share of parental leave. Men take significantly more leave when there is a "use it or lose it" paternal allocation, rather than a shared pool of leave that can be divided however the family wishes. In Spain, researchers found that after a 2007 paternal leave reform, most fathers used the entirety of their nontransferable, fully paid paternity leave, but used little transferable or unpaid leave, while mothers used all forms.[5] In Sweden, the introduction of nontransferable "daddy months" also increased men's parental leave.[6] A nontransferable extra month of paternity leave in Norway increased uptake among fathers and had positive spillover effects on the fathers' coworkers and brothers.[7]

And even short periods of leave can lead to longer-term "norm" shifts. Remember that promising evidence from Spain discussed in chapter 10, showing just two weeks of paternity leave led to moms working more? Well, they also found that kids whose fathers were eligible for paternity leave have more gender egalitarian attitudes themselves. I love the study design here—because fathers were eligible for leave based on their children's birth date, the authors surveyed kids born before and after the cutoff date, all of whom were seventh graders at the time of the survey. The researchers found that kids born after the cutoff date, who had fathers eligible for leave, were more likely to think fathers should work part-time, and in fact do chores within the household that are less gendered. They also show less gender stereotypical attitudes about their *own* labor market expectations, with boys expecting to be less likely to work full-time when they have kids, and girls expecting to be more likely to work full-time.[8] These results show that paternity leave doesn't only have positive impacts on the health of moms and babies[9] but can also be an important part of the social change we need to create the same gender revolution at home that we've seen in the workplace.

How do we avoid the unintended consequences that occurred in academia, where men took tenure clock extensions and used them to write more papers and books? Well, the first answer is that academia is unique because the criteria for promotion—research—is only a part of what universities pay us to do. Taking the leave and clock extension was *costless* from a career perspective and only created more time to accumulate the currency of our job, publications. Taking leave at a law firm, on the other hand, comes with career costs, even if not financial ones when the leave is paid. Which is perhaps the reason plenty of research on paternity leave shows that men often don't take it, even when it's 100 percent paid.[10] Whereas, I'd be willing to bet almost all academic men jumped at the clock extension opportunity (and can empirically confirm this in my own department). So outside of very specific kinds of jobs, I don't think offering paternity leave will naturally create perverse incentives. Nonetheless, I do think it makes sense to offer different benefits to "child bearers" compared to "child rearers." People who give birth might need additional time to recover from it, as well as more time with their new baby to breastfeed. (And this provides a way to account for the on-average gender differential impacts of having children without penalizing LGBTQ couples or making benefits explicitly linked to gender, which employers worry may constitute a form of discrimination.)

Changes like these won't necessarily close the gender wage gap, but they can help attract women to careers that otherwise wouldn't be feasible for them and potentially ensure that they are able to stay in the workforce without feeling as though they must make impossible choices between their job and their family.

Flexibility Across the Life Cycle

The timeline of a modern career was largely built around the needs of married, heterosexual men whose wives handle all the home production. It's not a system that typically acknowledges the needs of women, and, increasingly, since most men now also exist in a two-income household, it doesn't really serve *anyone*. The time has come for employers to not only understand this reality but to prioritize making care work economically feasible for all their employees.

We've already discussed, in chapter 7, how workplaces need to rethink the idea of "flexibility" as the be-all and end-all of a "woman-friendly" workplace and instead think about boundaries on nighttime and weekend work, as well as limits on face time to childcare hours. Now I want to talk about a different kind of flexibility.

The reproductive constraint women face—that the most rapid time of salary appreciation generally aligns with the most rapid depreciation of our reproductive capital—is the squeeze that can make the notion of "having it all" feel like a setup. But this constraint could be alleviated, in part, if employers offered flexibility across the life cycle of a career. There is no reason women shouldn't be able to have children at their reproductive peak, and then "lean in" to their careers when their kids are school-aged. This is especially true now that people are living and working longer than ever before. Changing this trajectory means that employers will need to identify opportunities that aren't off-ramps for women during the period they're likely to have children, and on-ramps and accelerators for women after this point.

Too often, the only option we offer women when excessive career demands aren't working *right now* is to switch to a role that changes their career trajectory *permanently*. I've seen women change tracks from working as litigators to becoming recruiters at law firms, or change from client-facing work to behind-the-scenes research at consulting firms, or step back from working full-time as teachers to working part-time as substitutes. In each of these switches, there's rarely a way to easily "reenter" the higher-paying track once you have more time to devote to your career.

And so I meet women with loads of human capital and boundless potential who are pouring it all into the parent-teacher association, keeping up a beautiful home, and managing their kids' schedules. I don't think any of these women made the wrong choice—they usually uniformly report feeling grateful that they can invest in their kids and acknowledge the financial privilege of being able to pay the "motherhood penalty" at work to maximize their holistic utility. But once their kids are older, they are often frustrated by the lack of options available to them. Take, for example, a parent at my son's school who worked as a finance VP, outearning her husband, until she took a break to care for two kids through their toddler years. With her youngest in first grade, she started job searching and found herself interviewing for entry-level jobs, despite an incredibly impressive CV.

The feeling of impossibility of working greater than full-time while caring for small children, around the clock, is a *temporary* problem. So we need employers to start creating temporary solutions. What would this look like? An ability to slow down a partner track without hopping off it—for example, working a 60 percent client load. Temporary "fellowship" type roles that come with slightly lower pay and lower productivity expectations, but allow you to hit "go" and rejoin the mainstream path at any moment. When I talk about this in my class and to companies, I compare this to highways that have a local route parallel to the express—it's a little slower, yes, but ultimately gets you to the same place, and allows you to re-join the express at multiple points, instead of being forced down an exit that lets you off in a small town in the middle of nowhere. We need more "local" routes and fewer exits for women's careers.

This means reforming traditional paradigms like residencies, partner tracks, tenure tracks, and so on, so that they don't have to start as soon as someone finishes grad school at thirty and the biological clock starts ticking faster. A qualified worker should be able to take a kind of "holding pattern" job and then decide *when* they want to hit go on the investment period that will take them to the next stage of their careers. Tenure, for example, is a simple formula of publications over six or seven years, but who says it has to be the six years after your PhD? Similarly, going up for partner at a law or consulting firm is about your productivity over a certain period—there's plenty you could do to be productive during a phase of life that you don't want to count as your "how much work can you jam into a short time" judgment period. Residency is an intensive training period in a particular specialty—but could doctors work in a less intensive role until they're ready to start it? Doing so would hopefully make a dent in disparities like the fact that only 60 percent of female surgeons have children, while 92 percent of male surgeons do.[11] There's a reason that jobs with a simple seniority basis—such as nursing—and pensions based on total years served—such as teaching and government jobs—tend to be more attractive to women.

Policies around the world have failed to provide incentives for firms to make career timelines work for women. But that doesn't mean we have to accept the status quo. For example, governments could offer employers wage subsidies for employing parents who have been outside the workforce for several years, or offer job training and workforce reentry programs to parents right as their youngest kid starts kindergarten, a time when we see women's labor supply often increases.[12] If you're a decision-maker for your employer, I encourage you to consider what practical changes you can make that allow for flexibility across the life cycle and boundaries during the workweek. The key mantra is that investments in making your career path and working hours compatible with the demands of life outside of work are investments in retaining *talent*. And in the modern economy, that applies to male and female talent, since few workers have the benefit of a spouse solely focused on home production.

Discrimination and Other Hazards

Early in my time at Wharton, I was asked to organize a seminar where we brought in outside speakers to discuss their research, something that is super important to academics' careers. I asked each of my colleagues to give the names of two people they'd be most interested in seeing. Putting the names together, I discovered to my shock and horror that I had an entirely male list. I don't think any one of my colleagues would have suggested we book only men for the semester-long seminar series. But the two economists who were top of mind for each of them individually were men. All men.

233

We cannot ignore the impact of bias on women's chances at equally paid careers. Employers invested in creating a more equal workplace also need to address their hiring practices to ensure women are getting an equal shot at getting in the door. The lessons of my research are that the slower, more objective, and less ambiguous hiring practices are, the less bias they create. This means that it's better to set objective criteria for an initial stage than name candidates "off the top of our heads." We all want to believe that our hiring practices are grounded in merit, but these subtle biases often undermine that goal. Adopting anti-discrimination measures can bring us closer to a meritocracy.

Not only is this a noble goal, it is a practical one as well; if bias is factoring into our hiring, it means hiring *worse* people. Recall my research with STEM firms, who gave a white male candidate with a 3.75 the same rating as a female or minority candidate with a 4.0. Bias and discrimination are distortionary forces, pushing us away from the meritocracy. A paper that helps illustrate this is Conrad Miller's work on affirmative action, which focused on a different nexus of discrimination: race instead of gender. Miller looked at federal contractors who were legally required by the Johnson administration to "take affirmative action" to hire employees that represented the racial makeup of their surrounding area. The neat trick exploited by Miller was that firms moved into and out of being federal contractors. Some won contracts and were then required to comply with affirmative action, and some didn't continue being contractors and were no longer under this regulation. The first part of his finding might be expected: when firms became federal contractors, subject to regulation, their hiring of Black employees increased substantially. What do you think happened when firms discontinued their federal relationship and were then free to hire as they chose? A cynical take might be that the firms would immediately fire these employees, especially if one expected them to be a drag on productivity, which is the rhetoric of people who oppose proactive measures to promote equality. Instead, Miller found that the percentage of Black employees at a firm *continued to increase* post-regulation. The only plausible explanation for these data is that the firms actually found their new employees to be beneficial to their organizations. So while they were forced to make hiring more equal, they maintained that equality by choice.[13] These results are in line with a host of other research showing that when people make biased decisions, they make worse decisions.[14] In which case, a forced correction can be more equitable *and* efficient.

So how can firms create fair hiring policies? First, set objective standards for initial screens, but ensure that they depend on factors that are markers of ability to do the job going forward, rather than having done the job in the past. For example, if you set your criteria for your new VP role in a STEM industry as "previously served as a STEM VP," you're building in whatever preexisting discrimination and lack of opportunity is keeping women out of other places. And remember, diversity-promoting practices can be a competitive edge precisely by allowing us to get talent that others are ignoring.

We're aware that using algorithms in hiring can cause problems by being trained on historical decisions. A famous cautionary tale is when Amazon scrapped its AI hiring tool after it turned out to be eliminating candidates from all-women colleges and other obvious signs of bias.[15] What I think we're less aware of is the way that human brains are also historically trained algorithms. When we make decisions in a more automatic way, what Daniel Kahneman called "System one thinking," we aren't carefully and objectively weighing all possible factors in the most optimal way. We're going with our gut—and our gut has been trained by millions of data points of the deeply biased world around us, where men are CEOs, women are nurses but not doctors, and computer nerds rarely wear skirts. Paul Graham, a well-known start-up investor, once said, "I can be tricked by anyone who looks like Mark Zuckerberg," despite evidence showing that successful start-up founders are in fact often over forty.[16] As someone once said when I presented these results: *Vibes are biased.*

The more you can keep your hiring process tethered to objective reality, the more you'll stay in the zone of "System two thinking," the more rational, objective part of our brains. Confirming this is research by Iris Bohnet and coauthors that shows evaluations of résumés are more biased when male and female candidates are compared sequentially, rather than side by side.[17] Side-by-side evaluation forces you to stay grounded in the facts being presented: who has better educational achievements, better work experience, better leadership skills, and so on. Sequential evaluation, on the other hand, allows your brain to bend the facts to fit your theories. This candidate "seems better" than the last one. Or you can even change how much you care about certain factors to make your brain's secretly preferred candidate come out ahead—for example, valuing education when the male candidate is better there, but focusing on work experience when that's where the male candidate leads.

In my own research, I've seen how biased recall and sequential evaluation can be. We found that employers evaluating résumés sequentially rated candidates immediately following a white male candidate lower. Why? It was driven by evaluations immediately following *low-quality* white male candidates. When rating high-quality white male candidates, employers' unconscious bias showed up, and these candidates were given unjustifiably high scores. But when rating low-quality white male candidates, employers may have experienced dissonance: to give a high score would make them *feel* biased, out of step with their own self impressions. So they didn't—we find no bias toward white men when the résumés are of low quality (poor grades, work experience, etc.). Instead, these employers retroactively (and again, most likely unconsciously) favor these candidates by lowering the score of the following candidate. They remember them as better than they actually were and lower the next candidate's score in response.

So if employers are seeking fair résumé evaluations, the best strategy is: piece by piece, side by side, and as slowly as possible.

When evaluating interviews, the same principles can be adapted. Instead of eliciting "gut feelings" and answers to questions such as, "Did you like them?" immediately after the fact, ask hiring managers to fill out a rubric asking about specific elements of the interview, one that compares candidates on a fixed set of criteria, which also means the goalposts can't be moved to suit a preordained outcome. Remember that super-subjective metrics like "culture fit" are breeding grounds for bias. If an industry is male dominated, of course folks are likely to feel like a male candidate is more of a "fit". Does that make them more qualified? Back in my consulting days, a common post-interview question used to be if someone passed the "airport test," which was whether you'd want to be stuck waiting for a delayed flight with them. But if men don't want to sit at an airport with women, is that an acceptable reason not to hire them? In Ellen Pao's (unsuccessful) gender discrimination lawsuit against Kleiner Perkins, she claimed she was excluded from a ski trip because "women kill the buzz." The defendants pushed back that they'd never said this; they'd merely excluded women to make the logistics of room-sharing easier, as though that excuses it.[18] The absurdity of wildly subjective evaluations is perhaps best embodied by a lawsuit against Google by April Curley, a Black ex-employee who received the feedback on a performance review that she was "not Googly enough."[19] The use of the made-up word really brings it home. What is *Googly*? Who knows! The problem is that its definition can be adjusted subjectively to align with who we're used to seeing in the workplace, and not necessarily who's the best or most productive worker.

Shutting down discrimination helps get women in the door, but firms also have to create cultures in which women thrive. What does this mean? Make self-promotion play a smaller role in hiring and promotion, distribute non-promotable work equally and include it on performance reviews and evaluations, get rid of toxically competitive atmospheres, and, perhaps most importantly, enforce real consequences for sexual harassment. This means creating channels for reporting, fostering a culture of social enforcement against those that mistreat women, and having a zero-tolerance policy for any behavior that violates codes of conduct.

Take a lesson from a hiring debacle I've used as a cautionary tale, that of the new *Jeopardy!* host to replace Alex Trebek. The hiring managers basically did everything wrong: they identified candidates based on previous experience hosting game shows (a job mostly exclusive to white men), they filled their short list with what I call "straw diversity"—candidates like Katie Couric who probably didn't want the job; they created an unequal evaluation process with opaque metrics (LeVar Burton's guest-host week was aired opposite the Olympics), and then they let a person leading the process become a candidate.[20] *Jeopardy!* executive producer Mike Richards, who had been heading the selection committee, suddenly threw his hat into the ring as a candidate and shortly thereafter was chosen as the permanent host.[21] Nine days later, however, he was out, after reports surfaced of two gender discrimination and sexual harassment suits against him from a previous job, as well as a record of offensive comments against women and Asians on a podcast he'd hosted.[22] By failing to vet Richards, *Jeopardy!* execs didn't just hire another white man, they hired a hostile work environment. An individual's contributions to diversity and inclusion aren't just their demographic characteristics—it's their actions, their decisions, and their leadership, which you can still screen for, even when a white man happens to be the best person for the job.

Policies That Invest in Women

Any consumer of Western media has seen articles fretting about falling birth rates in richer countries. There are both the legitimate reasons for concern—pension plans like Social Security become insolvent if the number of retirees exceeds the number of workers—and the more sinister and sometimes racist ones. Then there's the constant "marriage panic" in the media, worrying that people not getting married will spell the end of society. The latest example is *The Two-Parent Privilege* by economist Melissa Kearney.[23] Kearney's book seems to argue that women just don't understand how *great* marriage is for them. But I think women are pretty smart. And I think if they're choosing not to get married and not to have children, it's for one simple reason: that it's not working for them. So instead of scolding women, maybe we can reconsider the infrastructure that is no longer serving them.

If I'm trying to rewrite the policy agenda to work for women, in addition to paid family leave, and some reforms to protect against bias and discrimination in hiring, I would also want to reconsider the laws that have transformed divorce in many developed countries over the last 60 years. As a society, one of the goals of marriage is to create a legally binding agreement that protects the family unit, which allows two people to make mutually beneficial investments, ultimately creating value. It's similar to a business contract that would allow two companies to share confidential information—it can create value, but without legal binding, the risk would be prohibitive. In the past, the main "risky decision" these contracts protected was women investing in the family and homelife instead of their own careers. For this contract to provide this protection, the institution of marriage had to be protected—it is not meant to be entered into casually—but not enforced to such a degree that any party is forced to stay in an abusive situation. The absence of an ability to divorce—the lack of an "outside option"—puts women in an awful bargaining position in their marriage, and has a multitude of negative consequences. But, lost in this conversation has been the idea that divorce can also leave women worse off, especially those that invest in homemaking at the expense of their careers.

It would seem that one way to solve for this limitation would be to return to bilateral divorce (in which both parties must consent to the divorce) except in the case that fault—abuse, infidelity, and so on—can be shown. The problem with this approach is that it's reliant on a court system we already know is too lenient in holding abusers to account. So another approach might be to increase the amount of spousal support awarded when one individual specialized in domestic labor, the so-called homemaking provision that Ho-Po Crystal Wong has studied—making payments explicitly tied to contributions to home production, rather than just being the lower-earning partner.[24] And, a surprising policy lever, as shown in my work with Jeanne Lafortune, is make it easier for couples to accumulate marital property that will be shared in the case of divorce. Making home ownership easier through government subsidies, guarantees for low-income buyers, and reduced barriers to building housing will also help by providing the additional security of collateralized marriages to more families.

The next set of policies I would focus on would be those that govern a woman's reproductive rights. This means increasing resources for reproductive control at the beginning of the life cycle—when preventing unintended pregnancies is critical—as well as later in life, when the ability to have children may rely on fertility-extending technologies mostly available to the wealthiest women or those whose jobs offer premium insurance. *Both* of these forms of reproductive control have been shown to increase women's educational investments and career outcomes.[25]

But even these policy changes cannot be expected to serve as a magic bullet for falling fertility rates, as some women who delay having children due to access to new technologies may end up not being successful, or having smaller families as a result, as my research regarding Israel's free IVF showed. If we want to tackle falling birth rates, we need to make it possible for women to have children without giving up their ability to be full citizens. When I compare birth rates across the world, I always pay attention to how much women have to give up to become mothers. If there is a social norm against mothers working, for example, as there is in some East Asian countries, but even in places like Western Germany, women give up a lot of social and economic freedom to have children.

Government policies can make this trade-off less stark by reducing how much women have to lose by becoming mothers—including their lives. Researchers Stefania Albanesi and Claudia Olivetti found that the fall in maternal mortality and rise of formula use in the second half of the twentieth century allowed for a simultaneous increase in birth rates *and* women's labor supply. These changes made it less costly for women to have kids. But giving birth to a child in the United States is still shockingly dangerous. Our maternal mortality rate is almost three times that of France and Canada, and four to five times the UK and Australia, with devastatingly worse numbers for Black women. And restrictions on reproductive care are making childbirth *more* dangerous, as well as potentially making it more difficult to conceive in the first place, both by regulating assisted reproductive technology and increasing maternal morbidity—injuries and illnesses—that can affect future fertility. We can harness the powers of the mid-century decline in maternal mortality again. We can invest in reducing maternal mortality and supporting mothers. We *can* make childbirth as safe as in other developed countries. We just have to put the funds into 1) research and 2) implementing the best practices we already know work by equalizing health care access across rich and poor areas. And lastly, we cannot tie doctors' hands when it comes to saving women's lives.

And then after birth? How do we support making having children feel like part of a rich, rewarding, and sustainable life? One way is through subsidies for childcare, which we've discussed has risen in price enormously, due to a combination of changing standards and worker shortages. Keeping childcare costs affordable lowers the "price" of having children and allows for women to reenter the workforce before their children are school-aged.[26] We know these policies work—evidence from France extending its half-day (free) school to full day, for example, shows that it increased women's workforce participation.[27] In the Netherlands, increased childcare subsidies saw a 6.2 percent increase in women's work hours.[28]

But as I have emphasized throughout this book, women's participation in the workforce is not the be-all and end-all of policy. *Happiness* is. Or, as economists call it, *welfare* (the term for collective utility). So if women get a greater utility gain from staying home with their kids than from rejoining the work-force, I believe they should be able to access the same childcare subsidy as if they purchased childcare "on the market" from a day care provider or nanny. After all, the *same* economic activity is still taking place—caring for the physical, emotional, and developmental needs of a child—something all too rarely acknowledged when work is provided in the household rather than in exchange for money. This is something various US states have recently realized when it comes to elder care—family care providers can receive similar payments from Medicaid as what it would cost to pay an agency or other care provider.[29] How-ever, policies like this for childcare are rare, even in countries with otherwise generous family benefits. These suggestions go beyond the "basics" of a social safety net, and instead think about *incentives*—for firms to hire women, for women to have children, and for men to invest in families.

These kinds of policy reforms that support women as they work *and* invest in the next generation benefit everyone economically by creating an educated workforce to pay our social security or pensions when we need it.[30] And they're a fundamental part of living in a just society, where all parents can spend time with their babies and invest in the human capital of the next generation, not just white and wealthy ones. We like to complain about problems that stem from underinvestment in parenting, yet balk at making it possible for parents who *want* to make these investments but have zero paid leave and don't have the privilege of working part-time while still managing to make ends meet. Women invest in the next generation. A healthy society must invest in women.

The Agenda for Men

Investing in support structures that make it easier for families to have children also means investing in men learning how to be good parents, partners, and homemakers, something I rarely hear mentioned in the policy agenda about falling birth and marriage rates. And it means investing in education, job training, and job opportunities for lower-income men and men of color, so that fewer women are facing a marriage market where they can expect to be winning the bread and baking it too.

But while we wait for those policy interventions, there's plenty that individual men can do to be allies in the workplace *and* at home. So, men: this part is for you.

Priority number one is for men to increase their effectiveness and participation in home production. I urge the men in my life to become an expert in several of their household's most time-consuming tasks—not just cooking special meals but prepping lunch boxes, batch cooking weeknight dinners, and so on. Don't just assume you "do about half"—actively track your time. You might be doing half the tasks *you know about*. Understand outsourcing as an investment in later earning power, especially for your wife. If you're saying you can't afford help, ask if the best person to "hire" for the task is really your wife. Also remember that outsourcing creates its own mental load and management work. Can you reset the defaults so you're the go-to with the babysitter, cleaner, school, and so on? And if you do have children, please take your paternity leave.

More generally, though, I encourage you to find opportunities to lean in to your wife's career. Don't take for granted that she will always be the one to stay home with the sick kid, cancel the meeting, or absorb a childcare shock. Remember that today's decisions are tomorrow's constraints: if you always rely on her to be the one to reduce her extra time—and thus career investments—now, her wages won't grow as fast and it will "just make sense" for her to pick up more home production later. You can prevent this! You can invest in her career growth! And if you do, I bet you're more likely to stay happily married, and think about how much better *that* would be for your utility function.

To be an ally at work, remember that a male (especially white) voice tends to get amplified naturally. Actively use your voice to lift up female voices: "What were you saying?" when someone gets interrupted. "___ had a good idea; I'll let her explain it." "I think that's similar to the point ___ was making." And keep women from being excluded from "the room where it happens": "Maybe we should pause this conversation until ___ is here." Don't schedule meetings after childcare closes. And turn down the "world's best dad" award that's implicitly awarded every time a man with kids does any form of parenting.

Remember that biases often slip in when we are unaware, and sometimes in the language that we use. Read evaluations aloud with a male name. If you wouldn't write what you wrote about a man, you shouldn't say it about a woman, either (e.g., "Chad can be shrill when making a point"). When you find yourself using a term that couldn't be applied to a white male, reflect on hidden attitudes and biases. Ask yourself, *Why am I thinking of this person this way?*

Stop people who make sexist (or racist) comments within earshot: "No, sorry, I don't know what you mean." Stop worrying about making it awkward; *they* made it awkward. Return the awkward to sender (as advice blogger Jennifer Peepas, Captain Awkward, says)! Let them deal with that awkwardness! Say, "Wow—what?" Go ahead and socially exclude people who have committed sexual harassment. "Beyond a reasonable doubt" is for the court of law, not for who you have a beer with or chum around with at a conference.

Speaking of beer, drink beer (or the beverage of your choice) with women! Informal social events are opportunities, and women are all too often excluded. I sometimes hear men say they worry about socializing with women being "misunderstood"— trust me that we are able to tell the difference between well-meaning gestures to include us and sexual overtures! The men who pretend these are indistinguishable are acting in bad faith to cover up their own malfeasance. On the same topic, recognize that romantic overtures to women at work create massive externalities. If you're really meant to be together, it can wait until you're not working closely with each other.

Better yet, start businesses with women! The incredible women surrounding you at school and work are your *network*. If you always turn to people who look just like you when there's a business opportunity, ask yourself why. When it comes to hiring, if there are no women on your short list, think harder. If you find there are a lot of unwritten rules at the place where you work, teach them to a woman or someone else who is being excluded. Make the "it goes without saying" stuff explicit. Shut down gossip that focuses on people not fitting in or not getting the unwritten stuff right, and *definitely* gossip that focuses on women's dress, speech patterns, or sexual history. Introduce women with first name, last name, accomplishment.

See about the catering. Pick up the non-promotable tasks. My absolute favorite male colleague at work is the one who's always game to co-plan the happy hour, advise the student who is struggling, and write up the notes after the meeting. I haven't seen any of this hold him back in the slightest, possibly because the default level for non-promotable work assigned to men is so much lower. But I have seen it build up an enormous well of gratitude and loyalty from his female colleagues, who are all too used to being expected to be the ones to take on these tasks.

Improving the World for Others

When I talk about policymaking, I'm usually referencing organizations whose choices affect a large population—governments, executives. But really, anyone who makes choices that impact a number of other people is their own sort of policymaker. So one of the things I now want you to do is explore the areas where you hold influence, and consider how *you* might be able to use that influence for the greater good.

Leading a life that contributes to the well-being of others can be a cornerstone of our own utility. Staying connected to your role of producing utility for other people can help you find meaning and fulfillment at work, and therefore enhance your job's efficiency at converting your time into money. If work doesn't suck, you can sometimes get some utility out of the money machine at the same time. But these types of contributions to collective well-being can extend beyond your work. It might be that you prefer to keep the job that's the most efficient at converting your time into money, but pursue making the world a better place through your volunteer work or hobbies.

If you are someone who has been historically marginalized, your mere presence in places designed to exclude you is transformational. Persisting and succeeding in a system that is not set up for your success is making a difference structurally and at the individual level. There may be opportunities where you're able to "lift as you climb," but sometimes, the act of living your best life is in itself revolutionary.

On the other hand, if you benefit from some degree of privilege, it is imperative to consider how you might transform your workplace and community for the better. It can feel like such a slog to navigate our careers that we often lose sight of the power and privilege we do have. Always ask yourself: *Who has less access than I do? Who has less power in this situation?* Think about how you can ensure that person's life is a little bit better.

At work, this might mean fighting for more inclusive hiring practices, offering to mentor junior staff, and finding ways to give people with less privilege visibility and credit. At home, this might mean considering the broader impacts of your educational choices. I've observed, in others as well as myself, that having kids tends to make us selfish in a specific way: it narrows the scope of our altruism from the broad ecosystem we're part of to the specific little people who are reliant on us. It is an understandable impulse, but it often creates pathways for privileged people to defend not sharing what they have with others in the name of looking out for *their* kids, their families. One way to bring more meaning into our lives is to use our specific interests that relate to our families to champion broader change that improves the system for everyone, rather than just using our money or privilege to solve it privately.

If you find ways to live your life in a way that sprinkles a little extra fairy dust—help, comfort, smiles, support, and every now and then, cash—to others who need it, you yourself will feel more at peace and sustained, while contributing to changes that benefit everyone.

*

Together, I hope this agenda—for policymakers, for managers, for men, and for ourselves—will lead to a world where women will no longer feel squeezed from all sides—exhausted, with nothing left to give. A society where we acknowledge care work as economic production and make it possible for all employees, give women on-ramps to reenter or accelerate their careers later in life, eliminate the barriers standing in the way of hiring and retaining women in male-dominated fields, acknowledge the value of women's unique skills like collaborative negotiation, and make non-promotable tasks promotable. This means recognizing the tremendous economic resource women represent as workers, spouses, and parents and how that resource is currently being taxed beyond its capacity.

We're tired. Something's gotta change. And this one time, I'll dare to dream it can be the world.

Acknowledgments

First I'd like to thank my wife, Sondra, for showing me that there is indeed love after love, and for being my fiercest cheerleader and protector, even, and especially, when what I need protecting from is myself. And thank you to my kids—A, who first made me a mom, K, who makes me laugh every day, and baby H, who is my dream come true.

Thank you to my mom, Kira, for being my first writing teacher, and for telling me not to settle for anything less than I deserved. And my grandmother, Aloma, for showing me exactly what home-making women were worth in divorce, and sister Gwen, my oldest friend. A huge thank you to my friends, who have stood by me through thick and thin, celebrated successes and picked up the pieces of failure, and welcomed K and me into their homes when I needed it most: Jo, Moriah, Christin, Melissa, Lawrence, Gwyn, Michael and Michelle, Clayton and Krista, Jonathan and Amy, Alex and Liz, Shing-Yi and Santosh, Ben and Amy, Jenique, Kate, May, Eva, the friends who got me through grad school, Maya, Jonathan, Toko, and Virginia, and my new and now lifelong friends in Philadelphia, Tiffany, Chelsea, Emily, Monique, Dorit and Sylvia.

A special thanks to my literary agent, Celeste Fine, for being a champion of this story being told, right from the beginning, and Jaidree Braddix for her feedback whenever we needed a different perspective. Thank you to my UK editor, Kirty Topiwala, who has been a huge fan and advocate of this work at every stage, and US editor, Julie Will, whose edits helped me say exactly what I wanted to, better than I could, and the entire Hodder and Flatiron production teams. A huge thank you also to my research assistant Stephanie Dodd, whose attention to detail never fails to amaze me, and without whom this book, and its 160-some endnotes, would not have happened.

I owe an enormous debt of gratitude to the women who made this work possible: those who let me share their stories, those who did the research that makes up its pages, and those who have surrounded me in an extraordinary community of female economists. Most importantly, I need to thank my coauthors, whose incredible ideas are woven throughout this book, and who have become friends, confidants, and co-conspirators: Alessandra Voena, Jeanne Lafortune, Naomi Gershoni, Natalie Bau, Nava Ashraf, Bryce Steinberg, Kathleen McGinn, Christine Exley, Jennie Huang, and Xiaoyue Shan. But also, the trailblazing women in economics whose research has inspired me: Muriel Niederle, Lise Vesterlund, Claudia Goldin, Claudia Olivetti, Raquel Fernández, Valerie Ramey, Shelly Lundberg, and Shoshana Grossbard, and the mentors who have shown me so much kindness in a profession that is too often cold: Ilyana Kuziemko, Martha Bailey, Sandy Black, Janet Currie, Seema Jayachandran, and, at Wharton, Katy Milkman, Olivia Mitchell, and Nancy Rothbard. A special thanks also to Lena Edlund who first taught me gender economics, and from whose ideas I still draw so much. And, the biggest thanks to all the women around the world, past and present, who have crafted their own paths and found their constrained optimums, who make up the data, and thus beating heart of this book.

Finally, in a book that has many examples of men standing in the way of women's progress, I'd like to thank the men who have championed mine: my undergraduate advisor, Connel Fullenkamp, who told me to write a thesis and yelled at me when I didn't believe in myself, and my PhD advisors, Kiki Pop-Eleches, who first took me under his wing at Columbia, and Pierre-André

Chiappori, who first encouraged me to try theory, letting me borrow his confidence in me when I lacked my own, and always treated me as a *scientist* whose ideas deserved to be heard. My colleague, coauthor, and friend Judd Kessler, who has been an advocate of my career in little and big ways from the moment I met him. And my colleague and friend Ben Lockwood, who is always willing to see about the catering (or the campfire). Two excellent department chairs, Rob Jensen and Joe Harrington. My dad, Ron, who has always been proud of me, and my grandfather, Marshall, who may not have fully believed in women in the sciences, but who loved me fiercely and supported me nonetheless (and mailed me *Wall Street Journal* articles titled "Grandpa blog").

Endnotes

Introduction

1 L. Babcock, B. Peyser, L. Vesterlund, and L. Weingart, *The No Club: Putting a Stop to Women's Dead-End Work* (New York: Simon & Schuster, 2022).
2 K. Hancock, J. Lafortune, and C. Low, "Winning the Bread and Baking It Too: Gendered Frictions in the Allocation of Home Production" (working paper no. w33393, National Bureau of Economic Research, Cambridge, MA, 2025).
3 J. Pepin, L. Sayer, and L. Casper, "Marital Status and Mothers' Time Use: Childcare, Housework, Leisure, and Sleep," *Demography* 55, no. 1 (2018): 107–33.

Chapter 1

1 K. Engemann and M. Owyang, "Social Changes Lead Married Women into Labor Force," *Federal Reserve Bank of St. Louis*, April 1, 2006, https://www.stlouisfed.org/publications/regional-economist/april-2006/social-changes-lead-married-women-into-labor-force.
2 G. Becker, "A Theory of Marriage: Part I," *Journal of Political Economy* 81, no. 4 (1973): 813–46. G. Becker, "A Theory of Marriage: Part II," *Journal of Political Economy* 82, no. 2 (1974): S11–S26.
3 S. Albanesi and C. Olivetti, "Gender Roles and Medical Progress," *Journal of Political Economy* 124, no. 3 (2016): 650–95; J. Greenwood, A. Seshadri, and M. Yorukoglu, "Engines of Liberation," *Review of Economic Studies* 72, no. 1 (2005): 109–33.
4 V. Ramey, "Time Spent in Home Production in the Twentieth-Century United States: New Estimates from Old Data," *Journal of Economic History* 69, no. 1 (2009): 1–47; L. R. Ngai, C. Olivetti, and B. Petrongolo, "Gendered Change: 150 Years of Transformation in US Hours" (working paper no. w32475, National Bureau of Economic Research, Cambridge, MA, 2024).

5 M. A. Bronson, *"Degrees Are Forever: Marriage, Educational Investment, and Life Cycle Labor Decisions of Men and Women"* (working paper, Georgetown University, 2015).

6 R. Fernández and J. C. Wong, "Free to Leave? A Welfare Analysis of Divorce Regimes," *American Economic Journal: Macroeconomics* 9, no. 3 (2017): 72–115; H. Foerster, "Untying the Knot: How Child Support and Alimony Affect Couples' Decisions and Welfare," *Review of Economic Studies* (2024), rdae105.

7 J. Lafortune and C. Low, "Collateralized Marriage," *American Economic Journal: Applied Economics* 15, no. 4 (2023): 252–91.

8 B. Stevenson and J. Wolfers, "Bargaining in the Shadow of the Law: Divorce Laws and Family Distress," *Quarterly Journal of Economics* 121, no. 1 (2006): 267–88.

9 S. Albanesi and C. Olivetti, "Gender Roles and Medical Progress," *Journal of Political Economy* 124, no. 3 (2016): 650–95; J. Greenwood, A. Seshadri, and M. Yorukoglu, "Engines of Liberation," *Review of Economic Studies* 72, no. 1 (2005): 109–33.

10 G. Ramey and V. Ramey, "The Rug Rat Race," *Brookings Papers on Economic Activity* (2010).

11 A.M. Slaughter, "Why Women Still Can't Have It All," *The Atlantic*, July–August, 2012, https://www.theatlantic.com/magazine/archive/2012/07/why-women-still-cant-have-it-all/309020/.

12 K. Fisher, J. Gershuny, S. Flood, J. G. Roman, and S. L. Hofferth, "American Heritage Time Use Study Extract Builder: Version 1.2 [dataest]" (Minneapolis, MN: IPUMS, 2018); Institute for Social Research, "Panel Study of Income Dynamics, public use dataset" (Ann Arbor, MI: University of Michigan, 2024)

13 I. Kuziemko, J. Pan, J. Shen, and E. Washington, "The Mommy Effect: Do Women Anticipate the Employment Effects of Motherhood?" (working paper no. w24740, National Bureau of Economic Research, Cambridge, MA, 2018).

14 J. Jessen, S. Schweighofer-Kodritsch, F. Weinhardt, and J. Berkes, "Separate Housework Spheres" (discussion paper no. 17134, IZA, Bonn, Germany, 2024).

15 C. Goldin and L. Katz, "The Power of the Pill: Oral Contraceptives and Women's Career and Marriage Decisions," *Journal of Political Economy* 110, no. 4 (2002): 730–70.

Chapter 2

1 S. Flood, L. C. Sayer, D. Backman, and A. Chen, "American Time Use Study Data Extract Builder: Version 3.2 [dataset]" (College Park, MD: University of Maryland and Minneapolis, MN: IPUMS, 2023).

2 M. Iyigun and J. Lafortune, "Putting the Husband Through: The Role of Credit Constraints in the Timing of Marriage and Spousal Education," *Journal of Labor Economics* 41, no. 1 (2023): 245–89.

3 S. Levitt, "Heads or Tails: The Impact of a Coin Toss on Major Life Decisions and Subsequent Happiness," *Review of Economic Studies* 88, no. 1 (2021): 378–405.

4 N. Bhattacharjee, A. Schumacher, A. Aali, Y. H. Abate, R. Abbasgholizadeh, M. Abbasian, M. Abbasi-Kangevari, H. Abbastabar, S. A. ElHafeez, S. Abd-Elsalam, et al., "Global Fertility in 204 Countries and Territories, 1950–2021, with Forecasts to 2100: A Comprehensive Demographic Analysis for the Global Burden of Disease Study 2021," *Lancet* 403, no. 10440 (2024): 2057–99.

5 J. Davidson and D. Hannaford, eds., *Opting Out: Women Messing with Marriage Around the World* (New Brunswick, NJ: Rutgers University Press, 2023).

6 B. S. Lee, S. Jang, and J. Sarkar, "Women's Labor Force Participation and Marriage: The Case of Korea," *Journal of Asian Economics* 19, no. 2 (2008): 138–54.

7 M. Rich, "Craving Freedom, Japan's Women Opt Out of Marriage," *New York Times*, August 3, 2019, https://www.nytimes.com/2019/08/03/world/asia/japan-single-women-marriage.html; M. Rich, "Japan's Working Mothers: Record Responsibilities, Little Help from Dads," *New York Times*, February 2, 2019, https://www.nytimes.com/2019/02/02/world/asia/japan-working-mothers.html?action=click&module=RelatedCoverage&pgtype=Article&region=Footer.

8 L. Ungar, "More Women Had Their Tubes Tied After Roe v. Wade Was Overturned," AP News, September 11, 2024, https://apnews.com/article/abortion-tubal-ligations-tying-tubes-dobbs-roe-jama-2ec56d7f2707d-b083e513bdc74a5016d.

9 European Commission, *Low Fertility in the EU: A Review of Trends and Drivers* (Joint Research Centre, 2024), https://publications.jrc.ec.europa.eu/repository/handle/JRC137492; J. Hellstrand, J. Nisén, V. Miranda, P. Fallesen, L. Dommermuth, and M. Myrskylä, "Not Just Later, but Fewer: Novel Trends in Cohort Fertility in the Nordic Countries," *Demography*, 58 no. 4 (2021): 1373–99.

10 "Germany Birth Rate Drops Rapidly, New Report Says," DW, October 23, 2024, https://www.dw.com/en/german-birth-rate-drops-rapidly-new-report-says/a-70573468.

11 "Only a Quarter of Millennials Who Want Children Are Trying for Them," UCL Centre for Longitudinal Studies, October 4, 2024, https://cls.ucl.ac.uk/only-a-quarter-of-millennials-who-want-children-are-trying-for-them/.

12 "Hungary Tries for Baby Boom with Tax Breaks and Loan Forgiveness," BBC, February 11, 2019, https://www.bbc.com/news/world-europe-47192612; I. Dominioni, "Italy Introduces Kids' Check in Support of Fam-

ilies (and Family-Making)," *Forbes*, March 31, 2021, https://www.forbes.com/sites/irenedominioni/2021/03/31/italy-introduces-kids-check-in-support-of-families-and-family-making/.

13 J. Calarco, *Holding It Together: How Women Became America's Safety Net* (New York: Penguin Random House, 2024).

14 B. Stevenson and J. Wolfers, "The Paradox of Declining Female Happiness," *American Economic Journal: Economic Policy* 1, no. 2 (2009): 190–225.

15 D. Blanchflower and A. Bryson, "The Female Happiness Paradox," *Journal of Population Economics* 37, no. 1 (2024): 16.

Chapter 3

1 R. Thaler and C. Sunstein, *Nudge: Improving Decisions About Health, Wealth, and Happiness* (New York: Penguin, 2009).

2 D. Kahneman, *Thinking, Fast and Slow* (New York: Macmillan, 2011).

3 A. Gopnik, *The Gardener and the Carpenter: What the New Science of Child Development Tells Us About the Relationship Between Parents and Children* (New York: Macmillan, 2016).

Chapter 4

1 C. Goldin and L. Katz, "The Power of the Pill: Oral Contraceptives and Women's Career and Marriage Decisions," *Journal of Political Economy* 110, no. 4 (2002): 730–70.

2 C. Myers, "The Power of Abortion Policy: Reexamining the Effects of Young Women's Access to Reproductive Control," *Journal of Political Economy* 125, no. 6 (2017): 2178–24.

3 O. Judson, *Dr. Tatiana's Sex Advice to All Creation: The Definitive Guide to the Evolutionary Biology of Sex* (New York: Macmillan, 2003).

4 R. L. Trivers, "Parental Investment and Sexual Selection," in *Sexual Selection and the Descent of Man 1871-1971*, ed. B Campbell (Chicago: Aldine Publishing Company, 1972).

5 L. Edlund, "The Role of Paternity Presumption and Custodial Rights for Understanding Marriage Patterns," *Economica* 80, no. 320 (2013): 650–69.

6 N. Gershoni and C. Low, "The Power of Time: The Impact of Free IVF on Women's Human Capital Investments," *European Economic Review* 133 (2021): 103645; N. Gershoni and C. Low, "Older yet Fairer: How Extended Reproductive Time Horizons Reshaped Marriage Patterns in Israel," *American Economic Journal: Applied Economics* 13, no. 1 (2021): 198–234.

7 L. Kenny, T. Lavender, R. McNamee, S. O'Neill, T. Millis, and A. Khashan, "Advanced Maternal Age and Adverse Pregnancy Outcome: Evidence from a Large Contemporary Cohort," *PLOS ONE* 8, no. 2 (2013): e56583; S. Lean, H. Derricott, R. Jones, and A. Heazell, "Advanced Maternal Age and Adverse Pregnancy Outcomes: A Systematic Review and Meta-Analysis," *PLOS ONE* 12, no. 10 (2017): e0186287.

8 C. Low, "The Human Capital–Reproductive Capital Trade-Off in Marriage Market Matching," *Journal of Political Economy* 132, no. 2 (2024): 552–76.

9 C. Low, "Pricing the Biological Clock: The Marriage Market Costs of Aging to Women," *Journal of Labor Economics* 42, no. 2 (2024): 395–426.

10 L. Aldén, L. Edlund, M. Hammarstedt, and M. Mueller-Smith, "Effect of Registered Partnership on Labor Earnings and Fertility for Same-Sex Couples: Evidence from Swedish Register Data," *Demography* 52, no. 4 (2015): 1243–68.

11 S. Mullainathan and E. Shafir, *Scarcity: Why Having Too Little Means So Much* (New York: Macmillan, 2013).

12 For example, "Credit Card Calculator," Calculator.net, https://www.calculator.net/credit-card-calculator.html.

Chapter 5

1 M. Bertrand, C. Goldin, and L. Katz, "Dynamics of the Gender Gap for Young Professionals in the Financial and Corporate Sectors," *American Economic Journal: Applied Economics* 2, no. 3 (2010): 228–55.

2 L. Bennetts, "First Lady in Waiting," Vanity Fair, December 27, 2007, https://www.vanityfair.com/news/2007/12/michelle_obama200712.

3 S. Jayachandran, L. Nassal, M. Notowidigdo, M. Paul, H. Sarsons, and E. Sundberg, "Moving to Opportunity, Together" (working paper no. w32970, National Bureau of Economic Research, Cambridge, MA, 2024).

4 H. Antecol, A. Jong, and M. Steinberger, "The Sexual Orientation Wage Gap: The Role of Occupational Sorting and Human Capital," *ILR Review* 61, no. 4 (2008): 518–43; D. Black, H. Makar, S. Sanders, and L. Taylor, "The Earnings Effects of Sexual Orientation," *ILR Review* 56, no. 3 (2003): 449–69; L. Jepsen, "Comparing the Earnings of Cohabiting Lesbians, Cohabiting Heterosexual Women, and Married Women: Evidence from the 2000 Census," *Industrial Relations: A Journal of Economy and Society* 46, no. 4 (2007): 699–727; M. Klawitter, "Meta-Analysis of the Effects of Sexual Orientation on Earnings," *Industrial Relations: A Journal of Economy and Society* 54, no. 1 (2015): 4–32.

5 S. Kliff, "The Truth About the Gender Wage Gap," Vox, September 8, 2017, https://www.vox.com/2017/9/8/16268362/gender-wage-gap-explained.

6 H. Antecol, K. Bedard, and J. Stearns, "Equal but Inequitable: Who Benefits from Gender-Neutral Tenure Clock Stopping Policies?," *American Economic Review* 108, no. 9 (2018): 2420–41.

7 H. Kleven, C. Landais, and J. Søgaard, "Children and Gender Inequality: Evidence from Denmark," *American Economic Journal: Applied Economics* 11, no. 4 (2019): 181–209.

8 H. Kleven, C. Landais, and G. Leite-Mariante, "The Child Penalty Atlas," *Review of Economic Studies* (2025), rdae104.

9 A. Uribe, C. Vargas, and N. Bustamante, "Unintended Consequences of Maternity Leave Legislation: The Case of Colombia," *World Development* 122 (2019): 218–32.

10 M. A. Bronson and P. Thoursie, "The Wage Growth and Within-Firm Mobility of Men and Women: New Evidence and Theory" (working paper, Georgetown University, 2019).

11 M. Bertrand and S. Mullainathan, "Are Emily and Greg More Employable Than Lakisha and Jamal? A Field Experiment on Labor Market Discrimination," *American Economic Review* 94, no. 4 (2004): 991–1013.

12 J. Kessler, C. Low, and C. Sullivan, "Incentivized Résumé Rating: Eliciting Employer Preferences Without Deception," *American Economic Review* 109, no. 11 (2019): 3713–44.

13 O. Folke and J. Rickne, "Sexual Harassment and Gender Inequality in the Labor Market," *Quarterly Journal of Economics* 137, no. 4 (2022): 2163–212.

14 R. Traister, "Why the Harvey Weinstein Sexual-Harassment Allegations Didn't Come Out Until Now," *The Cut*, October 5, 2017, https://www.thecut.com/2017/10/why-the-weinstein-sexual-harassment-allegations-came-out-now.html.

15 X. Shan, "Essays on Peer Effects, Gender Disparities, and Skill Formation," (University of Zurich, Faculty of Economics, 2021).

16 C. Exley, R. Fisman, J. Kessler, L. P. LePage, X. Li, C. Low, X. Shan, M. Toma, and B. Zafar, "Do Optimal Information Policies Increase Equity? Evidence from Two Large-Scale Grading Experiments" (working paper no. w32350, National Bureau of Economic Research, Cambridge, MA, 2024).

Chapter 6

1 E. Klein, "Mitt Romney Flashback: Stay-at-Home Moms Need to 'Learn Dignity of Work,'" *Washington Post*, April 15, 2012, https://www.washingtonpost.com/blogs/ezra-klein/post/mitt-romney-flashback-stay-at-home-moms-need-to-learn-dignity-of-work/2012/04/15/gIQAhmbZJT_blog.html.

2 V. Burbano, N. Padilla, and S. Meier, "Gender Differences in Preferences for Meaning at Work," *American Economic Journal: Economic Policy* 16, no. 3 (2024): 61–94.

3 R. Fisher, W. Ury, and B. Patton, *Getting to Yes: Negotiating Agreement Without Giving In* (New York: Penguin, 2011).

4 W. Ury, *Getting Past No: Negotiating in Difficult Situations* (New York: Bantam, 1993).

Chapter 7

1 B. Auyeung, S. Baron-Cohen, E. Ashwin, R. Knickmeyer, K. Taylor, G. Hackett, and M. Hines, "Fetal Testosterone Predicts Sexually Differentiated Childhood Behavior in Girls and in Boys," *Psychological Science* 20, no. 2 (2009): 144–48; M. Hines, "Sex Steroids and Human Behavior: Prenatal Androgen Exposure and Sex-Typical Play Behavior in Children," *Annals of the New York Academy of Sciences* 1007, no. 1 (2003): 272–82; M. Hines, "Prenatal Endocrine Influences on Sexual Orientation and on Sexually Differentiated Childhood Behavior," *Frontiers in Neuroendocrinology* 32, no. 2 (2011): 170–82.

2 A. Kentner, A. Abizaid, and C. Bielajew, "Modeling Dad: Animal Models of Paternal Behavior," *Neuroscience & Biobehavioral Reviews* 34, no. 3 (2010): 438–51.

3 I. Alger, "On the Evolution of Male Competitiveness," *Journal of Economic Behavior & Organization* 190 (2021): 228–54.

4 D. Thomas, "The Distribution of Income and Expenditure Within the Household," *Annales d'Economie et de Statistique* no. 29 (1993): 109–35; A. Quisumbing and J. Maluccio, *Intrahousehold Allocation and Gender Relations: New Empirical Evidence* (Washington, DC: World Bank, 1999); E. Duflo, "Grandmothers and Granddaughters: Old Age Pensions and Intrahousehold Allocation in South Africa," *World Bank Economic Review* 17, no. 1 (2003): 1–25.

5 M. Walter, H. Abele, and C. Plappert, "The Role of Oxytocin and the Effect of Stress During Childbirth: Neurobiological Basics and Implications for Mother and Child," *Frontiers in Endocrinology* 12 (2021): 742236; N. Scatliffe, S. Casavant, D. Vittner, and X. Cong, "Oxytocin and Early Parent-Infant Interactions: A Systematic Review," *International Journal of Nursing Sciences* 6, no. 4 (2019): 445–53.

6 M. Niederle and L. Vesterlund, "Do Women Shy Away from Competition? Do Men Compete Too Much?," *Quarterly Journal of Economics* 122, no. 3 (2007): 1067–101.

7 C. Lagarde, "Ten Years After Lehman—Lessons Learned and Challenges Ahead," *IMF Blog*, September 5, 2018, https://www.imf.org/en/Blogs/Articles/2018/09/05/blog-ten-years-after-lehman-lessons-learned-and-challenges-ahead.

8 J. Huang and C. Low, "The Myth of the Male Negotiator: Gender's Effect on Negotiation Strategies and Outcomes," *Journal of Economic Behavior & Organization* 202 (2022): 517–32.

9 C. Exley, O. Hauser, M. Moore, and J. H. Pezzuto, "Believed Gender Differences in Social Preferences," *The Quarterly Journal of Economics* (2024), 1–56.

10 C. Exley, M. Niederle, and L. Vesterlund, "Knowing When to Ask: The Cost of Leaning In," *Journal of Political Economy* 128, no. 3 (2020): 816–54.

11 A. Leibbrandt and J. List, "Do Women Avoid Salary Negotiations? Evidence from a Large-Scale Natural Field Experiment," *Management Science* 61, no. 9 (2015): 2016–24.

12 L. Babcock, M. Recalde, L. Vesterlund, and L. Weingart, "Gender Differences in Accepting and Receiving Requests for Tasks with Low Promotability," *American Economic Review* 107, no. 3 (2017): 714–47.

13 L. Babcock, B. Peyser, L. Vesterlund, and L. Weingart, *The No Club: Putting a Stop to Women's Dead-End Work* (New York: Simon & Schuster, 2022).

14 C. Exley and J. Kessler, "The Gender Gap in Self-Promotion," *Quarterly Journal of Economics* 137, no. 3 (2022): 1345–81.

15 K. Kay and C. Shipman, *The Confidence Code: The Science and Art of Self-Assurance—What Women Should Know* (New York: HarperCollins, 2014).

16 D. Card, S. DellaVigna, P. Funk, and N. Iriberri, "Are Referees and Editors in Economics Gender Neutral?". *The Quarterly Journal of Economics* 135, no. 1 (2020): 269–327.

17 A. Kugler, C. Tinsley, and O. Ukhaneva, "Choice of Majors: Are Women Really Different from Men?," *Economics of Education Review* 81 (2021): 102079; B. Ost, "The Role of Peers and Grades in Determining Major Persistence in the Sciences," *Economics of Education Review* 29, no. 6 (2010): 923–34.

18 X. Jiang, "Women in STEM: Ability, Preference, and Value," *Labour Economics* 70 (2021): 101991; D. Beede, T. Julian, D. Langdon, G. McKittrick, B. Khan, and M. Doms, *Women in STEM: A Gender Gap to Innovation* (Washington, DC: Economics and Statistics Administration, US Department of Commerce, 2011).

19 Author's calculation based on data including employed, college-educated individuals between the ages of 23 and 65 from the 2024 Current Population Survey Annual Social and Economic Supplement. Data: S. Flood, M. King, R. Rodgers, S. Ruggles, J. R. Warren, D. Backman, A. Chen, G. Cooper, S. Richards, M. Schouweiler, "IPUMS CPS: Version 12.0 [dataset]" (Minneapolis, MN: IPUMS, 2024); STEM Classifications: U.S. Census Bureau, "2018 Census STEM, STEM-Related and Non-STEM related Code List" (Washington, DC: United States Census Bureau, September 11, 2024).

20 A. Mas and A. Pallais, "Valuing Alternative Work Arrangements," *American Economic Review* 107, no. 12 (2017): 3722–59.

21 C. Goldin, "A Grand Gender Convergence: Its Last Chapter," *American Economic Review* 104, no. 4 (2014): 1091–119.

22 C. Goldin, "The Economic Status of Women in the Early Republic: Quantitative Evidence," *Journal of Interdisciplinary History* 16, no. 3 (1986): 375–404.

23 S. Karlamangla, "Male Doctors Are Disappearing from Gynecology. Not Everybody Is Thrilled About It," *Los Angeles Times*, March 7, 2018, https://www.latimes.com/health/la-me-male-gynos-20180307-htmlstory.html.

24 S. Cheryan, V. Plaut, P. Davies, and C. Steele, "Ambient Belonging: How Stereotypical Cues Impact Gender Participation in Computer Science," *Journal of Personality and Social Psychology* 97, no. 6 (2009): 1045.

25 "Is the American strip club dying out?" BBC, July 5, 2019, https://www.bbc.com/news/world-us-canada-48667681.

Chapter 8

1 G. Loewenstein, "Hot-Cold Empathy Gaps and Medical Decision Making," *Health Psychology* 24, no. 4S (2005): S49.

2 S. Peele and A. Brodsky, *Love and Addiction* (New York: Taplinger, 1975); A. Redcay and C. Simonetti, "Criteria for Love and Relationship Addiction: Distinguishing Love Addiction from Other Substance and Behavioral Addictions," *Sexual Addiction & Compulsivity* 25, no. 1 (2018): 80–95.

3 S. Flood, L. C. Sayer, D. Backman, and A. Chen, "American Time Use Survey Data Extract Builder: Version 3.2 [dataset]." (College Park, MD: University of Maryland and Minneapolis, MN: IPUMS, 2023).

4 M. C. Inhorn, *Motherhood on Ice: The Mating Gap and Why Women Freeze Their Eggs* (New York: NYU Press, 2023).

5 b. hooks, *Feminism Is for Everybody: Passionate Politics* (London: Pluto Press, 2000).

6 R. Fernández, A. Fogli, and C. Olivetti, "Mothers and Sons: Preference Formation and Female Labor Force Dynamics," *Quarterly Journal of Economics* 119, no. 4 (2004): 1249–99.

7 D. Del Boca, M. Locatelli, and S. Pasqua, "Employment Decisions of Married Women: Evidence and Explanations," *Labour* 14, no. 1 (2000): 35–52.

8 S. Jayachandran, L. Nassal, M. Notowidigdo, M. Paul, H. Sarsons, and E. Sundberg, "Moving to Opportunity, Together" (working paper no. w32970, National Bureau of Economic Research, Cambridge, MA, 2024).

9 E. Rodsky, *Fair Play: A Game-Changing Solution for When You Have Too Much to Do (and More Life to Live)* (New York: G. P. Putnam's Sons, 2019).

Chapter 9

1 N. Folbre, The Invisible Heart: Economics and Family Values (New York: The New Press, 2001).

2 H. Allcott, L. Braghieri, S. Eichmeyer, and M. Gentzkow, "The Welfare Effects of Social Media," *American Economic Review* 110, no. 3 (2020): 629–76.

3 L. Bursztyn, B. Handel, R. Jimenez, and C. Roth, "When Product Markets Become Collective Traps: The Case of Social Media" (working paper no. w31771, National Bureau of Economic Research, Cambridge, MA, 2023).

4 G. Keren and P. Roelofsma, "Immediacy and Certainty in Intertemporal Choice," *Organizational Behavior and Human Decision Processes* 63, no. 3 (1995): 287–97.

5 O. Giuntella and F. Mazzonna, "Sunset Time and the Economic Effects of Social Jetlag: Evidence from US Time Zone Borders," *Journal of Health Economics* 65 (2019): 210–26; M. Gibson and J. Shrader, "Time Use and Labor Productivity: The Returns to Sleep," *Review of Economics and Statistics* 100, no. 5 (2018): 783–98; "*What Are Sleep Deprivation and Deficiency?*" National Heart, Lung, and Blood Institute, updated March 24, 2022, https://www.nhlbi.nih.gov/health/sleep-deprivation; "*Sleep,*" Center for Disease Control Chronic Disease Indicators, June 3, 2024, https://www.cdc.gov/cdi/indicator-definitions/sleep.html; "Lack of Sleep in Middle Age May Increase Dementia Risk," National Institutes of Health Research Matters, April 27, 2021, https://www.nih.gov/news-events/nih-research-matters/lack-sleep-middle-age-may-increase-dementia-risk.

6 M. Avery, O. Giuntella, and P. Jiao, "Why Don't We Sleep Enough? A Field Experiment Among College Students," *Review of Economics and Statistics*, 107, no.1 (2025): 65-77.

7 K. Milkman, *How to Change: The Science of Getting from Where You Are to Where You Want to Be* (New York: Portfolio/Penguin, 2021).

8 S. Ambec and N. Treich, "Roscas as Financial Agreements to Cope with Self-Control Problems," *Journal of Development Economics* 82, no. 1 (2007): 120–37.

9 N. Augenblick, M. Niederle, and C. Sprenger, "Working Over Time: Dynamic Inconsistency in Real Effort Tasks," *Quarterly Journal of Economics* 130, no. 3 (2015): 1067–115.

10 C. Rampell, "Outsource Your Way to Success," *New York Times Magazine*, November 5, 2013.

11 P. Cortés and J. Pan, "Outsourcing Household Production: Foreign Domestic Workers and Native Labor Supply in Hong Kong," *Journal of Labor Economics* 31, no. 2 (2013): 327–71.

12 S. J. Kwon, "Grandparents and Parental Labor Supply During the COVID-19 Pandemic," *Review of Economics of the Household* 22, no. 3 (2024): 935–64; J. Posadas and M. Vidal-Fernandez, "Grandparents' Childcare and Female Labor Force Participation," *IZA Journal of Labor Policy* 2 (2013): 1–20.

13 M. Carlin, "Fast Food and Urban Living Standards in Medieval England," in *Food and Eating in Medieval Europe*, ed. M. Carlin and J. T. Rosenthal (London: Hambledon Press, 1998).

14 R. Perez-Truglia, "The Effects of Income Transparency on Well-Being: Evidence from a Natural Experiment," *American Economic Review* 110, no. 4 (2020): 1019–54.

15 N. Bottan and R. Perez-Truglia, "Choosing Your Pond: Location Choices and Relative Income," *Review of Economics and Statistics* 104, no. 5 (2022): 1010–27.

16 V. Robin and J. Dominguez, *Your Money or Your Life: 9 Steps to Transforming Your Relationship with Money and Achieving Financial Independence* (New York: Penguin Books, 2008).

Chapter 10

1 B. Spock, *The Common Sense Book of Baby and Child Care* (New York: Duell, Sloan and Pearce, 1946).

2 J. Traig, *Act Natural: A Cultural History of Misadventures in Parenting* (New York: HarperCollins, 2019).

3 S. Fomon, "Reflections on Infant Feeding in the 1970s and 1980s," *American Journal of Clinical Nutrition* 46, no. 1 (1987): 171–82.

4 G. Wall, "Is Your Child's Brain Potential Maximized?: Mothering in an Age of New Brain Research," *Atlantis: Critical Studies in Gender, Culture & Social Justice* 28, no. 2 (2004): 41–50.

5 R. Ferber, *Solve Your Child's Sleep Problems* (New York: Simon & Schuster, 1985).

6 K. Pickhert, "The Man Who Remade Motherhood," *Time*, May 21, 2012, https://time.com/606/the-man-who-remade-motherhood/.

7 B. Pan, M. Rowe, J. Singer, and C. Snow, "Maternal Correlates of Growth in Toddler Vocabulary Production in Low-Income Families," *Child Development* 76, no. 4 (2005): 763–82; F. Cunha, M. Gerdes, Q. Hu, and S. Nihtianova, "Language Environment and Maternal Expectations: An Evaluation of the LENA Start Program," *Journal of Human Capital* 18, no. 1 (2024): 105–39.

8 P. Blackwell, "The Influence of Touch on Child Development: Implications for Intervention," *Infants & Young Children* 13, no. 1 (2000): 25–39.

9   T. Vanderbilt, "What Ever Happened to the Playpen?: How the Kiddie Enclosures Fell Out of Favor," Slate, August 7, 2009, https://slate.com/human-interest/2009/08/how-the-playpen-fell-out-of-favor.html.

10 J. Currie and D. Almond, "Human Capital Development Before Age Five," in *Handbook of Labor Economics*, vol. 4 (San Diego: Elsevier, 2011).

11 D. Almond and B. Mazumder, "Health Capital and the Prenatal Environment: The Effect of Ramadan Observance During Pregnancy," *American Economic Journal: Applied Economics* 3, no. 4 (2011): 56–85; D. Almond, B. Mazumder, and R. Van Ewijk, "In Utero Ramadan Exposure and Children's Academic Performance," *Economic Journal* 125, no. 589 (2015): 1501–33; B. Mazumder, D. Almond, K. Park, E. Crimmins, and C. Finch, "Lingering Prenatal Effects of the 1918 Influenza Pandemic on Cardiovascular Disease," *Journal of Developmental Origins of Health and Disease* 1, no. 1 (2010): 26–34.

12 J. Heckman, "Skill Formation and the Economics of Investing in Disadvantaged Children," *Science* 312, no. 5782 (2006): 1900–1902; J. Heckman, R. Pinto, and P. Savelyev, "Understanding the Mechanisms Through Which an Influential Early Childhood Program Boosted Adult Outcomes," *American Economic Review* 103, no. 6 (2013): 2052–86; T. Havnes and M. Mogstad, "No Child Left Behind: Subsidized Child Care and Children's Long-Run Outcomes," *American Economic Journal: Economic Policy* 3, no. 2 (2011): 97–129.

13 "Data Finds Child Care Prices Continue to Rise Ahead of Midterm Elections, Outpacing Inflation," First Five Years Fund, October 13, 2022, https://www.ffyf.org/2022/10/13/data-child-care-prices-continue-to-rise-ahead-of-midterm-elections-outpacing-inflation/.

14 S. Abbott, "Child Care Prices, Inflation, and the End of Federal Pandemic-Era Aid in Five Charts," Washington Center for Equitable Growth, May 8, 2023, https://equitablegrowth.org/child-care-prices-inflation-and-the-end-of-federal-pandemic-era-aid-in-five-charts/.

15 S. Hays, *The Cultural Contradictions of Motherhood* (New Haven, CT: Yale University Press, 1998).

16 K. Boyse, A. Wojciechowski, K. Orringer, S. Laule, and S. Ryckman, "Feeding Your Baby and Toddler (Birth to Age Two)," University of Michigan Health, C. S. Mott Children's Hospital, 2022, https://www.mottchildren.org/posts/your-child/feeding-your-baby-toddler; "Bottle Feeding Babies FAQ for Parents," Ann & Robert H. Lurie Children's Hospital of Chicago, July 18, 2023, https://www.luriechildrens.org/en/blog/bottle-feeding-faq/.

17 N. Butte, C. Jensen, J. Moon, D. Glaze, and J. Frost Jr., "Sleep Organization and Energy Expenditure of Breast-Fed and Formula-Fed Infants," *Pediatric Research* 32, no. 5 (1992): 514–19; N. Jafar, E. Tham, W. Pang, "Association Between Breastfeeding and Sleep Patterns in Infants and Preschool Children," *American Journal of Clinical Nutrition*

114, no. 6 (2021): 1986–96; M. Treeby, "When Do Babies Start Sleeping Through the Night?," Pampers, June 19, 2022, https://www.pampers. com/en-us/baby/sleep/article/when-do-babies-sleep-through-the-night; "Breastfeeding vs. Formula Feeding," Nemours KidsHealth, June 2018, https://kidshealth.org/en/parents/breast-bottle-feeding.html.

18 R. Wong, "Infants Wake Up More Today Than They Did 40 Years Ago," Joyful Parenting SF, August 4, 2024, https://joyfulparentingsf.com/p/in-fants-wake-up-more-today-than-they.

19 A. Isen, M. Rossin-Slater, and W. R. Walker, "Every Breath You Take—Every Dollar You'll Make: The Long-Term Consequences of the Clean Air Act of 1970," *Journal of Political Economy* 125, no. 3 (2017): 848–902.

20 E. Frank, "The Economic Impacts of Ecosystem Disruptions: Costs from Substituting Biological Pest Control," *Science* 385, no. 6713 (2024).

21 D. Anderson, M. Binder, and K. Krause, "The Motherhood Wage Penalty: Which Mothers Pay It and Why?," *American Economic Review* 92, no. 2 (2002): 354–58; R. Glauber, "Marriage and the Motherhood Wage Penalty Among African Americans, Hispanics, and Whites," *Journal of Marriage and Family* 69, no. 4 (2007): 951–61.

22 J. Guryan, E. Hurst, and M. Kearney, "Parental Education and Parental Time with Children," *Journal of Economic Perspectives* 22, no. 3 (2008): 23–45.

23 L. Buzard, L. Gee, and O. Stoddard, "Why You Gonna Call? Gender Inequality in External Demands for Parental Involvement" (working paper, Social Science Research Network, 2024).

24 P. Persson and M. Rossin-Slater, "When Dad Can Stay Home: Fathers' Workplace Flexibility and Maternal Health," *American Economic Journal: Applied Economics* 16, no. 4 (2024): 186–219.

25 L. González and H. Zoabi, "Does Paternity Leave Promote Gender Equality Within Households?" (working paper no. 9430, CESifo, 2021).

Chapter 11

1 R. Fernández and J. C. Wong, "Free to Leave? A Welfare Analysis of Divorce Regimes," *American Economic Journal: Macroeconomics* 9, no. 3 (2017): 72–115; H. Foerster, "Untying the Knot: How Child Support and Alimony Affect Couples' Dynamic Decisions and Welfare," *The Review of Economic Studies*, (2024), rdae105.

2 D. Meyer, M. Cancian, and S. Cook, "The Growth in Shared Custody in the United States: Patterns and Implications," *Family Court Review* 55, no. 4 (2017): 500–512; D. Meyer, M. Carlson, and M. Ul Alam, "Increases

in Shared Custody After Divorce in the United States," *Demographic Research* 46 (2022): 1137–62.

Chapter 12

1 N. Ashraf, N. Bau, C. Low, and K. McGinn, "Negotiating a Better Future: How Interpersonal Skills Facilitate Intergenerational Investment," *Quarterly Journal of Economics* 135, no. 2 (2020): 1095–151.
2 M. Oliver, "The Summer Day" in *New and Selected Poems* (Boston: Beacon Press,1992).
3 C. Manning and A. Gregoire, "Effects of Parental Mental Illness on Children," *Psychiatry* 5, no. 1 (2006): 10–12; C. Kamis, "The Long-Term Impact of Parental Mental Health on Children's Distress Trajectories in Adulthood," *Society and Mental Health* 11, no. 1 (2021): 54–68.

Afterword

1 E. Andres, S. Baird, J. Bingenheimer, and A. R. Markus, "Maternity Leave Access and Health: A Systematic Narrative Review and Conceptual Framework Development," *Maternal and Child Health Journal* 20 (2016): 1178–92; M. Rossin, "The Effects of Maternity Leave on Children's Birth and Infant Health Outcomes in the United States," *Journal of Health Economics* 30, no. 2 (2011): 221–39.
2 A. Uribe, C. Vargas, and N. Bustamante, "Unintended Consequences of Maternity Leave Legislation: The Case of Colombia," *World Development* 122 (2019): 218–32.
3 M. Rossin-Slater, "Easing the Burden: Why Paid Family Leave Policies Are Gaining Steam," Stanford Institute for Economic Policy Research, February 2018, https://siepr.stanford.edu/publications/policy-brief/easing-burden-why-paid-family-leave-policies-are-gaining-steam.
4 M. Hansen and N. Nohria, "How to Build Collaborative Advantage," *MIT Sloan Management Review* 46, no. 1 (2004): 22.
5 C. Castellanos-Serrano, L. Escot, and J. Fernández-Cornejo, "Parental Leave System Design Impacts on Its Gendered Use: Paternity Leave Introduction in Spain," *Family Relations* 73, no. 1 (2024): 359–78.
6 J. Ekberg, R. Eriksson, and G. Friebel, "Parental Leave—A Policy Evaluation of the Swedish 'Daddy-Month' Reform," *Journal of Public Economics* 97 (2013): 131–43.

7   D. Avdic and A. Karimi, "Modern Family? Paternity Leave and Marital Stability," *American Economic Journal: Applied Economics* 10, no. 4 (2018): 283–307.

8   L. Farré, C. Felfe, L. González, and P. Schneider, "Changing Gender Norms Across Generations: Evidence from a Paternity Leave Reform" (discussion paper no. 163412023, IZA, Bonn, Germany).

9   P. Persson and M. Rossin-Slater, "When Dad Can Stay Home: Fathers' Workplace Flexibility and Maternal Health," *American Economic Journal: Applied Economics* 16, no. 4 (2024): 186–219.

10 T. Jørgensen and J. Søgaard, "The Division of Parental Leave: Empirical Evidence and Policy Design," *Journal of Public Economics* 238 (2024): 105202.

11 "Women Surgeons and the Challenges of 'Having It All,'" Clayman Institute for Gender Research, November 17, 2015, https://gender.stanford.edu/news/women-surgeons-and-challenges-having-it-all.

12 E. Cascio, "Maternal Labor Supply and the Introduction of Kindergartens into American Public Schools," *Journal of Human Resources* 44, no. 1 (2009): 140–70.

13 C. Miller, "The Persistent Effect of Temporary Affirmative Action," *American Economic Journal: Applied Economics* 9, no. 3 (2017): 152–90.

14 V. Angelova, W. Dobbie, and C. Yang, "Algorithmic Recommendations and Human Discretion" (working paper no. w31747, National Bureau of Economic Research, Cambridge, MA, 2023); D. Arnold, W. Dobbie, and P. Hull, "Measuring Racial Discrimination in Algorithms," in *AEA Papers and Proceedings*, vol. 111 (Nashville, TN: American Economic Association, May 2021).

15 J. Dastin, "Insight—Amazon Scraps Secret AI Recruiting Tool That Showed Bias Against Women," Reuters, October 10, 2018, https://www.reuters.com/article/world/insight-amazon-scraps-secret-ai-recruiting-tool-that-showed-bias-against-women-idUSKCN1MK0AG/.

16 C. C. Miller, "The Next Mark Zuckerberg Is Not Who You Might Think," *New York Times*, July 2, 2015, https://www.nytimes.com/2015/07/02/upshot/the-next-mark-zuckerberg-is-not-who-you-might-think.html.

17 I. Bohnet, A. Van Geen, and M. Bazerman, "When Performance Trumps Gender Bias: Joint vs. Separate Evaluation," *Management Science* 62, no. 5 (2016): 1225–34.

18 N. Bowles and L. Gannes, "All-Male Ski Trip and No Women at Al Gore Dinner: Kleiner's Cien Takes the Stand in Pao Lawsuit," Vox, February 25, 2015, https://www.vox.com/2015/2/25/11559418/all-male-ski-trip-and-no-women-at-al-gore-dinner-kleiners-chien-takes.

19 M. Nayak and Bloomberg, "Not 'Googly' enough: Google sued by Black ex-employee over 'racially biased' culture," Fortune, March 19, 2022, https://fortune.com/2022/03/19/not-googly-enough-google-sued-by-black-ex-employee-over-racially-biased-culture-april-curley-san-diego-alphabet-inc/.

20 A. Westenfeld, "An Expert on Hiring Bias Weighs In On Jeopardy!'s Mike Richards Controversy," *Esquire*, September 15, 2021, https://www.esquire.com/entertainment/tv/a37596556/jeopardy-mike-richards-hiring-bias-expert-opinion/.

21 M. Grynbaum and N. Sperling, "'Like Choosing a Pope': How Succession Got Messy at 'Jeopardy!,'" New York Times, August 14, 2021, https://www.nytimes.com/2021/08/14/business/media/jeopardy-mike-richards-ken-jennings.html; McNear, "A Smile with Sharp Teeth": Mike Richards's Rise to 'Jeopardy!' Host Sparks Questions About His Past," The Ringer, August 18, 2021, https://www.theringer.com/2021/08/18/tv/mike-richards-jeopardy-host-search-process-past-comments.

22 C. Littleton, "Mike Richards Out as 'Jeopardy!' Host Amid Cascade of Scandals," Variety, August 20, 2021, https://variety.com/2021/tv/news/mike-richards-jeopardy-host-fired-1235045394/.

23 M. Kearney, *The Two-Parent Privilege: How Americans Stopped Getting Married and Started Falling Behind*, (Chicago, IL: The University of Chicago Press, 2023).

24 H. C. Wong, "When Homemakers Are Compensated: The Effect of Homemaking Provisions on Spousal Time Allocation," *Journal of Legal Studies* 52, no. 1 (2023): 107–36.

25 C. Goldin and L. Katz, "The Power of the Pill: Oral Contraceptives and Women's Career and Marriage Decisions," *Journal of Political Economy* 110, no. 4 (2002): 730–70; C. Myers, "The Power of Abortion Policy: Reexamining the Effects of Young Women's Access to Reproductive Control," *Journal of Political Economy* 125, no. 6 (2017): 2178–24; N. Gershoni and C. Low, "The Power of Time: The Impact of Free IVF on Women's Human Capital Investments," *European Economic Review* 133 (2021): 103645.

26 E. Cascio, "Maternal Labor Supply and the Introduction of Kindergartens into American Public Schools," *Journal of Human Resources* 44, no. 1 (2009): 140–70.

27 E. Duchini and C. Van Effenterre, "School Schedule and the Gender Pay Gap," *Journal of Human Resources* 59, no. 4 (2024): 1052–89.

28 L. Bettendorf, E. Jongen, and P. Muller, "Childcare Subsidies and Labour Supply—Evidence from a Large Dutch Reform," *Labour Economics* 36 (2015): 112–23.

29 "Medicaid Structured Family Caregiving Program: Paying Loved Ones as Caregivers," American Council on Aging, August 1, 2024, https://www.medicaidplanningassistance.org/structured-family-caregiving/.

30 N. Folbre, "Children as Public Goods," *American Economic Review* 84, no. 2 (1994): 86–90.

Index